PASCAL
PRECISELY

PASCAL
PRECISELY
Third Edition

JUDY BISHOP
UNIVERSITY OF PRETORIA

 **Addison-Wesley Publishing Company**

Wokingham, England · Reading, Massachusetts
Menlo Park, California · New York · Don Mills, Ontario
Amsterdam · Bonn · Sydney · Singapore · Tokyo · Madrid
San Juan · Milan · Paris · Mexico City · Seoul · Taipei

Cover designed by Hybert Design and Type, Maidenhead
and printed by The Riverside Printing Co. (Reading) Ltd.
Camera-ready copy prepared by the author using Microsoft Word 5.0 on an Apple Macintosh IIci with camera-ready copy produced on a LaserWriter IIf.
Printed and bound in Great Britain by William Clowes, Beccles, Suffolk.

First printed 1993

ISBN 0–201–62402–8

British Library Cataloguing-in-Publication Data
A catalogue record for this book is available from the British Library.

Library of Congress Cataloging-in-Publication Data is available

Preface

This third edition represents a departure from the original *Pascal Precisely* mould. The four previous texts under the *PP* banner – the first and second editions, the *Scientists and Engineers* version, and the *Turbo Pascal* version – have stuck to a ten-chapter format, with minor shuffles in topics between the different editions. *PP 3E* has broken free to spread the material more widely, and is presented in 15 chapters, in three parts.

Ordering of topics

The advantage of the new model is that the reader has definite milestones – Part I covers the Fundamentals, Part II the Power and Part III the Applications. The topics have been regrouped to be more coherent within a chapter, without compromising the easy introduction to programming right at the beginning, nor the growing complexity of the examples tackled towards the end. The key points of the order of the material in the new edition are:

- Rapid entry to genuine programming problems;
- Early introduction to procedures and parameters;
- Delayed mention of variables as such;
- Number and character data treated side by side from the start;
- Spiral approach to types, with an easy introduction in Part I followed by a detailed study in Part II;
- Grouping of 'advanced features' in one chapter in Part III;
- Recognition that recursion is *not* an advanced feature – it appears in Part II.

As before, *PP3E* does not just introduce a feature, give an example, and then ignore it thereafter. Every feature is used and reused, reinforcing the notion that Pascal is an holistic language: every feature is necessary and the whole language is sufficient for solving quite sophisticated problems.

Increased coverage

In terms of additional coverage, *PP3E* makes two major departures. First, objects and graphics are now covered. How, one might well ask? After all, Standard Pascal provides for neither. However, the beauty of Pascal is its inherent versatility. I have written a small package in Standard Pascal which provides all the features of screen management that one expects at the character level on a modern computer. This is introduced in Part II and used extensively thereafter. The package itself is based on an object-oriented approach and therefore provides a vehicle for the discussion of objects in Part III.

The second enhancement is in the increased treatment of sorting and searching algorithms, and classical data structures. To selection sort has been added Quicksort, to linear search, binary search, and to lists and queues, stacks and trees. This gives *PP3E* readers a direct entry into the CSII syllabus.

Teaching aids

The examples have been extensively revised and all the case studies replaced by fresh, up-to-date ones. Gone are most of the shape printing examples, to be replaced by financial modelling (histograms), desk top publishing of a sensible sort and a wider choice of subjects, from train travel to games. Each chapter is rounded off with a summary of *What we have learnt*, followed by the ever-popular quiz (mostly completely new questions) and expanded problem sections. Great care has been taken in the reshuffle to ensure that the problems are still directly related to the material in the chapter, and can be solved completely correctly using only the features covered up to that point.

Acknowledgements

I acknowledge sincerely the equipment and time provided by my new department in Pretoria; the help and support of Simon Plumtree and Alan Grove (editors, Addison-Wesley); and the understanding and love of my family – Nigel, William and Michael.

Judy Bishop
Pretoria, South Africa
February 1993

Contents

List of examples

1 Computers and Programming

1.1 Computers

What is a computer? A straight answer might be:

> A computer is an electronic machine.

This does not tell us very much – no more than saying that a refrigerator is an electric machine. If we ask 'What is a refrigerator?', the answer would be:

> A refrigerator is an electro-thermal machine for
> making and keeping things cold.

This defines the object in terms of the *function* that it performs – in this case, it is a built-in function to cool things. The difference between a computer and most other machines is that a computer is not confined to performing a specific built-in function. Functions are supplied by means of **programs**.

Let's try again: what is a computer?

> A **computer** is an electronic machine which can be programmed to perform a variety of functions.

What functions? Look around and you will see computers in most walks of life these days. If one had a brain-storming session in class and asked everyone to name one use of computers, the list could well be something like:

banking	airline reservations
controlling spaceships	controlling washing machines
solving equations	newspaper publishing
pay-rolls	controlling chemical plants
advising doctors	calculating engineering constraints
stock control in shops	marking examinations
playing games	monitoring heart beats

and so on. Computers in general have a seemingly endless range of functions, but there are limits to what any one computer can do, and these limits are imposed by:

- the **hardware** of the computer, whether it is extensive or minimal, fast or slow;

- the **software** that is provided in the form of programs;

- the **devices** to which the computer is connected, such as automatic money dispensers, cash registers, optical card readers, chemical equipment, volt meters, laser printers and so on.

Thus, any one computer cannot perform any function – it must be suited to the task in terms of its hardware, and it must have the appropriate devices and software.

The vocabulary of computers is many and varied. What follows is a guide to the most common computer terms.

Multi-user computers

Mainframe computers are usually large in terms of their memory and the number of devices that can be connected to them. They are usually very fast, and are used by hundreds or thousands of people in big organizations. A mainframe computer can be located in one city, and by using **telecommunications** via land lines or satellite, it can receive and transmit data to and from **remote** sites or devices in other cities. Examples of such computers would be those used by banks, with their automatic tellers all over the country, or by a university, with **terminals** all over the campus.

Large machines are **multi-programmed**, in that they can deal with several functions and many users, seemingly all at once. Of course, there is still only one computer, but it is so fast that it can share its time between tasks, without humans noticing this sharing process – at least most of the time. When one does notice degradation in the visible performance of any one device connected to a mainframe (such as a wait before a balance slip is printed) then it means that the computer could well be getting congested, with too many things to do.

There are two different kinds of large machines, depending on the tasks that they mainly perform. By far the largest number of computers in the world are concerned with **information processing** (formerly **data processing** or DP), and the applications they are involved in tend to use very large amounts of information stored in a **database**. For example, a bank keeps a database of all its accounts, their owners' names and addresses, recent transactions, balances and so on. The other kind of mainframe is used for very complex and lengthy calculations such as weather prediction or nuclear physics research. These **supercomputers** are extremely fast at numerical computations and usually employ several processors working at the same time using **parallel processing**.

Personal computers

For the past three decades, computer hardware has been getting smaller and cheaper, thus bringing computers within the range of individuals, for their businesses, home organization or pleasure. **Minicomputers** were the first of the affordable computers and they tended to be used by 10 to 20 people, performing much the same tasks as a mainframe, but on a smaller scale. They were thus often found in small businesses or university departments.

Next came the **microcomputers**, which were distinct in that they were intended to be used by one person at a time – enter the **personal computer**. Personal computers meant an explosion in usable, friendly software, with games, word processors and spreadsheets being the most popular. Nowadays, microcomputers often have very sophisticated devices for performing graphics, high quality typesetting or even speech synthesis.

Following on from the micros are the **workstations**, which have hardware that rivals that of many mainframes, but that are still meant to be used by only a few people. Their function was originally to provide the increased power demanded by more sophisticated applications in research and software development, such as expert systems or image processing. However, workstations are increasingly replacing microcomputers as standard desk equipment.

Microprocessors

Mainframes and workstations are quite visible – one can walk into an office or computer room and see the metal cabinets containing the electronic machinery. Probably far more populous are the computers which reside inside other machinery – often known as **microprocessors** or even just **chips**. Such a computer is manufactured with its software built in, and this would consist of a dedicated program for performing a specific task, such as controlling a washing machine or an arcade game.

Microprocessors are relatively cheap to manufacture, but they are not intended for use by people directly. They are embedded in the machine they control and essentially form part of it. The software for embedded computers is developed on some other, larger, computer, and then may be **down-loaded** to the chip. It could well be that the chip in a household machine or a car is the same as one in a microcomputer – the difference is that the microcomputer has additional devices that enable it to communicate directly with people, and to be programmed afresh to carry out new tasks.

Networks

Computers of different makes and capabilities can be connected together to provide communication or to enhance the capabilities of one by using the facilities of another. Networks can be created within a small area such as a building or a campus where the physical connections between the machines can be made relatively easily. Such networks are known as **local area networks** or LANs). On a larger scale, computers can be connected right around the world using satellites, provided a common **network protocol** is observed during communication.

The beauty of networks for the ordinary user is that communication is often initially via a telephone, so that very little special equipment is needed. Of course, it is not legal to gain access to another computer unless one has permission, and this is the area of concern of **computer security**.

1.2 Hardware and software

The machinery of a computer is known as the **hardware**. When learning to program, one is most often faced with the hardware of a microcomputer, for use by one person at a time, or a terminal connected to a mainframe being used by many people. We shall describe a microcomputer here, since it includes all the important computer components. The situation for a terminal would be similar, but some of the devices of the computer may be in other rooms. Figure 1.1 shows a typical microcomputer.

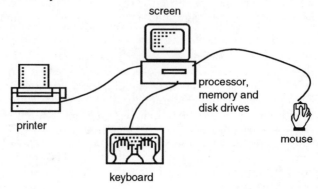

Figure 1.1 Components of a typical microcomputer.

While the arrangement of the boxes may vary, virtually every microcomputer will have a keyboard, screen, processor, memory, disk drive(s) and access to a printer. The mouse is optional, but is becoming increasingly popular. Let us look at each component in turn.

Keyboard

The keyboard enables one to type in instructions, programs and data to the computer. It resembles a typewriter, but has many more keys. The keyboard is an **input** device.

Screen

The screen enables one to see what is typed on the keyboard, and is also used by the computer for presenting results, messages, and so on, in the form of text and graphics. For the text, screens usually allow 80 characters across, and some 25 lines down. Modern screens also allow **graphics** (pictures) to be shown. For this, the screen is treated as a rectangular grid of dots or **pixels**. The brightness and colour of each pixel can be controlled. The detail which can be shown depends on the size of the pixels – the smaller the size, the greater the detail. On IBM and compatible personal computers the size depends on the **graphics adapter** used. A range of adapters is available, including CGA, EGA, VG, **Super** VGA and **Hercules**. The screen is an **output** device.

Processor

The processor performs the actual work of the computer, calculating or processing data according to instructions, and producing results. Processor throughput can be measured in Mips (millions of instructions per second) and typically a microcomputer might run at 0.5 to 1 Mips. This figure will depend on the underlying speed of the computer's clock which is measured in MegaHertz (MHz), with typical clock rates being 8 or 16 MHz.

Memory

While it is working, the processor keeps the current program and much of the data and results in its memory. Memory is usually volatile in that the contents are erased when the power is switched off. Memory is measured in terms of **bytes** consisting of 8 binary digits (**bits**) and may in addition be organized in units called **words** which may be 16 or 32 bits long. Typically, a microcomputer will have 1 Mbyte (where M stands for Mega or 1 048 576 = 2^{20}). Some memory is termed RAM (**randomly accessible memory**) and can be used freely by a program; other memory known as ROM (**read-only memory**) is used by software provided with the computer and cannot be overwritten.

Disk drives

In order for programs and data to be reusable, they must be stored on some permanent medium. **Disks** are the most suitable magnetic medium, though some larger computers may use magnetic tapes as well. A microcomputer will have a **hard disk drive** built in, which will be capable of storing from 40 Mbytes upwards. On the hard disk will be all the system software and spaces for the user to put applications and data. The hard disk can be partitioned into sub-disks, and these would be known by the letters C drive, D drive, E drive and so on. For saving software and data, and for moving it from one computer to another, the most popular method is to use small removable **diskettes**. Most microcomputers have one or two such diskette drives, and they come in two sizes: 3.5 inch and 5.25 inch. The older 5.25 inch disks are usually known as **floppies** because they are encased in a flexible cardboard cover, whereas the newer 3.5 inch disks have a hard plastic cover and are sometimes known as **stiffies**. The amount of information that can be stored on a disk depends on the density and quality of the magnetic covering and most floppies and stiffies can store over a megabyte.

Printer

Printers produce the **hard copy** of programs or results that can be taken away and studied. The printer may be connected directly to a microcomputer, or it may be shared by several over a network. The two most popular types of printer are:

- **dot matrix printers** which give reasonable quality printing, and are versatile in being able to output a reasonable selection of fonts and graphics;
- **laser printers** which can produce output of typeset quality, complete with font changes and graphics.

Mouse

A mouse is a pointing device which acts as an assistant to the keyboard. It enables parts of the screen and the instructions that manipulate it to be selected more easily. To operate a mouse, one rolls it around on a flat table top, and the motion is reflected on the screen. When the correct place is found, a button on the mouse is clicked, to indicate that the computer can go ahead and perform the selected operation. Some mice have one button, some have two or even three. Mice on portable computers are often integrated into the keyboards as tracker balls. They operate in exactly the same way as a mouse.

Software

As **hardware** is the name for the electronic components discussed above, so **software** is the name for the programs that reside in the computer In addition to hardware, computers also possess resident software, and additional software can be obtained and written. Figure 1.2 gives an impression of the different layers of software.

The main piece of resident software in a computer is its **operating system** which controls all the peripherals and provides an interface to the user. It generally handles access to the compiler and to utilities which can include an editor, a filer (or finder), and a debugger.

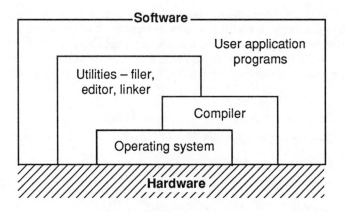

Figure 1. 2   Layers of software.

The **editor** is a program that enables one to type in a program, store it on a disk file, edit it, and add to it at will. The **filer** is there to keep track of all the names and properties of the files and disks being used. On a multi-programming system, further components of the operating system keep track of the amount of time and resources consumed by each user. Sometimes these are budgeted to users, and one has to take care to keep within one's allotted budget since the system could deny access if a budget is exceeded.

A system may have several **compilers**, one for each computer language. The compiler's task is to translate a program into a form that the computer can then execute. In the process, it checks the program for incorrect spelling, grammar and usage, and reports any errors to the user.

As you gain practical experience with using a computer, you will become familiar with the features for your particular computer. Although operating systems for different machines are superficially different, underneath they all provide the same sorts of functions, and after a while it becomes relatively easy to move from one computer to another.

1.3 Problem solving

As we have already discussed, the crucial difference between computers and other machines is that computers can be **programmed**. What is a program?

> A **program** is a set of ordered
> instructions which can be
> understood by the computer.

The purpose of the program is to provide a new capability to the computer – a capability to solve a new problem. The process of developing the program is called **programming** but in reality it involves all the skills relevant to **problem solving** as well. In the context of programming, problem solving involves several stages, each with its own particular difficulties and skills.   The stages are:

- defining the problem,
- outlining a solution,
- developing an algorithm,
- programming the algorithm,
- testing the program,
- documenting the solution,
- maintenance.

Problem definition

The first step is naturally to define the problem. This is surprisingly difficult in practice. Problems that are intended for solution by a computer can be phrased at any level from the wishful:

'Theatre reservations are too slow in this town.'

to the specific:

'What is the standard deviation of the following 100 numbers?'

The purpose of the problem definition phase is to pin down the problem more exactly. To do this, we try to define what the **data** will look like, and what the expected **results** will be. It is often useful to work through an example with the person who set the problem, thus bringing to light any misconceptions or misunderstandings.

For example, suppose one is asked to arrange a file of student records 'in order'. The questions to be asked would include the following:

- What is the basis for the ordering – surnames or student numbers or years and then surnames, or whatever?
- Must the old file be replaced by the new one, or must it remain?

Despite the importance of this phase of problem solving, it is nevertheless the case that a problem can seldom be completely defined *a priori*. There will always be aspects which only become clear as a solution is being worked out, and this is quite acceptable. It is actually better to leave some questions open until more information is available, rather than to make pre-emptive assumptions which may spoil the solution at a later stage.

Outlining a solution

The very first question to be asked is 'Do we need a computer at all?' There are times when using a computer is not appropriate, although it seems attractive at first. For example, deciding to put one's car mileage, consumption and service record on a computer could turn out to be more of a nuisance than an aid, because the computer is not available in the car, where most of the questions about its state will probably be asked. It would be better to stick to a note-book and calculator.

However, given that a computerized solution is required, it is necessary at this stage to set up the parameters within which the solution must work. Must the solution be fast? Are answers required on a terminal? Must results be stored on disk as well? In fact, is all the necessary equipment available? For example, if we need to print a graph of a function, it will make quite a difference to the solution whether we have a graph plotter connected, or whether we have to simulate plotting by printing dots on a printer.

At this stage, too, one should be thinking of past solutions. Has this problem been solved before, or even something very like it? Time can be saved by reusing tried and tested methods, rather than starting from scratch. If the problem is in a particular domain, such as mathematics or biology, we should make sure that we have all the essential equations and methods worked out, and be aware of any constraints that apply to the numbers and arithmetic involved. As we shall see later on, computers have bounds on their arithmetic capabilities, and as a result errors can creep in.

Algorithms

It is at the algorithm stage that the logical thought processes must start, and the outline of a solution be worked out into a step-by-step method. Algorithms have been around since long before computers were first thought of and are visible in many walks of life. For example, in cooking, one might find the following recipe for meringues:

> Beat the egg whites until
> stiff. You will know that they
> have been beaten enough if they
> don't fall out when the bowl is
> turned over.

This is an unhelpful algorithm, since the test for completion will not allow the process to continue!

In general, algorithms in computer programming must have certain properties, if they are to be used as starting points for a program. These properties all relate to preciseness and are: unambiguous, finite, brief, self-checking and deterministic. An algorithm for summing positive and negative numbers together and separately would be as in Figure 1.3.

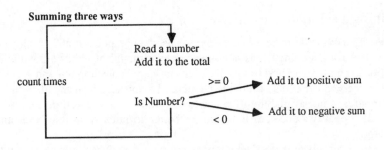

Figure 1.3   An algorithm as a pseudo-code chart.

How to achieve good algorithms, and how to write them down, is looked at more closely in Section 1.5. Moreover, this whole book is a case study in algorithm development: there are over 60 worked examples where a problem is taken through a draft solution to an algorithm, and from there to a program which is tested on the computer.

1.4   Programming

The next phase in the problem-solving process is that of programming itself. In older days, programming was regarded as the main activity of computing, but now it is only part of the process, which also involves design, maintenance and documentation, among other phases.

Languages

Now we have to write the algorithm down in a programming language. There are many, many such languages in use throughout the world, but relatively few that are available on all kinds of computers. These are known as the **high-level languages**, and include Pascal, Ada, Fortran, COBOL, BASIC, C, Lisp, Prolog and Modula-2. These languages are also **general purpose** in that they can, by and large, be used to solve a wide range of problems. They do have their special areas of application though, with COBOL being business-oriented, Fortran being for scientific use, and Prolog being very good for artificial intelligence. Pascal is named after Blaise Pascal the seventeenth century French mathematician and philosopher.

　　　The choice of which language to use for a particular application will depend on what is available, and whether it has any specific features that give it an edge over others. For learning to program, educators usually choose a language that:

- is **modern, easy to understand**, and

- has **good protection against mistakes**.

Pascal fulfils all these goals. It was devised in 1970 by a Swiss professor, Niklaus Wirth, and is now used throughout the world in universities and colleges as a first teaching language.

Part of a Pascal program that implements the algorithm depicted above is:

```
PROCEDURE Summation3;
   VAR
      number  :real;
      i       : 1..10000;  {say}
   BEGIN
     Total := 0;
     PosTotal := 0;
     NegTotal := 0;
     FOR i := 1 to count do begin
        read (number);
        Total := Total + number;
        if number > 0 then PosTotal := PosTotal + number
                      else NegTotal := NegTotal + number;
     END {for};
     readln;
   END; {Summation3}
```

The program is written in a stylized, yet fairly readable, English. Each step in the program is written on a new line, and the lines are indented to achieve certain effects. For example, the lines between the FOR and END {for} constitute a loop, and this is emphasized by the indentation.

High-level languages are **machine-independent** in that they can be run on any computer for which a compiler is available. Every computer also has its own specific **machine language** which it can execute directly. Programming is not usually done at this level, though sometimes it is necessary to use a symbolic form of the machine language, known as **assembly language** or just **assembler**.

Programming languages fulfil many of the properties of algorithms discussed above, but there are good and bad ways of using them, just as there are good and bad ways of using English. One of the goals of this course is to teach the correct way of using a programming language, so that the resulting program is both efficiently executable by the computer and easily understandable by humans.

Testing

Once a program has been written down in a programming language, it has to be submitted to the computer in some way, **compiled** into that computer's machine language and then executed. On the way, things may go wrong, and steps may need to be repeated. This is all summed up in Figure 1.4.

The programmer takes the sheets of paper to a terminal and types the program in. The program, often known as **source code**, is sent to the compiler, which checks it for correct grammar or **syntax**. If anything is wrong, a list of **compilation** errors will be produced, or the errors could be indπicated as they occur. The errors must be attended to by changing the program, and then the source is resubmitted to the compiler. This process continues until there are no more compilation errors. The program is then translated by the compiler into a machine-executable form, called **object code**.

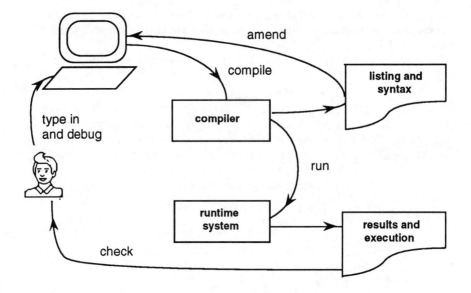

Figure 1.4   Life cycle of a program.

The object code can then be **run** on the computer, by a runtime system which is either part of Pascal or part of the computer's **operating system**. The program will produce results, and it may also produce **execution errors**. In either case, the results must be carefully scrutinized, a process which is usually better done away from the computer in peace and quiet.

If the program is not executing correctly, then the necessary changes must be made, and the process begun again. Unfortunately, it is sometimes unclear what is causing an error, in which case, more information must be gained by putting additional instructions in the program. This process is known as **debugging**. Once a program runs without errors and produces the correct results, it can be released for production use. In the case of student programs, this usually implies handing them in for marking.

Documentation

When a program is running, it can provide instructions to the user as to what it expects in the way of data or other responses. However, it is not always possible to provide all information about the operation of a program in this way, and it is then necessary to write a **product manual** or **user's guide** to go with it. Such a document should be written primarily in the terminology of the problem domain, not in computer terms.

On the other hand, there is also a need for a **system manual** or **implementor's guide** which does go into the technical details of the program, and can be used particularly by people who may need to modify the program later.

With modern environments such as Turbo Pascal, it is usual to find that the documentation is **on-line** and available on the screen while the program is running. It is also possible to write one's own programs with this sort of facility built in.

Maintenance

Finally, the program is up and running, and like any piece of equipment, it needs to be maintained. It is not that parts of the program might 'wear out', but that the environment might change, such as a new kind of disk being added, or even a new processor. It is also true that **requirements** change over time, and because programs are so adaptable, people have come to expect an instant reaction to any desire for change. Thus, programs are modified, expanded, speeded up or otherwise altered all the time, and this **maintenance** is a large part of any company's software budget.

As a student, you will be involved in relatively little maintenance, because once a program works, you move on to the next assignment. Nevertheless, it is worth remembering that the care that is put into writing clear programs and documentation to go with them will reduce the effort required to maintain such programs in the future.

1.5 Algorithm development

The development of a good algorithm is central to the process of transforming a problem into a computer program which solves it. Unfortunately, there is no science of algorithms that can be studied formally: much has to be learnt by experience and practice. Nevertheless, there are a few key techniques which we can follow, and which will guide us in the early stages of setting down methods in an orderly way. We shall illustrate these techniques by considering the example of summing the first 20 positive numbers in a list.

Notations

The first issue we must settle is the notation for writing down an algorithm. There are many notations, some proprietary, some informal and some more suited for business data processing. Commonly used notations are **flow charts** and **pseudo-code**.

Consider the example of summing the first 20 numbers in a list. A flow chart to do this is shown in Figure 1.5. Flow charts have found their way into everyday life, and by their familiarity are reasonably easy to read. Their disadvantages, though, are numerous. They are complicated to draw, and almost impossible to amend; they tend to encourage too much detail immediately, and, most of all, they do not foster the algorithm techniques which good programming practice now promotes. The flow chart is already more detailed than the corresponding Pascal program would be.

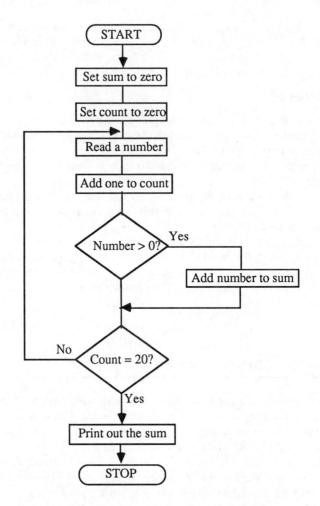

Figure 1.5   A flow chart for summing 20 positive numbers.

The other popular alternative is pseudo-code, which is a stylized English more akin to modern programming. Pseudo-code treats algorithms at a higher level than flow charts. It employs indented levels to indicate structure and grouping, and enables us to see the algorithm at different levels of detail. The disadvantage of pseudo-code is that it loses the visual impact that lines and boxes convey. The same example in a pseudo-code would be:

(1) Set sum to zero
(2) Do 20 times
        (2.1) Read a number
        (2.2) If it is positive, add it to sum
(3) Print the sum

Pseudo-code charts

In this book, we have chosen to use both charts and pseudo-code in an informal notation called **pseudo-code charts**. The form of pseudo-code charts is as simple as possible, making them easy to draw on paper, freehand. The chart starts off with a **title** which indicates the overall intention of the algorithm. Thereafter, instructions are given in plain, though abbreviated, English, and lines are used to show alternative and repetitive paths. A pseudo-code chart for summing is given in Figure 1.6.

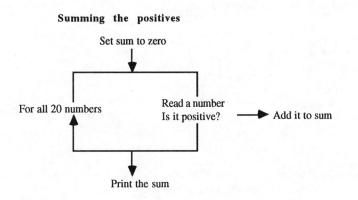

Figure 1.6   A pseudo-code chart for summing 20 positive numbers.

The box indicates that the instructions must be repeated: the action is given on the right-hand side, and the information about how many times it must be done, on the left-hand side. The question 'Is it positive?' is followed by an arrow that indicates what should be done in this case. After this choice has been taken, we proceed on and around the chart. The advantage of an informal notation such as this is that an algorithm can be expressed in greater or lesser detail: we are not restricted to the kinds of instructions that we write down. Some may be at a very high level, such as 'Solve the first equation for x', whereas others are almost atomic actions, such as 'Set sum to zero'. In all other ways, the charts combine the advantages of the other two methods with few of the disadvantages.

Top-down development

Having settled on a notation, we can now discuss some of the algorithm development techniques we shall need in the chapters that follow. The first is as old as the hills – or at least as old as Caesar's invasion of Gaul – and is termed **top-down development**. It involves viewing a problem in its entirety, and then breaking it up into **subproblems**. We then solve the subproblems in the same way, just by breaking them up, until such time as we reach a subproblem that can be solved by an existing technique, or by a simple sequence of instructions. (Caesar called this **divide and conquer**.)

So, if we were taking our previous example from the top down, we would start off thus:

Summing the positives
    Set sum to zero
    Read and add the positive numbers
    Print the sum

The first and last instructions are already as simple as we can make them, but the middle one can be tackled further, giving:

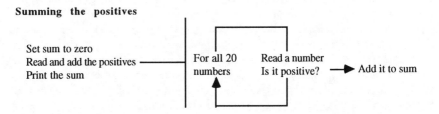

The line-and-bar notation indicates a refinement of the instruction 'Read and add the positives'. Since we do the refinement step by step, this process is also known as **step-wise refinement**.

Structured programming

Within the field of computer programming, there was a revolution in the 1970s, as computer scientists sought to convert people from programming according to flow charts into something less error-prone. The key to the new methodology, which was known as **structured programming**, was the use of a restricted set of constructs, which in themselves were simple, safe, and yet powerful. The three constructs are called:

- sequencing,
- selection,
- repetition.

Sequencing acknowledges that computers follow instructions in an ordered sequence, so that in the absence of any other information, sequencing prevails. Pascal features that support sequencing are the assignment (Section 4.3), input/output (Sections 2.2, 4.4) and the begin-end statements (Section 5.1).

    Selection enables choices to be made, based either on some **condition** or on a **key value**. The idea is that the actions associated with a choice form a closed sequence in themselves, and when they are completed, control returns automatically to after the choice. This is why in our pseudo-code chart we show the following:

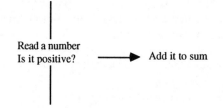

and do not bother to draw a line from 'Add it to sum' back to the main stream. Pascal statements which implement selection are the if-then-else (Section 5.1) and the case-statement (Section 5.2).

Repetition involves doing a sequence of actions several times, with either a count or a condition governing the number of the repetitions. Once again, the important point is that the sequence to be repeated forms a whole, and may not be split up, except by another of the structured constructs. We saw this even in our small example. Within the repeated read-add cycle, there are two paths: one has a read and a question, the other has a read, question and add. The distinction between the two is based on a selection construct in a proper way. Pascal features that implement repetition are the for-loop (Section 2.4), the while and repeat-loops (Section 5.3, 5.4) and recursion (Section 8.4).

Modular decomposition

Techniques of algorithm development are intimately entwined with good programming practice. Where structured programming helps in the lower levels of programming, a technique called **modular decomposition** assists in the higher levels.

Suppose we have a large, complex problem to solve, and in fact several people – maybe twenty or even a hundred – involved in the project. We would start by dividing up the tasks – but where do we draw the boundaries? How do we decide which subproblems go together, and which depend on the results from others? A complex problem may well not devolve into a simple hierarchical structure as explained in the discussion under top-down development.

The key here is to decompose the problem into modules based on **interfaces**, whilst keeping the interaction between the modules to a minimum. We start with the different sorts of data in the solution and consider the operations that will be needed to manipulate them. For each sort of data, we parcel it up with its operations into a **module**. The module then decides on which parts of the data and operations it will export to the rest of the program, and reserves for itself those that it does not deem to be of public concern.

In this way, we keep interfaces to a minimum, and lessen the chances of confusion and errors. Even in our little summing example, we can see the benefits of modular decomposition. Suppose this algorithm forms part of a very much larger system. We would set the interface up to be only that data that was necessary to be seen outside – the **black box** approach. Thus the interface could be defined as:

```
PROCEDURE PositiveSums (var sum : integer);
```

The program that used this black box would therefore only be concerned with the data in the sum: it would not have to know anything about number or count, which remain private to the workings of the algorithm.

Pascal features that support modular decomposition are procedures (Section 3.1, 8.3), functions (Section 8.2) and parameters (Sections 3.2, 8.1, 13.2, 13.3).

Generalization

An essential technique for launching an algorithm into the wide world of a programming project is to ensure that it is sufficiently general to be used in all the necessary cases. Take our example. We stipulated that 20 numbers would be read: what if there were 10 instead, or 400? Looking at the algorithm, it is clear that it will not change if there are more or fewer numbers. Thus, we can generalize it to handle n numbers, making this part of the interface:

```
PROCEDURE PositiveSums (n:integer; var sum:integer);
```

Generalization is supported in Pascal by means of parameters (Sections 3.2, 8.1, 13.2, 13.3).

Bottom-up and reusable programming

It would be incorrect to believe that top-down is the only way to develop algorithms. We can also start at the opposite end and look for the small problems that can be easily solved. These can form building blocks for the problems higher up. It is all a question of scale: we developed the 'Summing 20 positive numbers' algorithm from the top down, but within a wider picture, it could be part of a bottom-up process to develop tools for later use. In practice, a little bit of both is required – top-down and bottom-up.

The important spin-off from bottom-up development is that algorithms can be reused in many different projects. Reuse is certainly a theme of this book. Many of the algorithms developed in the early chapters form essential tools for more complex problems later on. In all cases, we have taken care to express the algorithms with clear interfaces so that they are self-contained, and can be reused as is.

Data abstraction

Modern thinking is that proper attention to the structure of data in a program is as important as attention to the control constructs. Indeed, we have seen above that the vital technique of modular decomposition depends on the way in which the data is viewed in a program. Knowledge of data structuring techniques is an essential part of any programmer's repertoire. Pascal has a rich choice of such techniques, and these are covered in Chapters 6, 9 and 10.

WHAT WE HAVE LEARNT

*In this chapter we considered the different types of **hardware** that make up a personal computer, and the options available for other computer configurations. Thereafter, we concentrated on **software** and **programming**, emphasizing in particular the development of **algorithms** and the **notations** that can be used to express them. We considered the **life cycle** of a program including the phases of debugging, maintenance and documentation. We showed that we preferred the informal **pseudo-code charts** and explained the few features that go into them. Moving to more general issues, we defined briefly the major **software development** strategies, indicating where they will be covered later in the book.*

QUIZ

1. What limits the capabilities of a particular computer?
2. What is meant by multi-programming?
3. Explain the difference between the terms microcomputer , microprocessor, personal computer and chip.
4. In what units is the speed of computers measured?
5. What is the difference between RAM and ROM?
6. What does a compiler do?
7. List five desirable properties of algorithms.
8. What is the difference between a compilation error and an execution error?
9. If a computer does not have a mouse, what takes its place?
10. What is meant by machine language?

PROBLEMS

1.1   List the input devices and output devices for the computer you are familiar with.
1.2   What is the clock speed of the computer you are using?
1.3   How much memory does your computer have?
1.4   What is the capacity of the disks you are using?
1.5   Would this textbook (including all the spaces) fit on your disk, assuming one printed character per byte of memory?
1.6   List all the software that you encountered when getting your first Pascal program running on your computer.
1.7   List all the computer applications that you come into contact with in the course of an ordinary week.

1.8 What algorithms do you come into contact with in an ordinary day? Do they match up to the criteria discussed in this chapter?

1.9 Have you ever been on the wrong end of a computer error? If so, could you tell whether the mistake was in the program or in the data that was fed in?

1.10 Devise an algorithm for choosing the three shortest people from a group.

1.11 Devise an algorithm for getting from your lecture room to a place for lunch in any weather.

1.12 Find out the name, version and creation date of the computer, operating system and compiler that you will be using.

2 Simple Programs

2.1 Programs

A Pascal program consists of:

- **declarations** which describe the objects of a program – its constants, types, variables, functions and procedures;

- **statements** which provide the step-by-step algorithm, making use of the objects.

The **objects** in a program are associated with the data that the program is intended to manipulate. Objects need **identifiers** by which the statements can refer to them. In keeping with the properties of algorithms, the statements are executed in sequence, one after the other. Some statements are specifically designed to alter this sequence, and are sometimes known as **control statements**, because they alter the flow of control of the program. A program that is solving a real problem will also usually require input and produce output:

- **input** is the actual information or data that the program will process;

- **output** forms the results of the program's endeavours.

The data and results are considered to be in **files**. Files are held on a device such as a disk, and the particular files required by a program can be specified for each run of the program.

The form of a program

These elements are combined in the program in the following form.

```
Program

    PROGRAM  name   (files);
       declarations
       BEGIN
          statements
       END.
```

The plain words such as PROGRAM, BEGIN and END are Pascal **keywords** which indicate the structure of the program. The words in italics describe parts of the program that must be supplied by the programmer. The program name is compulsory, but the files, declarations and statements are optional. Thus the following is a valid Pascal program which does nothing.

```
PROGRAM DoNothing;
   BEGIN
   END.
```

There are many kinds of declarations and many kinds of statements. Throughout this book we shall be introducing the various declarations and statements in easy stages, until the whole language is covered. We start in this chapter by looking at statements for writing, then we look at expressions and constants, and finally the statement for a counting-loop. By the end of the chapter, enough will be known about Pascal to perform simple repetitive tasks involving printing, in the best possible programming style.

2.2 Output with writeln and write

The simple form for the Pascal statements to print a piece of text are:

```
Simple output statements

    write (list of items );
    writeln (list of items);
    writeln;
```

where the list of items in parentheses consists of values to be printed, and the items are separated by commas. For the time being, we shall only consider items which are strings. A **string** is any sequence of characters enclosed in apostrophes, for example

```
'London'      'USA'      '$5.95 per lot'      'User''s Guide'
```

To include an apostrophe itself in a string, it is given twice, as in the last example.

A **writeln statement** prints out the list of items and ends the line of print. Thus, the statements

```
writeln('Mr John Smith');
writeln('33 Westridge Road');
writeln('Greenwood');
```

will cause the following to be written out:

Mr John Smith
33 Westridge Road
Greenwood

(In examples from now on, Pascal statements are given in plain type, and the corresponding output is shown in bold.)

The **write statement** works in a similar way except that it does not end the line of print, so that a subsequent write or writeln will continue to print on the same line from the last point reached.

The list of items is optional for a writeln statement and, if it appears on its own, then it will finish off the current line. This can be used to obtain a blank line, as in:

```
writeln('Mr John Smith');
writeln('33 Westridge Road');
writeln('Greenwood');
writeln;
writeln('********************');
```

which would give as output:

Mr John Smith
33 Westridge Road
Greenwood

****

To obtain several blank lines, we use several writelns in a row, as in:

```
writeln;  writeln;  writeln;
```

EXAMPLE 2.1   Printing a label _____

Problem   Mr John Smith would like a nice address label printed for a parcel.

Program   This first program is very simple:

```
PROGRAM AddressLabel(output);
```

```
BEGIN
   writeln   ('-------------------------------');
   writeln   ('|                              |');
   writeln   ('|   Mr John Smith              |');
   writeln   ('|   33 Westridge Road          |');
   writeln   ('|   Greenwood                  |');
   writeln   ('|                              |');
   writeln   ('-------------------------------');
END.
```

The program name clearly indicates what the program is to do. The word output after the program name indicates that the program is going to make use of an output device such as a screen to do some writing. The keyword BEGIN indicates the start of the statements. After the keyword END, there is a full stop.

Testing   The output produced by this program would be:

```
---------------------------------
|                               |
|   Mr John Smith               |
|   33 Westridge Road           |
|   Greenwood                   |
|                               |
---------------------------------
```

Notice that we can use dashes, bars and other such symbols for effect, in the same way as one would on a typewriter. There are many such printing tricks, and computers are particularly good at them. Further examples in this chapter and the next illustrate some more of these.

Layout

How the program is written down, in terms of lines and spaces, does not have an effect on how the output appears. Only what is inside the apostrophes is actually written out. When writing strings, there is no gap caused by splitting them up into different items or into different write statements, nor do blank lines in the program have any effect. Therefore, the following statements will cause Mr Smith's name and address to be printed as before.

```
writeln ('Mr ', 'John Smith');

                          write ('33 ');
writeln   ('Westri',
               'dge Road');
write('Green');                    write('woo');
writeln('d');
```

The point is that the instructions given to the computer do not have to be in any special layout. We usually write them neatly one underneath each other, and we shall also use **indenting** to make groups of statements stand out, but there is no formal rule that says this should be so. Other points about the form of the program which we can make right now are:

- more than one statement can be written on a line;
- statements can be split over several lines;
- statements are separated by semicolons.

The effect of this last point is that a semicolon is placed at the end of virtually every statement. The semicolon is optional before an END, but in this book we shall include it.

Field widths for strings

An item to be printed can be followed by a colon and an indication of the number of spaces in which the item is to appear, right justified. Right justification is useful for lining up columns, as illustrated in the next example.

Field widths are particularly useful for getting gaps of the correct size, using the string with a single space in it, instead of counting out the spaces explicitly. So

```
write (' ':15);
```

will write 15 spaces.

EXAMPLE 2.2   Metric units

Problem   Some people have trouble remembering the main metric units and we would like to print a poster to help them.

Solution   We want to print out the physical concept (for example, distance), the name of the unit (for example, metres) and its abbreviation (for example, km). This is going to form a table of three columns, so we shall use field widths to line them up nicely.

Algorithm   We tackle the solution by looking at the kind of output we would like, and then emulating it. The important decision is the width of each column. We shall choose 20, 15 and 5 to start with.

Program   The program looks like this:

```
PROGRAM Units (output);
   BEGIN
      writeln(' ':10, 'The Metric Units');
      writeln(' ':10, '================');
      writeln(' ':12, 'Unit          Abbreviation');
      writeln ('Distance':12, 'metres':14,'m':5);
      writeln ('Mass':12, 'kilograms':14,'kg':5);
      writeln ('Time':12, 'seconds':14,'s':5);
   END.
```

Testing   Running the program will produce:

```
       The Metric Units
       ================
     Unit            Abbreviation
 Distance     metres      m
     Mass   kilograms     kg
     Time     seconds      s
```

2.3 Simple expressions

The examples so far have used the write and writeln statements to print **strings**. It is also possible to print **numbers** and, indeed, to print the results of calculations. For example, to print the cube of 23 less 54, we would have

```
writeln (23 * 23 * 23 - 54);
```

which would print out

12113

Such calculations are called **expressions** in Pascal. The way in which expressions are written in computer languages is slightly different to the normal way of writing them. The three main differences are that:

- multiplication is indicated by an asterisk *
- division is indicated by a slash /
- everything is on one line.

For example, consider some simple formulae and their Pascal equivalents:

$$\frac{1}{2} \qquad => \qquad 1 / 2$$

$$6\,(7-3) \qquad => \qquad 6 * (7-3)$$

The implication of the last point – writing on one line – is that we use more parentheses in Pascal expressions than we would normally. Division that would usually be written as a fraction has to be split into two parenthesized parts separated by a slash. For example, consider the following:

$$\frac{100 - 9.99}{15 + 0.1} \qquad => \qquad (100 - 9.99) / (15 + 0.1)$$

As another example, to print 15°C converted to Fahrenheit, using the formula

$$\frac{9t}{5} + 32$$

we would say

```
writeln ((15 * 9 / 5) + 32);
```

which would print out

```
5.900000E+01
```

Integers and reals

The output from the temperature conversion above is somewhat disconcerting: why is it printed as a decimal fraction with E+01, rather than just 59? The answer is that the expression involved division, and so the answer was considered to be a real number. Pascal distinguishes between **integer** numbers and **real** numbers and has different default output formats for each of them. The integers represent whole numbers and the reals permit fractional parts, but **also include the integers**. For integers, we have the operators

+	addition
−	subtraction
*	multiplication

(plus two others which we shall leave to Section 6.2). But the result of dividing two numbers is not always an integer, so the fourth operator

/	division

gives an answer which is a real number, even if the values are integers.

Real numbers span a wide range of values, and by default, Pascal prints them as a fraction and an exponent raised to the power of ten. This format is known as **scientific format**. There is one figure before the decimal point, and the resulting decimal exponent comes after an E, as we saw above. This is clearly messy for simple results, and there are two ways of overriding it:

1. Use field widths.

2. Convert the real back to an integer.

Field widths for numbers

Pascal has defaults for writing out numbers, which are usually:

Integers	12 figures,
Reals	scientific form with 6 decimal places.

In both cases, the numbers are written flush to the right. To change either default, we can indicate a **field width** which defines the size of the gap in which the number is to be written. The field width comes after the expression, preceded by a colon. One field width can be specified for integers, and one or two for reals. The effects are as follows:

Integer, one field width	print the number in that width,
Real, one field width	print the number in that width, using scientific form
Real, two field widths	print the number in the gap given by the first width, with the decimal places given by the second width.

If the overall width given is too small, Pascal overrides it and prints the number in as big a space as needed. If the decimal places are too few, the number is suitably rounded.

For the moment, we can use :6:2 for real numbers, which will serve most purposes. In Chapter 6, when we look at real numbers again, there will be some examples and exercises to find out more about the effects of field widths.

Numbers and strings can be written in the same write statements, so for example, we might have:

```
writeln('Today''s temperature will be 15 Celsius, that''s
',                 15*9/5+32:4:1, 'Fahrenheit.');
```

**Today's temperature will be 15 Celsius, that's 59.0
Fahrenheit.**

Notice that the first field width for a real should include space for the whole number, including the decimal point and sign.

Converting reals to integers

Although only the +, − and * are defined between integers to produce integer results, a division operator / can be used between integers and it will produce a real result. Real numbers are covered in detail in Section 6.5, but in some of the examples that follow, the use of real division is necessary. In order to convert the result to an integer, so that it can be used within the context of Pascal so far, there are two functions:

trunc (x)	truncates x to the next integer nearest zero
round (x)	rounds x to the nearest integer

These two functions take a real expression and produce an integer. Thus we have:

trunc (6.3)	6	round (6.3)	6
trunc (6.8)	6	round (6.8)	7

Named constants

In the real world, many values acquire names. For example, 3.141592 is known as *pi*, and a *decade* is 10. Giving quantities names makes them easier to remember and use. Pascal acknowledges this advantage by allowing values to be assigned to names. Constants are declared directly under the program statement in a special section which has the form:

Constant declaration

```
CONST
    identifier = value;
    identifier = value;
        . . .
    identifier = value;
```

It is helpful to follow a constant declaration with a comment on its units, where applicable. The comment is enclosed in curly brackets. Comments are there to explain parts of the program, but are not executed when the program runs. Examples of constant declarations are:

```
CONST
    pi          = 3.141592;
    space       = ' ';
    kmpermile   = 1.609;
    speedlimit  = 90;        {km/hour}
    kilo        = ' K'
    pa          = 'per annum'
    taxrate     = 10;        {%}
```

Named constants aid readability and make program changes easier. Once the declaration has been made, the name of the constant can be used wherever the number is required. The name should convey more information than a plain number, and if the value has to change, then the change need only be made once – in the declaration. If, for example, the tax rate were to be raised to 15%, then only this one declaration would need to be altered, not all occurrences of the number 10. Since there may be occurrences of the number 10 which are not related to taxrate, confusion is also avoided.

EXAMPLE 2.3   Calculating interest

Problem The bank in the country of Zanyland – called ZanBank – quite often changes its interest rate for savings accounts. We would like to know what difference the change will make to the interest we may receive for the rest of the year.

Solution In this, our first real problem, we have to start by asking:

> What do we know?
> What do we want to know?
> How are we going to get there?

We know that the formula used for calculating interest is the usual one of

$$I = \frac{P\,T\,R}{100}$$

where P is the principal, T is the time in years and R is the rate per annum. In this case, we know our principal – let's suppose it is D1000. (The unit of currency in Zanyland is the dolly, abbreviated to D.) The time is going to be (12 – M)/12 where M is the month we are currently in. So if we are in May, the time left will be 7/12. Finally, we must know the old rate and the new rate, for example 12% and 12.5%.

What we want to know is whether we are better off or worse off under the new rate, and by how much. We find that out by calculating the interest under both rates and finding the difference.

Algorithm   The algorithm includes the names of all the values we have just been discussing.

> Print out the difference between
> > (P * (12 – M)/12) * newRate) / 100
> and
> > (P * (12 – M)/12) * oldRate) / 100

Program   The program does just that! It uses constants for all the values we know, and uses expressions in the writeln statement for the answer. Notice how careful use is made of writeln statements and field widths to get a pleasing output.

```
PROGRAM Interest (output);
  CONST
    P = 1000; {dollies}
    M = 4; {It is currently April}
    oldRate     = 12.5; {%}
    newRate     = 13.00; {%}

  BEGIN
    writeln('ZanBank Interest Calculation');
    writeln('============================');
    writeln('Given a change of interest rate from ',
            oldRate:4:1,'% to ', newRate:4:1,'%',
            'in month ', M);
    writeln('On a principal of D', P:1,
            ' the interest for the rest of the year');
    write('will change by dollies and cents: ');
    writeln((P * (12 - M)/12 * newRate)/100
            - (P * (12 - M)/12 * oldRate)/100 : 7:2);
  END.
```

Testing   If we run the program, the output will be:

```
ZanBank Interest Calculation
============================
Given a change of interest rate from 12.5% to 13.0% in month 4
On a principal of D1000 the interest for the rest of the year
will change by dollies and cents:    3.33
```

2.4   Repetition with counting-loops

Computers, like all machines, are very good at doing the same thing over and over again. In a program, such repetition can be formulated as a **loop**. There are two kinds of loops possible in Pascal – **counting-loops** and **conditional** loops. In this section we look at how counting-loops are achieved; the conditional ones are introduced in Chapter 5.

In order to get on with programming quickly, this section adopts a 'just do it this way' approach for the declarations that have to be associated with loops. The full discussion of how and why these work is given in Chapter 4.

The form of a counting-loop

A counting-loop is specified in two parts: the loop variable declaration and the corresponding for-statement.

Loop variable declaration

```
VAR loop variable  :  lower.. upper
```

For-statement

```
FOR loopvariable := lower  to upper DO BEGIN
    statements
END;
```

As before, the plain words form the template, and the ones in italics have to be appropriately filled in for an actual loop. The VAR declaration introduces a **loop variable** which is intended to operate between the values specified for `lower` and `upper`. These values may be numbers, or characters enclosed in single quotes, for example, the following would be valid loop declarations:

```
VAR i : 1..10;

VAR letter : 'a' .. 'z';
```

Additional possibilities for loop variables are discussed in Chapter 9.

About the form

The keyword FOR introduces the loop and states that the loop variable will start at `lower` and finish at `upper`. The keywords DO BEGIN introduce the **loop body** which consists of statements finishing off with the keyword END. Notice that the

END is aligned with the FOR and the statements in the body will be indented. As some variation on the position of the other keywords is possible, some textbooks place the BEGIN on a separate line underneath the FOR . The present formulation is, however, a neat one and is used throughout this book. In addition, we believe that too many capital letters in a program make it hard to read, so often we only put the first keyword on a line in capitals: in the above form, to is not in capitals for this reason. Because of the introductory keyword, these loops are also known as **for-loops.**

The action of the loop is to repeat the statements for each successive value of the loop variable.

EXAMPLE 2.4   Multiple labels _____

Problem   Mr John Smith would like to print out lots of labels which he is going to photocopy onto sticky labels.

Solution   We checked with Mr Smith, and confirmed that for the time being, he is happy to have them one underneath each other. (Later on we shall see how to fill a page with labels.) The solution is to take the body of the old AddressLabel program and put it in a loop.

Program   The program follows on quite easily. Note that we follow each label by two blank lines to separate them, and use a constant to specify how many labels there must be.

```
PROGRAM LotsofLabels (output);
  CONST
    max = 8;
  VAR counter : 1..max;

  BEGIN
    FOR counter := 1 to max do begin
      writeln  ('--------------------------------');
      writeln  ('|                              |');
      writeln  ('|   Mr John Smith              |');
      writeln  ('|   33 Westridge Road          |');
      writeln  ('|   Greenwood                  |');
      writeln  ('|                              |');
      writeln  ('--------------------------------');
      writeln;
      writeln;
    end;
  END.
```

Simpler loops

If there is only one statement in the loop body, then the keywords BEGIN and END can be omitted. For example, we could write out a blank label by using a loop to print the innermost lines:

```
VAR  line : 1..5;
```

```
writeln   ('------------------------------');
FOR line := 1 to 5 do
   writeln ('|                            |');
writeln   ('------------------------------');
```

The effect of this would be to write out the top line. Then the program starts the loop variable `line` at 1, writes the given string, goes around the loop, sets `line` to 2, writes the string again, goes around, sets `line` to 3, and so on, until the fifth time. At this point the values indicated for `line` have been exhausted, and the loop ends with the last line being written.

Using the loop variable

The loop variable serves to record the current iteration of a loop and its values can be used in various ways:

- in a write statement;
- in simple arithmetic;
- as part of the bounds of another loop.

Together, these three facilities make looping much more interesting. In order to focus on the looping operations themselves, we shall explore a few examples of loops of this sort. The examples are given as fragments of a Pascal program: it is assumed that the declarations and statements will slot into the appropriate parts of a full program.

Loops and integers

To print out the first ten even numbers, we can have a loop going from one to ten, and then write out double the loop variable, as in:

```
VAR number : 1..10;
FOR number := 1 to 10 do
   write(number * 2);
writeln;
```

which will produce:

```
2    4    6    8    10   12   14   16   18   20
```

To print the odd numbers requires a bit of thought. If `number*2` is an even number, then `number*2+1` or `number*2-1` is an odd number. Choosing one of these expressions, we have:

```
VAR number : 1..10;

FOR number := 1 to 10 do
   write(number * 2 - 1);
writeln;
```

which will produce:

```
1    3    5    7    9    11   13   15   17   19
```

Now let's look at an actual example.

EXAMPLE 2.5   Conversion table

Problem   An oceanography laboratory measures temperatures of lakes in Celsius, but some of the older technicians want the values in Fahrenheit. For the time being, the managers have agreed to put up conversion tables around the laboratory. Can you help?

Solution   Use a loop to go through the range of temperatures required, writing out the one temperature and then its conversion.

Algorithm   The algorithm for a conversion table needs a heading, and then a sequence-printing loop, as described in the discussion above. In diagrammatic form the table for Celsius to Fahrenheit is:

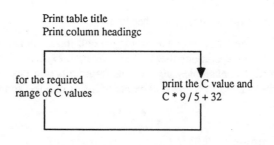

What will the required range of C values be?   Well, if these are water temperatures, they could range from 5 to 20.

Program   The program follows on easily. Notice that we use zero as our second field width and thereby get the answers out as integers.

```
PROGRAM ConversionTables(output);
   VAR
      C : 5 .. 20;
      F : 40 .. 70;

   BEGIN
      writeln('Conversion Table Celsius to Fahrenheit');
      writeln('===============================');
      writeln;
      writeln('  C        F');
      FOR C := 5 to 20 do
         writeln(c:8, round(C*9/5 + 32):8));
   END.
```

Testing   The program output follows. We could cut out the table and paste it up in the laboratory.

```
Conversion Table Celsius to Fahrenheit
=======================================

        C      F
        5     41
        6     43
        7     45
        8     46
        9     48
       10     50
       11     52
       12     54
       13     55
       14     57
       15     59
       16     61
       17     63
       18     64
       19     66
       20     68
```

Loops and real numbers

Loop variables cannot be real numbers, but they can be used in expressions which produce real numbers, as shown in the previous example. However, if we actually do want to run a loop over a real range, we have to use an equivalent integer range and apply the necessary scaling.

Character loops

A loop variable over characters can be used to print part of the alphabet, as in

```
VAR  letter : 'A' .. 'M';

FOR letter := 'A' to 'M' do
   write(letter,' ');
```

which would produce

```
A  B  C  D  E  F  G  H  I  J  K  L  M
```

Nested loops

A for-loop is a statement. Therefore, it can appear wherever a statement can appear, and one of these places is within a loop itself. An important consideration in nested loops is that the loop variables must be different. If we write:

```
for i := …
   for i := …
```

havoc will result, as the outer loop variable's value will be altered unexpectedly by the inner loop. Nested loops are shown in the next example, and explored in the problems at the end of the chapter.

EXAMPLE 2.6   Mountain viewing_____

Problem   We would like to draw a schematic of a mountain of a particular size.

Solution   Using write statements, we can produce a passable mountain as follows:

```
    **
   ****
  ******
 ********
**********
```

We can use loops to get the repetitive effect, with the varying number of stars in each row.

Algorithm   We develop the algorithm by looking at a simpler type of mountain first, and then improving it. Consider a right triangle of size 5 such as:

```
*
**
***
****
*****
```

The triangle consists of rows, where each row has a number of stars corresponding to the row number. Thus row 1 has 1 star, row 2, 2 stars and so on. Printing the triangle can be described by the following algorithm:

Right triangle

Print a row ⟶ Print a star
'size' times   'row' times

which translates into the nested Pascal loops:

```
VAR
   row, star : 1..size;

FOR row := 1 to size do begin
   FOR star := 1 to row do
      write('*');
   writeln;
END;
```

If we double the stars in each row, we get a wider, though still lopsided, mountain, thus:

```
    **
   ****
  ******
 ********
**********
```

To get the mountain upright, we need to print spaces before the stars in each row. How many? For the last row it is none. For the second last row, it is 1, moving up to the first row, when we need one less than the size, in this case 4.

Printing the spaces translates into the loop:

```
VAR
   gap : 1..size;

FOR gap := row +1 to size do
   write(space);
```

Program   Putting this all together, and choosing a value for the size, we have the program:

```
PROGRAM  Viewing (output);
   CONST
      space = ' ';
      size = 8;
   VAR
      row, gap, star : 1..size;
   BEGIN
      FOR row := 1 to size do begin
         FOR gap := row +1 to size do
            write(space);
         FOR star := 1 to row do
            write('*');
         writeln;
      END;
   END.
```

Testing   Testing this gives the expected output:

```
               **
              ****
             ******
            ********
           **********
          ************
         **************
        ****************
```

Counting backwards

Pascal has a further looping option, that of counting backwards. This is indicated by replacing the TO in the for-statement by the keyword DOWNTO. Thus, to print the sequence

```
10  9  8  7  6  5  4  3  2  1  0  -1 -2  -3  -4  -5  -6
```

we could say

```
FOR n := 10 downto -6 do
   write(n);
```

A nice example of counting backwards is found in the song 'One man went to mow', which is discussed in the next example.

EXAMPLE 2.7   Campfire song _____

Problem   A popular campfire song goes like this:

> 1 man went to mow, went to mow a meadow,
> 1 man and his dog, went to mow a meadow.
>
> 2 men went to mow, went to mow a meadow,
> 2 men, 1 man and his dog, went to mow a meadow.
>
> 3 men went to mow, went to mow a meadow,
> 3 men, 2 men, 1 man and his dog, went to mow a meadow.

We would like to print out the words up to a given number of men.

Solution   The way of tackling this problem is to take a verse from the output and underline those parts that change each time, that is:

> 3 men went to mow, went to mow a meadow,
> 3 men, 2 men, 1 man and his dog, went to mow a meadow.

We have carefully used digits rather than words for the numbers, to make programming easier.

Algorithm   We set up one loop for the verses, based on how many men there are, and one loop to repeat all the men in reverse order.

Program   A first attempt at a program for five men is:

```
PROGRAM MowaMeadow (output);
   VAR
      man, companions : 1 .. 5;
   BEGIN
      writeln('****** One man went to mow ******');
      FOR man := 1 to 5 do begin
         writeln(man,
               ' men went to mow, went to mow a meadow,');
         FOR companions := man downto 2 do
            write(companions, ' men, ');
         writeln('1 man and his dog, ',
                  'went to mow a meadow. ');
         writeln;
      end;
   END.
```

Testing   This will produce:

```
****** One man went to mow ******
1 men went to mow, went to mow a meadow,
1 man and his dog, went to mow a meadow.

2 men went to mow, went to mow a meadow,
2 men, 1 man and his dog, went to mow a meadow.

3 men went to mow, went to mow a meadow,
3 men, 2 men, 1 man and his dog, went to mow a meadow.
```

```
4 men went to mow, went to mow a meadow,
4 men, 3 men, 2 men, 1 man and his dog, went to mow a
meadow.

5 men went to mow, went to mow a meadow,
5 men, 4 men, 3 men, 2 men, 1 man and his dog, went to mow
a meadow.
```

The output has one defect: the first line is written as '1 men ...' rather than '1 man ...'. How could the program be altered to display correct grammar?

Skipping the body of a loop

When loop bounds consist of expressions, it may happen that when evaluated, the lower bound may already exceed the upper one. In this case, the loop body is not executed at all. In the above example, the statement

```
FOR companions := man downto 2 do
```

will be in this situation when man is 1. No 'men' phrases are written out for this verse, which is exactly what was intended.

WHAT WE HAVE LEARNT

In this chapter we learnt how to arrange a program and about its layout. We looked at strings, numbers and characters and used them in write and for statements. By using expressions for simple arithmetic, we were able to solve several problems of a repetitive nature. The solution processes we used in various combinations were:

1. Look at the output required and recreate it.
2. What have we got, what do we want, how do we get there?
3. Do it once, then do it lots of times, with a slight variation.
4. Simplify where possible, solve that, then add improvements.

QUIZ

1.   What comes first in a program – declarations or statements?

2.   What is special about the last END in a program?

3.   What must you do if the string you want to write is too long to fit on a line?

4.   Do the following statements have the same result?

```
writeln('Hello');
writeln('Hello':20);
```

5.   What is the value of $((7-2)/(4*5))$? Is it a real or integer result? What field width(s)

would you use to print it out?

6. What are the advantages of named constants?

7. How many stars would the following loops print out?

```
for star := 9 to 0 do write('*');
for star := -3 to 3 do write('*');
```

8. The following statements are meant to print a sequence consisting of a number and then that many equal signs followed by a plus, each on a new line. For example:

```
4 = = = = +
```

Can you work out what they actually print, and how to fix them?

```
for number := 1 to 5 do
    write(number);
    for sign := 1 to number do write(sign);
    writeln('+');
```

9. How would you display your name in the middle of a line 80 characters wide?

10. Write a loop to print out the first 20 even numbers.

PROBLEMS

2.1 **Scientific units** Extend Example 2.2 to print out more of the units, for example, joules, newtons. Use constants to specify the sizes of the three columns, and experiment with different widths to obtain a good layout.

2.2 **Fuel consumption** A motor car uses 8 litres of fuel per 100 km on normal roads and 15% more fuel on rough roads. Write a program to print out the distance the car can travel on a full tank of 40 litres of fuel on both normal and rough roads.

2.3 **Notepaper** Assume that your printer has 80 characters across a page. Write a program to print out notepaper with your address neatly right-justified, for example:

```
                              1 Green Road
                                 Seapoint
                                 Zanyland
```

2.4 **Interest changes** In Example 2.3, we looked at how the interest received would change depending on a change of rate in a given month. In order to plan ahead, we would like to know how the interest would change based on the month in which the rate change is announced. Write a program to print out a table showing how the interest would change from January to November. Use the same figures as Example 2.3.

2.5 **Another song** Another song that can go on a bit is:

> There were 10 green bottles hanging on the wall,
> 10 green bottles hanging on the wall
> And if one green bottle should accidentally fall
> There'll be 9 green bottles hanging on the wall.

9 green bottles hanging on the wall
And if one green bottle should accidentally fall
There'll be 8 green bottles hanging on the wall.
etc.

1 green bottle hanging on the wall
And if one green bottle should accidentally fall
There'll be 0 green bottles hanging on the wall.

Using the technique discussed in Example 2.7, design an algorithm to print out such a song, and program it starting with 5 green bottles.

2.6   **A number triangle** Write a program which uses for-statements and write statements to produce the following triangle:

```
1
2  2
3  3  3
4  4  4  4
5  5  5  5  5
```

Adapt the program to print the triangle so that the numbers are centred, as below. Adapt it again to print the triangle upside down.

```
      1
   2     2
3     3     3
4     4     4     4
5  5  5  5  5
```

2.7   **Shaded boxes** Write a program to print out boxes consisting of 'darker' and 'lighter' sides, like this:

```
+---
++--
+++-
++++
```

2.8   **Conversions** A conversion table can be viewed as a general algorithm. Establish this fact by adapting the program in Example 2.5 to print out the conversion from miles to kilometres (1 mile = 1.6 km) and again to print dollars to dollies (1 $ = 0.45 D). Choose suitable ranges and use named constants to control the loops.

3 Structuring with Procedures

3.4 Understanding error messages

3.5 Case study – financial modelling

3.1 Simple procedures

A **procedure** is a group of declarations and statements which is given a name and may be called upon by this name to perform a particular action. A procedure is therefore just like a program – it could in fact be called a **sub-program**. The simple form of a procedure declaration is:

Simple procedure declaration

```
PROCEDURE name;
   declarations
   BEGIN
      statements
   END;  {name }
```

The difference between this form and that for a program is essentially in the last

line, where the END is followed by a semicolon, not a full stop, and the name of
the procedure is repeated in curly brackets after it. (The name at the end is
optional, but conventional, and is used consistently thoughout this book.) An
example of a procedure would therefore be

```
PROCEDURE box;
   BEGIN
      writeln ('-----------');
      writeln ('|          |');
      writeln ('|          |');
      writeln ('|          |');
      writeln ('-----------');
   END; {box}
```

Creating a procedure like this is a **declaration.** The name box is declared to be
the action of performing the given statements.

Having been declared in the declaration part of a program, a procedure can
be **called** by mentioning its name thus:

Simple procedure call
name ;

So for example, to print a box, all we need to say is:

```
box;
```

the effect of which will be to print:

```
 ---------
|         |
|         |
|         |
 --------
```

This constitutes a **call statement.** When a call statement is executed, the
procedure is entered and its statements are performed until its END is reached,
whereupon execution continues with the statement after the call.

Defining procedures in this way will enable us to cut down on repetition,
but it also provides a means of creating a structure for a program, and the name of
a procedure can be carefully chosen to reflect the action it performs, thus
enhancing the readability of the program.

EXAMPLE 3.1   Large conversion tables

Problem The oceanography laboratory was so pleased with the table we
produced (Example 2.5) that they have asked us to do one for a larger range of
temperatures, but to arrange it so that the whole table fits nicely on the screen or
on a page.

Solution   We know how to do the conversion, so what we need to think about is how to arrange the layout of the table. A standard computer screen has lines 80 characters long. Each pair of temperatures occupies 14 characters (8 for the Celsius and 6 for the Fahrenheit). We can therefore fit 5 columns on the screen. For temperatures from 1 to 100, this gives 20 lines, which will fit nicely on a screen or a page. We can then use nested loops to get the desired effect.

Algorithm   We can tackle the solution from the top. We know how to print one line because we did it in Example 2.5. It is:

```
writeln (c:8, round(C * 9 / 5 + 32 : 8)
```

We can therefore set up a loop to print 20 lines. Let us define the following constants:

```
CONST
   colsperline = 5;
   maxlineno = 19;
```

The lines will be numbered from 0 to 19. Printing one line can be put in a procedure, `printline`, with its own loop and loop variable, say `col`. Then the expression for printing a number on a given line and column will be:

```
line * colsperline + col
```

We can also use the field width for strings feature, to set the column headings to line up on the same widths. This can be done in a separate `initialize` procedure, which also prints the table heading.

Program

```
PROGRAM LargeTable (output);
   CONST
      space = ' ';
      colsperline = 5;
      maxlineno = 19;

   VAR  line : 0 .. maxlineno;

   PROCEDURE initialize;
      VAR col : 1..colsperline;
      BEGIN
         writeln (space:15,
             'Conversion Table Celsius to Fahrenheit');
         writeln (space:15,
             '=======================================');
         writeln;
         FOR col := 1 to colsperline do
            write (' C':8, ' F':6);
         writeln;
      END; {initialize}

   PROCEDURE printline;
      VAR col : 1..colsperline;
      BEGIN
         FOR col := 1 to colsperline do
```

```
            write ((line * colsperline + col) : 8,
                round((line * colsperline + col)
                    * 9 / 5 + 32):6);
          writeln;
       END; {printline}

    BEGIN
       initialize;
       FOR line := 0 to maxlineno do
          printline;
    END.
```

Testing Running the program confirms that it does produce the required effect, and the right answers.

```
          Conversion Table Celsius to Fahrenheit
          =========================================
```

C	F	C	F	C	F	C	F	C	F
1	34	2	36	3	37	4	39	5	41
6	43	7	45	8	46	9	48	10	50
11	52	12	54	13	55	14	57	15	59
16	61	17	63	18	64	19	66	20	68
21	70	22	72	23	73	24	75	25	77
26	79	27	81	28	82	29	84	30	86
31	88	32	90	33	91	34	93	35	95
36	97	37	99	38	100	39	102	40	104
41	106	42	108	43	109	44	111	45	113
46	115	47	117	48	118	49	120	50	122
51	124	52	126	53	127	54	129	55	131
56	133	57	135	58	136	59	138	60	140
61	142	62	144	63	145	64	147	65	149
66	151	67	153	68	154	69	156	70	158
71	160	72	162	73	163	74	165	75	167
76	169	77	171	78	172	79	174	80	176
81	178	82	180	83	181	84	183	85	185
86	187	87	189	88	190	89	192	90	194
91	196	92	198	93	199	94	201	95	203
96	205	97	207	98	208	99	210	100	212

Step-wise refinement

The most important advantage of procedures is their ability to assist in the problem-solving process. A solution becomes more manageable when it is divided up into smaller pieces. Each of these can be viewed as a procedure, with a name which reflects its function. Then the work of each procedure can be further broken down, with another layer of procedures to solve the subproblems. This is known as the process of **step-wise refinement** and is an important problem-solving technique.

A program that is written in this way gives more information to the reader as to its function and its operation than one that consists of a single long sequence of statements.

There are other tangible advantages to procedures. If a procedure is carefully written, it may well be feasible to copy it for use in another program that requires the same functionality. Such a procedure is called **reusable**. Within a single program, procedures can also reduce repetition, thus making a program more compact. The smaller the program, the less memory it uses, and in certain circumstances memory may be at a premium. Thus, procedures contribute to **space efficiency**. Shorter programs, provided they are neatly laid out, are generally easier to read than longer ones, and procedures contribute substantially to the **readability** of a program.

EXAMPLE 3.2   Labels side by side

Problem   We wish to print out blank labels side by side, with suitable gaps between them.

Solution   There exists a procedure to print a rectangle, that is:

```
PROCEDURE rectangle;
  BEGIN
     writeln ('--------------------------');
     writeln ('|                        |');
     writeln ('|                        |');
     writeln ('|                        |');
     writeln ('--------------------------');
  END; {rectangle}
```

but if we call

```
      rectangle;   rectangle;   rectangle;
```

the labels will come out one underneath each other. This is because the Pascal write statements regard the output file as consisting of lines which are written in sequence. The contents of each line have to be composed and written out before going on to the next line. This model corresponds very closely to a class of printers of which matrix printers, line printers and daisy-wheel typewriters are good examples. It is possible to create a model whereby the screen or page can be drawn on freely, and this is discussed in Chapter 7.

However, given the sequential nature of ordinary output, the way to get the labels side by side is to have the outer loop being concerned with rows, then for each row, consider each label.

Algorithm   At the top level of the algorithm, we would have:

> Print the top horizontal line, and do it for each label
> Print the three vertical lines, for each label
> Print the bottom horizontal lines, for each label

Since printing the top horizontal lines is the same as printing the bottom lines, there are only two procedures to expand. The first one works out as a simple counting-loop. The other procedure is similar, but needs to be called three times, as shown in the program. Notice that printing a gap is easiest done simply by adding spaces on to the end of the line in each string. The pseudo-code chart for one of the loops is:

Print horizontals

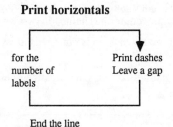

for the   Print dashes
number of   Leave a gap
labels

End the line

Program   The program uses constants to govern how many labels are to be printed alongside each other. In this case, we want four. Similarly, a constant indicates how deep the labels are, in this case three rows.

```
PROGRAM LittleBoxes (output);
  CONST
    labelsacross = 4;
    depth = 3;

  VAR
    row : 1..depth;

  PROCEDURE Printhorizontals;
    VAR box : 1..labelsacross;
    BEGIN
      FOR box := 1 to labelsacross do
        write('------------          ');
      writeln;
    END; {Printhorizontals}

  PROCEDURE Printverticals;
    VAR box : 1..labelsacross;
    BEGIN
      FOR box := 1 to labelsacross do
        write('|             |       ');
      writeln;
    END; {Printverticals}

  BEGIN
    writeln('****** Four blank labels ******');
    Printhorizontals;
    FOR row := 1 to depth do
      Printverticals;
    Printhorizontals;
  END.
```

Testing   Running the program will produce:

```
****** Four blank labels ******
----------      ----------      ----------      ----------
I        I      I        I      I        I      I        I
I        I      I        I      I        I      I        I
----------      ----------      ----------      ----------
```

To change the number of labels, all we need do is change the constant at the top. Notice that the use of procedures has helped in two ways:

- repetition: the horizontals loop is not repeated, as it is packaged up in a procedure;

- understanding: the nested loops are separated out, making the program easier to read.

3.2 Parameters

Procedures can be made more powerful by allowing the effect to differ slightly each time the procedure is called. For example, if we have a procedure that prints a 5 by 5 box, it would be useful if it were able to print a 10 by 10 box, or a 12 by 16 box, or whatever. In other words, the action of printing a box by means of writeln statements should appear to be independent of the number of writelns that are actually needed. This is called **generalizing** or **parameterizing** a procedure and the variables that are going to be different are known as **parameters**.

What we are aiming at is a means of being able to write:

```
box  (5,5);
box  (10,10);
box  (12,16);
```

This is achieved by declaring the procedure with parameters that are given names, like variables, and receive their values at the time the procedure is called. For the box, the declaration would become:

```
PROCEDURE box (length, breadth : integer);
```

There are actually three kinds of parameters in Pascal, but we shall just mention the simplest one – **value parameters** – at this stage. The others are covered in Chapters 8 and 13.

The form of a value parameter list

The parts of the procedure that are to be generalized are listed in the declaration, straight after the procedure name, together with their types. There are many different types in Pascal that we shall be discovering as we go along, but for now, we shall assume the existence of the three that we have seen already:

- **integer**, which has values that are whole numbers, both positive and negative, in some large range;

- **char**, which has values that include the letters, digits and special symbols such as those commonly found on a keyboard;

- **real**, which has values that are fractions over a very wide range, and which includes all the integers.

Given this, the form for a procedure declaration with parameters is:

Procedure declaration

```
PROCEDURE name (list of parameter declarations);
    declarations
    BEGIN
        statements
    END; {name}
```

The list of parameter declarations looks very much like a list of loop variable declarations, except that we cannot specify the range of the values, and must only give the type, which at this stage we would regard as being integer or char. Each declaration for value parameters has the form:

Value parameter declaration

```
list of parameters  : type ;
```

Then, somewhere in the body of the program, we would call the procedure with an appropriate list of parameter values for the particular version of the procedure that we want. The form of the call is:

Procedure call with value parameters

```
name (list of parameter values);
```

EXAMPLE 3.3 Mountain climbing _____

Problem Set up a procedure to display a mountain of any size, with any character.

Solution Use the mountain program from Example 2.5. Adapt it as a procedure with two parameters, `size` and `symbol`.

Procedure The procedure with its parameters is:

```
PROCEDURE Mountain (size : integer;  symbol : char);
   VAR row, piece : 1..20;
   BEGIN
      FOR row := 1 to size do begin
         FOR piece := row + 1 to size do
            write(' ');
         FOR piece := 1 to row do
            write(symbol, symbol);
         writeln;
      END;
END; {Mountain}
```

Testing Testing a procedure involves trying it out with various actual parameters. Calling ours in a program with:

`Mountain (3, '$');`	will give	$$ $$$$ $$$$$$

while:

`Mountain (5, '*');`	will give	** **** ****** ******** **********

as in our original examples. If we wanted to draw a mountain of zeros, we must be careful about using the *character* zero for the second parameter, not the number:

`Mountain (4, '0');`	gives	00 0000 000000 00000000

EXAMPLE 3.4   Price tickets

Problem Zanyland High School is having a fete and has set all food and drink at standard prices of two or five dollies. They would like to design suitable price tickets on the computer. The D5 tickets should be bigger and more impressive than the D2 ones.

Examples Some suggestions could be:

```
------------              ================
|2222222222|              =5555555555555=
|2222222222|              =5555555555555=
|2222222222|              =5555555555555=
------------              =5555555555555=
                          =5555555555555=
                          ================
```

Solution   We need a procedure that can print a box of any size, up to a maximum of 80 wide and 20 deep. Parameters should help here, but let us first simplify the problem by sticking to a standard hyphen and bar border. Then the only variable parts are the width and depth of the ticket, and the price.

In Example 3.2, we treated the 'horizontal' and 'vertical' lines of the box separately. In fact, by using generalization, we can regard them as the same, but with different first, middle and last symbols. In other words, we have:

Line type	First	Middle	Last
Horizontal	–	–	–
Vertical	ǀ	price	ǀ

Now we can define a further procedure to print a line with the symbols as parameters, and call it the required number of times.

Algorithm   Let us assume that the *width* and *depth* are the given measurements. Then each line consists of the following sequence:

> **Aline (first, middle, last);**
>> Draw the first symbol
>> Draw width–2 middle symbols
>> Draw the last symbol

The box itself consists of:

> **VaryBox (width, depth, price)**
>> Draw a line with parameters (–, –, –)
>> Draw depth–2 lines with parameters (ǀ, price, ǀ)
>> Draw a line with parameters (–, –, –)

Procedure   The procedure for the line can be nested inside the one for the box. Putting this all together gives:

```
PROCEDURE VaryBox (width, depth : integer; price : char);
   VAR  d : 1..20;

   PROCEDURE ALine (first, middle, last : char);
      VAR  w : 1..80;
         BEGIN
            write(first);
            FOR w := 2 to width - 1 do
               write(middle);
            writeln(last);
         END; {ALine}

   BEGIN
      ALine ('-', '-', '-');
      FOR d := 2 to depth - 1 do
         ALine ('|', price, '|');
      ALine ('-', '-', '-');
   END; {VaryBox}
```

Algorithm 2   Now we need to extend `Varybox` to include the two symbols to be used for drawing the border. This means adding on two more parameters, and using them in the calls to `ALine`.

Program   We can now test out the program for the two designs above. Others can be generated by varying the parameters.

```
PROGRAM PriceTickets (output);
   PROCEDURE VaryBox (width, depth : integer;
                      hori, verti, price : char);
      VAR d : 1..20;

      PROCEDURE ALine (first, middle, last : char);
         VAR w : 1..80;
         BEGIN
            write(first);
            FOR w := 2 to width-1 do
               write(middle);
            writeln(last);
         END; {ALine}

      BEGIN
         ALine(hori, hori, hori);
         FOR d := 2 to depth-1 do
            ALine(verti,price,verti);
         ALine(hori, hori, hori);
      END; {VaryBox}

BEGIN
   writeln('Suggested Price Tags for the fete');
   writeln;
   VaryBox(11,5,'-','|','2');
   writeln;
   VaryBox(15,7,'=','=','5');
END.
```

3.3 Basic syntax

Like any natural language (such as English or Spanish), Pascal has rules determining what is correct and what is not correct. The difference is that computer languages are more fixed, having relatively few permitted words and few ways of composing them into statements. This actually makes learning the language easier, and one expects to be able to master the rudiments of a computer language in a matter of weeks, whereas mastering a natural language may take years.

From the layout point of view, Pascal programs consist of:

- **words**, classified as keywords, identifiers, strings and comments;
- **punctuation**, such as semicolon and parentheses, and arithmetic symbols;
- **spaces** and **blank lines**.

Spaces and blank lines are important in aiding the readability of a Pascal program, and should be used freely. One word of caution – if a program has many blank lines, or has statements spread out over several lines, then the amount of information that can be displayed on a screen is limited, and it may be hard to understand a program that is presented in small fragments. In this book, we tend to use blank lines between procedures, and to keep statements fairly compact. Other books use other conventions, such as always putting BEGIN on a new line. The resulting spread over several pages of what could be a short program does not really aid readability.

Pascal programs are usually typed in small letters or **lower case** but free use can be made of capital letters (known as **upper case**) for emphasis. Some Pascal systems have built into them **pretty printers** which will reformat your program into a fixed style of indenting and mixture of cases, while some systems insist on lower-case letters only. We shall assume that you can control how your programs are written, and we shall adopt a neat, consistent style for laying them out.

Keywords

There are 48 words in Pascal which have special meanings and are reserved for use as **keywords**. Some of these are:

```
PROGRAM          PROCEDURE
BEGIN            to
END              do
FOR              VAR
```

Keywords can be written in small letters or in capitals, depending upon which looks better at the time. The convention we use is that the first keyword on a line, such as PROCEDURE or FOR, is written in capitals, while other less important words such as to and of can stay in small letters. Other textbooks have different conventions, sometimes putting all keywords in capitals, or using bold or italics for this effect. The point is that Pascal doesn't care about case, so that all the following are valid versions of a keyword:

```
PROCEDURE                     Procedure
pRoCeDuRe                     procedure
procedure
```

Two of Pascal's keywords – CONST and VAR – are abbreviations. They introduce the constant and variable sections of the declarations, and must be used in this abbreviated form. However, other keywords cannot be abbreviated. For example, PROC cannot be used for PROCEDURE.

Identifiers

The terms 'name', 'word' and 'identifier' have been used rather loosely up to now to describe sequences of letters. The proper Pascal term is **identifier**, and there is a precise definition of what constitutes an identifier:

> An **identifier** is a sequence of letters and digits that:
> - starts with a letter,
> - treats the lower- and upper-case letters as equivalent,
> - does not have the same spelling as any keyword.

Identifiers may not include spaces. This restriction becomes important when identifiers are formed from phrases rather than from single nouns or verbs. A convention often used is to employ the second property and put a capital letter at the start of each English word, thus serving to break up an otherwise confusing jumble of letters. For example, we could write:

> `ReduceToOne`   **rather than**   `reducetoone`

Mistakes in the formation of identifiers are detected by the compiler. Pascal normally shows the offending word and prints a message such as:

> **Error 2: Identifier expected**

without any explanation as to what exactly is wrong. The most common mistakes are using a keyword or starting an identifier with a digit. However, after a few weeks of programming, the rules become second nature.

Predefined identifiers

Pascal has certain identifiers which are predefined for all programs, but are not keywords. Some we have seen are:

```
integer
write
writeln
```

and others will be introduced later. The point about these identifiers is that they should be regarded as keywords from the point of view of not defining them as something else. If we declared the word `write` as a loop variable, say, then the original meaning of `write` would be lost, and trying to use it for writing would fail. Once again, conforming to this restriction should become natural after a while.

Since they are not keywords, `integer` and `writeln` should not be written in capitals.

Comments

Although Pascal is a precise language, parts of programs can sometimes be a bit cryptic. To make these parts easier to understand, comments can be added.

> A **comment** is any text enclosed in { },
> except curly brackets themselves.

Apart from explaining what is going on, comments are also used to amplify the bare syntax of Pascal in various ways. One such example is the practice of following the end of a procedure with its name, as in:

```
PROCEDURE Mountain (size : integer; symbol : char);
    ...
END;   {Mountain}
```

Other occasions for comments will be introduced later, but we note here that comments should only be used to amplify the Pascal, not to duplicate it.

Syntax

In Chapter 2, we introduced the *form* of various parts of a program with three such forms being given – for the program itself, for a procedure and for a counting-loop. To recall, the forms for procedure declarations and counting-loops are:

```
Simple procedure declaration

    PROCEDURE name;
        declarations
        BEGIN
            statements
        END; {name }
```

```
Loop variable declaration

    VAR loopid : lower.. upper;
```

```
For-statement

    FOR loopid  := lower  to upper do begin
        statements
    END;
```

These forms are ways of describing the **syntax** of Pascal. The syntax defines exactly which words are needed in what order to achieve a desired effect. In the notation we have used for the syntax, the plain words are those that *have* to be there, forming a **template**, while the words in italics represent syntactical elements that are filled in each time.

There are other more formal ways of representing syntax, one of which uses so-called bubble diagrams. In this notation, the counting-loop would be described as in Figure 3.1. Such diagrams are useful when writing a compiler or resolving difficult syntactical points, but for the purposes of learning the language, the template approach is adequate. Nevertheless, the complete diagrams for Turbo Pascal are given in Appendix 2.

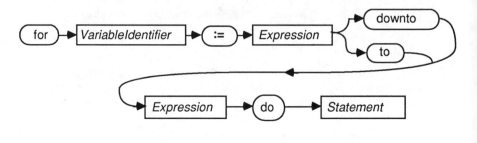

Figure 3.1 Syntax diagram for a for-loop.

Semantics

Whereas syntax gives the form of the Pascal construct, the semantics tell us how it works, or what it means. In most cases, it is sufficient to describe the semantics in clear English. Consider, for example, the description of the for-statement from Section 2.3:

> The action of the loop is to repeat the statements for each successive value of the loop variable within its given range.

This is followed by examples and further details of the special cases that may occur. In keeping with the tutorial style followed in this book, the semantics are discussed in the text and summarized at the end of each chapter. For a more succinct description of semantics, one should consult the Pascal Standard.

3.4 Understanding error messages

In the early stages of programming, many of the errors revolve around typing in the wrong thing. Unfortunately, compilers are excellent at spotting that something is wrong, but notoriously bad at identifying the cause! You are very likely to get cascading errors, where a simple mistake in one line causes havoc in

the next. Consider the following two lines from one of our programs, into which
I inserted **two** errors. The compiler has multiplied this to 20!

```
15    write(vwill change by dollies and cents: ');
              ^1        ^2                      ^3 ^4 ^5
(1)   Identifier not declared.
(2)   Error in variable.
(3)   Identifier not declared.
(4)   Illegal type of operand(s).
(5)   String constant must not exceed source line.

16    writeln((P * (12 - M)/12 * newrate/100 - (P * (12 - M)/12 *
oldrate)/100 : 7:2);
               ^1         ^2               ^3  ^4        ^5    ^6
       ^7 ^8 ^9
(1)   Unexpected symbol.
(1)   Identifier is not of appropriate class.
(2)   Error in variable.
(3)   Illegal type of operand(s).
(4)   Illegal type of operand(s).
(5)   Illegal type of operand(s).
(6)   Illegal type of operand(s).
(7)   Illegal type of operand(s).
(7)   Error in type of standard subprogram parameter.
(8)   Fixed point formatting allowed only for real types.
(8)   Error in type of standard subprogram parameter.
(8)   ')' expected.
(8)   Unexpected symbol.
(9)   'END' expected.
(9)   Unexpected symbol.
```

How are we to make sense of what is happening? Let's take it slowly. Line 15 is
shown as containing errors. Underneath it, there are little pointers and
numbers. The pointers indicate approximately where the error was spotted, and
the number refers to the list of possible causes given next.

    The first pointer highlights `vwill` as a possible error, and indeed it is. I
had meant to type `'will`. The next two errors are consequential, and number 4
starts off on a new problem: it thinks that a string begins here, does not find the
closing quote, and so starts complaining about the start of line 16. Although there
is an error in line 16, it is impossible to isolate among all the mistaken errors, so
the only thing to do is to correct line 15 and try again. The change is dramatic:

```
16    writeln((P * (12 - M)/12 * newrate/100 - (P * (12 - M)/12 *
              oldrate)/100 : 7:2);
                             ^1
(1)   ')' expected.
```

When the compiler reaches the colon for the field widths, it realizes that it had a
mismatched bracket pair. Of course, the actual spot where the bracket should be
inserted is a bit earlier, but we can work that out fairly easily.

So the moral of the story is not to be dismayed at having 100 error messages for your first program. Take it calmly, tackle lines one at a time initially, and watch the number come down to two or three. When this happens, you might then find that you cannot work out what is wrong. The line looks right to you, but the compiler is still complaining. To help you along, here are some typical mistakes you could make in the programs in this chapter, and their probable meaning.

1. **The disappearing program.** Sometimes a program produces no errors and then ends with the following:

    ```
    End of input encountered while reading a comment
    ```

    This is a helpful message. It tells you that you have started a comment with { and forgotten to close it, so the compiler ignored the rest of your program. Some compilers I know will merely say:

    ```
    Unexpected end of input
    ```

    which means the same thing.

2. **The missing semicolon.** One of the easiest errors for us to make, but the hardest for the compiler to work out, is a missing semicolon. Some compilers are good at finding them, others collapse, like this one:

    ```
    10    writeln('=============================');
          ^1                                ^2
    (1)   Unexpected symbol.
    (2)   'END' expected.
    (2)   Unexpected symbol.
    ```

    The writeln is unexpected because a semicolon was expected, but missing, on the previous line.

3. **END full stop.** Remember that the last END is followed by a full stop. If it isn't, then the error will be like this:

    ```
    16    END;
             ^1
    (1)   Unexpected symbol.
    ```

4. **Spelling!** Misspelled words are a common source of errors, and the compiler usually assumes that the identifier is a new one, and gives a message such as:

    ```
    9     writln('ZanBank Interest Calculation');
             ^1         ^2                          ^3
    (1)   Identifier not declared.
    (2)   Error in variable.
    (3)   ':=' expected.
    ```

These few examples show that finding errors improves with experience, and after a few days you should be able to decode your compiler's messages. Remember, that the important help the compiler gives you is detecting that there is an error and in finding the approximate position. The reason for the error is a puzzle for it, you and your instructor!

3.5   Case study – financial modelling

With the tools we have already, we can tackle a case study in simple financial modelling. ZanBank has a growth plan for savings which gives interest based on a novel formula. If the money is invested for a fixed period (say 10 years), then the interest is calculated as:

$$\frac{P \times (T+10\%) \times R}{100}$$

where P is the principal invested, T is the number of years, and R is the rate of interest. We would like to produce a diagram of how the principal will grow, given different investment periods, say from 5 to 15 years.

We could write a program similar to the temperature conversion one, listing the years versus the final principal. However, it would be much clearer for customers if the growth was shown in a graph. How do we draw a graph?

For financial modelling, a histogram is usually a good idea. We can show the number of years down the vertical axis, and draw the histogram going outwards, with dollies (the currency) on the x axis. The following is the effect we could achieve:

```
ZanBank Growth Plan for D1000 at 12.5%
==========================================

Years
  5 |****************** 1687.50
  6 |******************* 1825.00
  7 |********************* 1962.50
  8 |********************** 2100.00
  9 |*********************** 2237.50
 10 |************************* 2375.00
 11 |************************** 2512.50
 12 |*************************** 2650.00
 13 |***************************** 2787.50
 14 |****************************** 2925.00
 15 |****************************** 3062.50
       ==================================================
      +       +       +       +       +       +       +
           1000    2000    3000    4000    5000    6000
                           Dollies
```

In order to write a program to do this, we draw on all the techniques we have explored so far, and set up the following plan:

1. Decide how to print a single histogram for a given value *h*, including scaling *h* to fit on one line.

2. Express the interest formula in proper Pascal.

3. Set up a call to the histogram procedure with the calculated final principal as a parameter.

4. Put this in a loop over the number of possible investment periods

(years).

5. Design the write statements for the heading and final axis.

Put all together, the program is:

```
PROGRAM Interest (output);
   CONST
      P = 1000; {dollies}
      rate = 12.5; {%}
   VAR
      years : 5 ..15; {%}

   PROCEDURE axis;
      {Draws a horizontal axis labelled from
      0 to 6000 in steps of 1000}
      CONST
         gaps = 6;
         space = ' ';
      VAR
         D : 1..gaps;
         bar : 1..60; {10*gaps}
      BEGIN
         write(space:5);
         for bar := 1 to gaps*10 do write('=');
         writeln;
         write(space:4);
         for D := 1 to gaps do write('+',space:9);
         writeln('+');
         write(space:5);
         for D := 1 to gaps do write(D*1000:10);
         writeln;
         writeln(space:30,'Dollies');
      END;

   PROCEDURE histo(h : real);
      {Draws a histogram bar for values
      between 1 and 8000, scaled by 100}
      VAR
         star : 1..80;
      BEGIN
         write(years:2,'  |');
         for star := 1 to round(h/100) do
            write('*');
         writeln;
      END;

BEGIN
   writeln('ZanBank Growth Plan for D',P:1,' at 12.5%');
   writeln('========================================');
   writeln;
   writeln('Years');

   for years := 5 to 15 do
      histo(P * 1.1*years* rate/100+ P);
   Axis;
END.
```

The program makes good use of constants to achieve a certain degree of reusability, which is explored in the problems below.

WHAT WE HAVE LEARNT

In this chapter we saw how programs can be broken up into **procedures** *which serve a particular purpose. These procedures can be reused in other programs, and they can be generalised by adding* **parameters**. *We looked at* **value** *parameters for* **numbers** *and* **characters** *and wrote procedures with up to 5 different parameters, which were then called with a variety of values.*

We discussed the basic syntax of Pascal, defining **keywords**, **identifiers**, **predefined identifiers** *and* **comments**. *We looked at the minefield of syntax error messages, and how to negotiate it, and ended up with a case study which used all the features covered so far.*

The processes employed in this chapter were:

1. *Tackle it from the top.*
2. *Start simply, then elaborate.*
3. *Generalize, then specialize.*
4. *Adapt what we have already.*
5. *Look for work for loops to do.*

QUIZ

1. Is a procedure call a statement?

2. Is writeln a keyword?

3. Give three places where comments are useful.

4. The `VaryBox` procedure was defined as

    ```
    PROCEDURE VaryBox (width, depth : integer;
                       hori, verti, price : char);
    ```

    How would we call it to print empty boxes (such as labels)?

5. Why was the `price` parameter of `VaryBox` declared as char and not integer?

6. Which of the following are not valid identifiers?

    ```
    ReduceToOne              LastLimit
    t                        rectangles
    FirstValue               second_value
    1stvalue                 Hello!
    X                        MI5
    Maxsides                 end
    water-level              Number of lines
    ```

7. Given the declaration of the `Mountain` procedure, namely:

    ```
    PROCEDURE Mountain (size : integer; symbol:char);
    ```

    decide which of the following calls are valid or not, giving reasons:

    ```
    Mountain (10,10);
    Mountain (8, '8');
    Mountain (6);
    ```

8. Can a comment extend over more than one line?

9. Given the following declarations, which ones would cause the compiler to report errors and why?

```
CONST
    max      = 10;
    K        = 1,000;
    initials = 'JFK'
    Prize    = D50;
    2ndPrize = D25;

VAR
    maximum    : 0..max;
    i, j, k    : integer;
    start, end: char;
```

10. Draw a syntax diagram corresponding to the definition of an identifier given in Section 3.3.

PROBLEMS

3.1 **Printing names** Write procedures to print out the letters of the alphabet that form your name, in a large format using asterisks. Each letter is formed on a 7 by 9 grid and drawn downwards, so that when the letters are printed out underneath each other, the name can be turned sideways and read. For example, for William, we need five procedures, one to do each of the letters W, i, l, a and m and the letters might look like this:

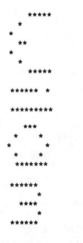

Then write a program to call the procedures in the right order to print your name.

3.2 **Labels** Adapt the program in Example 3.2 to print three labels with your name and address across the page, and do this 8 times to fill the page. If you line the output up carefully, you can photocopy this onto sticky labels.

3.3   **Clearer tables** The conversion table of Example 3.1 is not quite right because the values increase across the page, rather than down, which is more normal. Can you work out how to change the program so as to print the values increasing in columns?

3.4   **Times tables** In the olden days, exercise books used to have multiplication tables printed neatly on the back. These would be arranged 3 across and 4 down, with each row being of the form:

```
    4 times table       5 times table       6 times table
    1 x   4 =    4       1 x   5 =    5       1 x   6 =    6
    2 x   4 =    8       2 x   5 =   10       2 x   6 =   12
    3 x   4 =   12       3 x   5 =   15       3 x   6 =   18
    4 x   4 =   16       4 x   5 =   20       4 x   6 =   24
    5 x   4 =   20       5 x   5 =   25       5 x   6 =   30
    6 x   4 =   24       6 x   5 =   30       6 x   6 =   36
    7 x   4 =   28       7 x   5 =   35       7 x   6 =   42
    8 x   4 =   32       8 x   5 =   40       8 x   6 =   48
    9 x   4 =   36       9 x   5 =   45       9 x   6 =   54
   10 x   4 =   40      10 x   5 =   50      10 x   6 =   60
   11 x   4 =   44      11 x   5 =   55      11 x   6 =   66
   12 x   4 =   48      12 x   5 =   60      12 x   6 =   72
```

Write a program which makes good use of procedures and parameters to print out a complete set of all the 12 multiplication tables.

3.5   **Timetable** It is always useful to have a blank timetable to fill in for one's lectures. Write a program which will print out such a timetable, with Monday to Friday across the top, and the hours 8 to 15 down the left. The timetable should have suitable borders.

Changing the State

4.1 Declarations

A Pascal program, as we saw before, consists of:

- declarations, and

- statements.

The purpose of the declarations is to associate identifiers with the objects that are going to be used in the statements. There are five kinds of declaration, each of which is introduced by a special keyword, namely:

```
CONST
TYPE
VAR
PROCEDURE
FUNCTION
```

The first three introduce constant, type and variable declarations and the next two define procedures and functions. In Standard Pascal, there is a strict ordering of these sections, and the first three can occur only once each.

We have already seen three of the sections in our programs so far. To recall, the start of the program in the case study went like this:

```
PROGRAM Interest (output);
   CONST
      P = 1000; {dollies}
      rate = 12.5; {%}
   VAR
      years : 5 ..15; {%}

   PROCEDURE axis;
      {Draws a horizontal axis labelled from 0 to 6000 in
steps of 1000}
      CONST
         gaps = 6;
         space = ' ';

      VAR
         D : 1..gaps;
         bar : 1..60; {10*gaps}

      BEGIN
      ...
```

In this section we consider variable declarations in detail, together with assignment to variables and reading in values. Type declarations are covered in Chapters 9 and 10 and there are more details about procedures and functions in Chapters 8 and 13.

4.2   Variables

Put simply, a program's function is to transform some input data into some output results. In so doing, it moves through various states, representing steps in the transformation process. A fundamental need in computer programming, therefore, is to record the state of a process, and to be able to change that state. In the programs so far, state was:

- **maintained** in loop variables and parameters
- **changed** via for-loops and procedure calls.

The loop variable acquired different values as the loop progressed, and these values could actually be used to alter the effect of other statements. The parameter could acquire a different value each time the procedure was called. This idea of different values being represented by the same identifier at different stages in the execution of a program is generalized in the concept of a variable:

> A **variable** denotes a value that may change during execution. Every variable has associated with it an identifier and a type. The type determines the range of values of the variable and governs how the variable may be used.

Variables are declared in VAR declarations. After the keyword VAR, any number of variables may be declared, with their associated types, as in:

```
Variable declaration

VAR
    identifiers : type;
    identifiers : type;
       . . .
    identifiers : type;
```

If there is more than one identifier for a type, then they are separated by commas. The type may be one of the five predefined types, which are:

```
integer
real
char
boolean
text
```

or a user-defined type, as described in Chapters 9 and 10.

If the type is integer or char (for character), then we can indicate the actual range of values needed instead, using a **subrange** as follows:

```
Subrange type

lower..upper
```

Thus, instead of specifying:

```
VAR
    height : integer;
```

we try to be specific, as in:

```
VAR
    height : 0..5;   {metres}
```

It is a good idea to use a comment to give any other useful information such as physical units, currencies and so on.

For this chapter, we shall only deal with integers and characters. Within this limitation, examples of declarations are:

```
VAR
    side        : 1..3;
    grade       : 'A'..'F';
    line        : 1..10;
```

```
temperature : -50..60;     {in degrees Celsius}
initial     : char;
oldweight,
newweight    : 0..250;     {in kilograms}
x, y, z     : integer;     {unknowns}
```

It is worthwhile keeping declarations neat and tidy, with the identifiers and types
lined up.

4.3 Assignment

Having declared a variable, we can now use an assignment to give it a value. The
assignment statement has the form:

Assignment statement

```
variable  :=  expression;
```

The effect of an **assignment statement** is to evaluate the expression and to assign
the resulting value to the variable indicated by the identifier. The symbol which
indicates the assignment is read 'becomes'. Thus we can write:

```
temperature := 24;
```

and read it 'temperature becomes 24'. The value of the expression is 24, and
this is assigned to the variable temperature. In the next sequence:

```
oldweight := 65;
newweight := oldweight - 5;
```

oldweight is assigned the value 65, and this is then used to calculate the value
for the variable newweight which is 60.

To test that you understand this, what will be the values of p, q and r at the
end of the following sequence of assignments?

```
p := 8;
q := 5;
r := q;
q := q + 1;
p := p + q - 2 * r;
```

It is always useful in these cases to examine what is going on by simulating what
the computer would do, keeping track of the values of variables as each statement
is executed. We can construct such a 'trace' for the above statements by
recording each variable's values in a column, using ~ to mean that a value has not
yet been assigned.

statement	p	q	r
	~	~	~
p := 8;	8	~	~
q := 5;	8	5	~
r := q;	8	5	5
q := q + 1;	8	6	5
p := p + q - 2 * r;	4	6	5

Thus, the answers are 4, 6 and 5 respectively for p, q and r.

Some points about variables

The variables in a program together hold a record of the **state** of the program at any one instant. Reasoning about state, and its correctness, is difficult, so it is generally good practice to keep the number of variables to a minimum. However, variables are required when a state needs to be remembered for later use, or for transmitting values between statements. One way of keeping the number of variables to manageable proportions is to ensure that they are declared specifically in the procedures that need them, rather than all together at the start of a program. Two problems which illustrate the use of variables rather well are now discussed.

EXAMPLE 4.1 Swapping_____

Problem   The values in two variables need to be interchanged.

Solution   Write some assignment statements.

Algorithm   Suppose the variables are called x and y. A first stab at an answer might be:

```
x := y;
y := x;
```

What happens here? If x has the value 5 and y has the value 9, then a trace reveals:

statement	x	y
	5	9
x := y;	9	9
y := x;	9	9

The result is incorrect. The problem occurs in the first statement, when the value of y is put in x causing the original value of x to be lost. In order for the swap to work correctly, the value of x must first be copied, so that it can subsequently be used for setting up y. To do this, an additional variable is needed. Since it is only of temporary use, it will be called temp. The correct sequence of statements is:

```
temp  := x;
x    := y;
y    := temp;
```

and the trace would be:

statement	x	y	temp
	5	9	~
temp:= x;	5	9	5
x := y;	9	9	5
y := temp;	9	5	5

EXAMPLE 4.2   Train travel

Problem   A train starts with an acceleration of 0.5 m/s², which decreases uniformly to zero in 2 minutes. It then travels with uniform speed for 3 minutes, after which it is brought to rest by the brakes with a constant deceleration of 1 m/s². This is shown in the diagram:

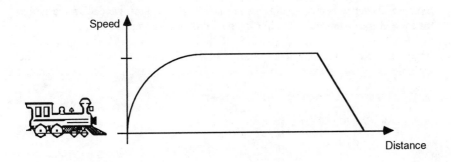

We want to find out how far the train travelled in kilometres.

Solution. Although we have been given precise figures for this journey, the problem could well come up again with different values, so we shall generalize, and refer to the various times, distances, velocities and accelerations as follows:

A, R The acceleration and deceleration rates.
$T_1\ V_1\ D_1$ The time, velocity and distance achieved at the point when acceleration stops.
$T_2\ D_2$ The time, and distance achieved at the point when deceleration starts.
D_3 The distance achieved when deceleration stops.

Given this, we can use the usual motion equations to get to the velocity and distance over the period of acceleration as:

$$V_1 = \frac{A\,T_1}{2}$$

$$D_1 = \frac{A\,T_2^2}{3}$$

The distance D_2 covered at constant speed depends on the velocity reached, and is simply $V_1 T_2$. For the final distance of deceleration, we have:

$$D_3 = \frac{V_2^2}{2R}$$

Algorithm   Armed with these equations, we simply have to calculate the three distances and add them up. Using Pascal identifiers corresponding to those defined above, the algorithm would be:

> **Train travel**
> Calculate V1 and D1 with t = 120.
> Calculate D2 based on V1.
> Calculate D3 based on V2 and R.
> The distance is D1 + D2 + D3.

Because D_2 depends on V_1, and just to make things clearer, we declare variables for each of the distances and do the calculations step by step.

Program   Note that constants cannot have expressions, so T1s and T2s must be variables.

```
PROGRAM TrainTravel (output);
  CONST
    A = 0.5;   {m/s/s}
    R = 1.0;   {m/s/s}
    T1 = 2;    {min}
    T2 = 3;    {min}
    kilo = 1000;

  VAR
    D, D1, D2, D3  : real;  {metres}
    V1             : real;  {m/s}
    T1s, T2s  : real;  {seconds}

  BEGIN
    writeln('****** Train travel ******');
    writeln;
    writeln(A:3:1,' m/s/s for ',T1:1,' mins, ');
    writeln('constant speed for ',T2:1, ' mins, ');
    writeln(' and ',R:3:1, ' m/s/s to rest');
    writeln;
    T1s := T1 * 60;
    T2s := T2 * 60;
    V1 := 0.5 * A * T1s;
    D1 := (A * T1s * T1s) / 3;
    D2 := V1 * T2s;
    D3 := V1 * V1 / (2 * R);
    D := (D1 + D2 + D3) / kilo;
    writeln ('The journey covers ', D:1:1, ' km');
  END.
```

Testing Running the program gives:

```
****** Train travel ******

0.5 m/s/s for 2 mins,
constant speed for 3 mins,
and 1.0 m/s/s to rest

The journey covers 8.3 km
```

We can verify by calculation that the answer is correct.

Initializing

When variables are declared, no value is specified for them. Thus, variables must always be initialized by the program before being used. This point is illustrated by the traces in Section 3.2 above, where variables which had not been touched had tildes (~) to indicate that they were undefined. The importance of remembering this property is brought out in Example 4.4.

Global and local variables

The variables that are declared at the program level are termed **global** and are available for use by all procedures within the program. If a global variable is changed by some procedure by mistake – perhaps because different people were writing different procedures – then errors will occur that will be difficult to trace. A procedure that changes a global variable is said to have a **side-effect**, and side-effects are generally a bad thing. Thus we would like to keep our procedures **self-contained** and limit, if not entirely avoid, side-effects.

At present, we have not learnt enough about Pascal to eliminate side-effects, but we can keep them to a minimum by declaring variables specifically in the procedures that need them, rather than all together at the start of a program. These variables are called **local** variables, and one can rely upon them being altered only by the statements within the procedure itself.

Using parameters does not in itself reduce the need for global variables, since one still needs to send a value into the procedure, and this could be in a variable. However, defining procedures with parameters makes them more self-contained and less reliant on globals.

4.4 Input with read and readln

A program will most often need to acquire values for its variables from the outside world. Such values form the **data** for the program and could consist of tables stored on disk, replies to questions or just lists of values to be typed in. Values for variables are acquired by means of the read and readln statements.

The form of read and readln statements

The three general forms of these statements are:

```
┌─────────────────────────────────────────────────────────┐
│  Input statements                                       │
├─────────────────────────────────────────────────────────┤
│     read (list of variables);                           │
│     readln (list of variables);                         │
│     readln;                                             │
└─────────────────────────────────────────────────────────┘
```

The list of variables consists of identifiers separated by commas, as in:

```
read(myweight, yourweight, temperature);
```

Data must be supplied which conforms with the types required. Thus, for this statement, suitable data would be:

```
65    70    23
```

The read statement picks off values to put into each variable in its list, and is quite happy to skip over spaces and blank lines when looking for a number. It will not usually skip over anything else, so that, using the ordinary read statement, we cannot put other information between numbers, such as:

```
65kgs        70kgs       23degrees C
```

The readln statement works just like the read statement except that when it has filled up all its variables, it looks for the end of line, skipping everything in its path.

EXAMPLE 4.3   Data-driven modelling _____

Problem   The directors of ZanBank were delighted with your growth plan program (Case study 3.5). However, they have just changed the interest rate, and anticipate that it will change again. They also feel it would be helpful to illustrate growth for amounts other than D1000.

Solution   Adapt the program so that the values for *P* and the rate can be read in.

Program   The reading in can be done right at the beginning, so that the specific values can be incorporated in the headings. Notice how we use a write-readln sequence to get the questions and answers neatly on a line. The Axis and Histo procedures remain exactly the same, so we do not reproduce them here.

```
PROGRAM Interest (output);
   VAR
      years : 5..15;
      P : integer; {dollies}
      rate : real; {%}
```

```
    PROCEDURE axis;
        {Draws a horizontal axis labelled from 0 to 6000 in
steps of 1000}
        ...
        END;

    PROCEDURE histo(h : real);
        {Draws a histogram bar for values between 1 and 8000,
scaled by 100}
        ...
        END;

    PROCEDURE GetValues;
        BEGIN
            writeln('ZanBank Growth Plan');
            writeln('=================');
            writeln;
            write('What is the current rate? ');
            readln(rate);
            write('How much is to be invested? ');
            readln(P);
            writeln;
        END;

    BEGIN
        GetValues;
        writeln('ZanBank Growth Plan for D',P:1,' at ',
                rate:4:1,'%');
        writeln('=======================================');
        writeln;
        writeln('Years');

        for years := 5 to 15 do
            histo(P * 1.1*years* rate/100+ P);
        Axis;
        END.
```

Testing The beginning of a typical run would be:

```
ZanBank Growth Plan
===================

What is the current rate? 12.0
How much is to be invested? 2000

ZanBank Growth Plan for D2000 at 12.0%
======================================
```

Now, what would happen if we put in a very large amount? The calculations would proceed, but the histogram would not be able to cope. Thus, with data input, we need to check that it is valid for our application. This point is taken up in the next chapter.

EXAMPLE 4.4 Summing a list of numbers

Problem There is a list of numbers that needs to be summed.

Solution It is quite straightforward to read the numbers into the computer, adding each one in turn to a total. The problem is how to know when the end of the numbers has been reached. There are actually four ways:

- **state in advance** how many numbers there must be and keep a running count;
- **precede the data by a count** of how many numbers there actually are, and keep a running count;
- put a **special terminating value** at the end of the numbers, such as zero or 999;
- make use of an **end-of-file property** to mark the end of the numbers.

The first two methods are applicable to counting-loops, since they rely on the number of numbers being known before reading starts. In the next two methods the number of numbers is not relevant; rather, the reading stops when a certain condition is achieved. These two are applicable to conditional loops, and are discussed in Sections 4.4 and 5.3 respectively.

Of the two methods for counting-loops, the second is more general, since the same program will be able to read in 10 numbers, or 55, or 1800, with just the data being changed.

Algorithm

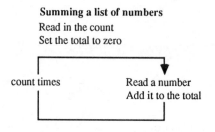

Summing a list of numbers
Read in the count
Set the total to zero

count times

Read a number
Add it to the total

The algorithm is fairly simple, but has one important feature: the total must be initialized to zero before adding commences.

Program In the program header, the parentheses now include `input` as well as `output`, since the program is going to be reading and writing.

```
PROGRAM Summation1 (input, output);
  CONST
    max = 10000;
  VAR
    count,
    i     : 1..max;
    total,
    number : integer;   {anything}
  BEGIN
    writeln('****** Summing numbers ******');
    read(count);
    total := 0;
    FOR i := 1 to count do begin
```

```
      read(number);
      total := total + number;
   END;
   writeln;
   writeln('The total is ', total);
END.
```

Testing   If this program was run, and we knew how to put in the data, then the screen might have the following on it:

```
****** Summing numbers ******
7   85   65   43   90   12   55   50
The total is 407
```

The plain type indicates the values that are typed in; bold type indicates output from the program. The problem is that not all users of a program will know how the data has to be entered, and therefore the program should give some guidance. Let's examine this issue in full.

4.5 Interactive programs

An **interactive program** is one that is run with the user sitting in front of a terminal and entering data as necessary. This is how most programs are run these days, and even large programs will start off with a bit of dialogue before starting on their computations. In interactive mode, it is the computer program, rather than the user, that is in control all the time. The program decides what needs to be read, and what will be written. The only way the user can alter the course of the program is by responding to set questions. In particular, the user can't just ask the program 'What should I do next?' or 'How do you want your data?'. It is the responsibility of the programmer to provide all the necessary information to guide the user and to anticipate any problems. As we learn more about Pascal, so this issue will be taken up again and again. Meanwhile, we can look at some basic techniques of dialogue and amend the summation program accordingly.

Dialogue

Dialogue with a user via a terminal should be precise, but friendly. Instructions should be quite clear, yet should not take up too much space. The reason for this is that it is not helpful if the instructions disappear off the top of the screen before the user has had time to respond to them. There are many ways of issuing instructions and choice depends on personal taste, but the following list of guidelines is a good start:

1.   **Introduction.** A program should introduce itself, so that the user knows it has started running. If there are different versions of a program, the version name or number should appear in the introduction. Examples are:

```
****** Summing numbers ******
****** Summing numbers (Version 2 - with dialogue) ******
```

The title of the program should remain on the screen throughout its lifetime, so that using the bottom few lines in a window is attractive for this purpose. We would say:

```
window (1, 22, 80, 25);
writeln('***** Summing numbers ****);
```

2.   **Prompts.** Data can be requested by a prompt being written out on the screen first. If the answer expected is a single item, then a `write-readln` sequence enables the answer to be written on the same line as the prompt. The user enters the reply ending up with a return. As an example:

```
write('How many numbers (1..10000)? ');
readln(count);
```

would produce:

How many numbers (1..10000)? 7

The return has two functions: it serves to terminate the number (a space would too) and it preserves the neatness of the dialogue. To coordinate the statements with the intended data format therefore, we recommend a readln rather than a read at this point.

3.   **Limits.** If a limit applies on the value to be read, then this should be made quite plain, as in the above example. It is equally helpful if the fact that there is no limit is also communicated, as in the next example.

4.   **Avoid 'screen creep'.** Bulk data should not be subject to individual requests. Thus, if a list of items is required, there need not be a prompt for each item, just one for the list. Further, to free the user from counting them, a writeln can be issued after the list, rather than the program waiting for a readln. So, reading numbers could go like this:

```
writeln('Type in ', count, ' numbers (any size).');

FOR i := 1 to count do begin
  read(number);
     ...etc....
END;

writeln; {To stop the typing}
writeln('That''s enough, thanks.');
```

which would run as:

Type in 7 numbers (any size).
65 34 -22 90 19 87 -15
That's enough, thanks.

5.   **Keeping track.** It may sometimes be more helpful to indicate which number is being read in, with a prompt inside the loop:

```
writeln('Type in ', count, ' numbers (any size).');
FOR i := 1 to count do begin
```

```
        write(i:4,': ');   readln(number);
            . . . etc . . .
    END;

    writeln('That''s enough, thanks.');
```

which would run as:

```
Type in 7 numbers (any size).
    1:  65
    2:  34
    3:  -22
    4:  90
    5:  19
    6:  87
    7:  -15
That's enough, thanks.
```

EXAMPLE 4.5 Summation revisited

Given all this advice, the summation program can be greatly improved:

```
PROGRAM Summation2 (input, output);
    VAR
        count , i      :1..10000; {say}
        total, number : integer;   {anything}

    BEGIN
        writeln('****** Summing numbers ',
                ' (Version 2 - with dialogue)******');
        write('How many numbers   (1..10000)? ');
        readln(count);
        writeln('Type in the ', count, ' numbers (any size)');
        total := 0;
        FOR i := 1 to count do begin
            write(i:4,': ');   read(number);
            total := total + number;
        END;
        writeln;
        writeln('That''s enough, thanks.');
        writeln('The total is ', total);
    END.
```

and a complete run would look like this:

```
****** Summing numbers (Version 2 - with dialogue) ******
How many numbers (1..10000)? 12
Type in the 12 numbers (any size).
    1:  65    2:  34    3:  -22    4:  90    5:  19    6:  87    7:  -15
    8:  0     9:  100  10:  6    11:  -1   12:  77
That's enough, thanks.
The total is 440
```

WHAT WE HAVE LEARNT

We learnt how to declare **variables** *in a program, and explored two different ways of changing their values:* **assignment**, *and* **reading**. *Through specific and general examples we practised how to choose and declare variables. Sometimes there are many variables (the train example) but they each get used once only, and in other programs there are only a few variables (summation) whose values are continually changing.*

We considered how to read in a **sequence** *of values and were able to make use of the first two of four suggestions, leaving the other two till later. Finally, we considered the important issue of* **interaction** *with the user, and looked at a list of* **guidelines** *for keeping input and output neat and readable on the screen.*

Programming processes used in this chapter are:

1. Temporary variables for keeping the state.

2. Making programs data driven.

3. Reading sequences of fixed numbers of data items.

4. Prompting users for data.

5. Avoiding screen creep.

QUIZ

1. Set up suitable declarations for the following variables: a roman numeral, a distance in track events in the Olympics, the weight of flour in a supermarket, the age of a child in a school, minutes in an hour, a bank balance in dollies.

2. Write assignment statements to interchange two times represented as three variables each – hours, minutes and seconds.

3. What is screen creep, and how can it be avoided?

4. Consider the program in Example 4.3 (data-driven modelling) and see whether constants could be introduced to make it easier to understand and modify.

5. What advantages does a write–readln sequence have over other options for interactive input?

6. Why did the program in Example 4.5 (summation revisited) use a write–read sequence instead?

7. Given the following statements and data, what will be printed out?

```
VAR                           Data:
   i, j, k : integer;          67    56
BEGIN                          98    91
   read(i);                    11    33
   readln;
   read(j);
   readln(k);
   writeln(i,j,k);
END;
```

8.   Investigate what happens on your computer system if you use a variable without first initializing it.

9.   What do you think should happen?

10.   If one wanted to read in amounts such as 65kg or 7s, how could the data be set up so that this could be done simply?

PROBLEMS

4.1   **Postage stamps.** Zanyland Mail has decided to have machines that print out postage stamps up to a maximum value of D99.99. The stamps have a basic design as follows:

```
---------------
|   ZANYLAND   |
|    D14.30    |
|    BY AIR    |
---------------
```

There are three zones of postage rates as follows:

A   50c per 10 grams

B   90c per 10 grams

C   D1.10 per 10 grams

and the postage is doubled for airmail. Write a program which prompts the user for the mass of an article, the zone to which it is going and whether it should go by air or not, and then prints out the correct stamp.

4.2   **Conversions.** Adapt the program for Problem 2.8 so as to read in the limits required for the table.

4.3   **Fibonacci.** The Fibonacci series consists of a series of numbers in which each is the sum of the two that precede it, that is:

1 1 2 3 5 8 13 21 34 55 ...

Write a program to print the first 50 terms of the series.

4.4   **Average ages.** A Cub Pack has 24 boys grouped in 4 'sixes'. The boys are aged 7 to 11. Write a program using the interactive methods explained in Example 4.5 to work out the average age per six for a group of 24 boys.

4.5   **Fuel consumption.** Adapt the program written for Problem 2.2 so as to read in all the values that may vary.

4.6   **Weighted averages.** A computer science course has three parts to it: a test, an assignment and an examination, which are weighted at 20%, 30% and 50% respectively. Write a program which prompts the user for the marks (out of 100) that were obtained for each part, and prints out the final mark using the weightings.

Controlling the Flow

5.1 Selection with if-then-else

Two methods of changing the values of variables have been covered so far, that is assignment and reading in. We now consider how to check the values in variables, and choose alternative actions based on the result of the check. Pascal has two **selection** statements known as the **if-statement** and the **case-statement**. The first is covered here, and the second in Section 5.4.

Form of the if-statement

The general form of the if-statement is:

```
If-statement

IF condition THEN statement
   ELSE statement;
```

where a condition, in its simplest form, consists of a comparison between two items or expressions of the same type, using one of the following six operations:

=	equals
<>	not equals
<	less than
<=	less than or equals
>	greater than
>=	greater than or equals

Examples of simple conditions are:

```
speed > speedlimit
age <= 16
year = 1066
day <> 29
initial = 'J'
```

More complex conditions are covered in Section 6.3.

In the if-statement we refer to the statement following the `then` as the **then-part** and similarly to the statement following the `else` as the **else-part**. The whole if-statement is executed as follows. First, the condition is evaluated. If this result is true, then the then-part is executed, and the else-part is skipped. If the result is false, the then-part is skipped and the else-part is executed. A simple example would be:

```
if number >= 0 then writeln('Positive')
            else writeln('Negative');
```

In the general form of the if-statement, the else-part is given in italics. This means that it is optional and the statement can be used in an `if-then` version. For example,

```
if day = 25 then writeln('Christmas, Hooray');
```

A consequence of this option is that if the else-part is present, the statement before the keyword `else` must not have a semicolon at the end. The reason for this is to enable Pascal to distinguish between if-then and if-then-else statements.

EXAMPLE 5.1 Summing three ways _____

Problem   A list of numbers needs to be summed, and separate sums kept of the positive and negative numbers as well.

Solution   Start with the summation program from the previous chapter. Add in two new totalling variables, and use an if-statement to cause values to be added to one or the other.

Algorithm   The loop in algorithm form is:

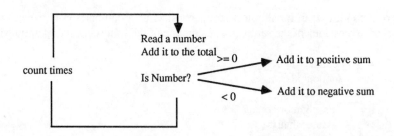

Program   Because the program is now more complex than Summation, we shall break it up into procedures.

```
PROGRAM ThreeSums (input, output);
   VAR
      i, count  : 1..10000;   {say}
      Total,
      PosTotal,
      NegTotal  : integer;

   PROCEDURE Initialize;
      BEGIN
         writeln('******Three sums *****');
         write('How many numbers (1..10000)? ');
         readln(count);
         writeln('Type in the ', count:1,
                 ' numbers (any size)');
         Total := 0;
         PosTotal := 0;
         NegTotal := 0;
      END; {Initialize}

   PROCEDURE ReadandTotal;
      VAR  number : integer;
      BEGIN
         write(i,': ');   read(number);
         Total := Total + number;
         if number > 0 then PosTotal := PosTotal + number
                       else NegTotal := NegTotal + number;
      END;   {ReadandTotal}

   PROCEDURE Finalize;
      BEGIN
         writeln('That''s enough, thanks.');
         writeln('The total is ', Total);
         writeln('The positive total is ', PosTotal,
                 ' and ','the negative total is ',
                 NegTotal);
      END;   {Finalize}

   BEGIN
      Initialize;
      FOR i:= 1 to count do
        ReadandTotal;
      Finalize;
   END.
```

Testing   A complete run would look like this:

```
***** Three sums *****
How many numbers (1..10000)? 12
Type in the 12 numbers (any size)
    1 : 65      2 : 34      3 : -22     4 : 90      5 : 19
    6 : 87      7 : -15     8 : 0       9 : 100    10 : 6
   11: -1      12 : 77
That's enough, thanks.
The total is 440
The positive total is 478 and the negative total is -38
```

Compound statements

There may be times when several statements are needed in the then- or else-parts
of an if-statement. These must be enclosed in `begin-end`, as was done with for-
loops. Such a group of statements enclosed in `begin-end` is called a **compound
statement**, and may be used in place of a statement. The form of a compound
statement is therefore:

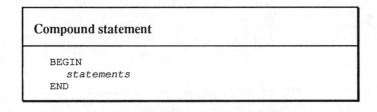

```
Compound statement

    BEGIN
        statements
    END
```

Suppose that in the `Threesums` program, it is also required to know how many
positive and negative numbers were read. Then two more counters are needed,
and, to each part of the if-statement, an extra statement is added to do the
counting. Thus, the if-statement would become:

```
if number >= 0 then begin
    PosTotal := PosTotal + number;
    PosCount := PosCount + 1;
end else begin
    NegTotal := NegTotal + number;
    NegCount := NegCount + 1;
end;
```

Successive else-ifs

Sometimes, there are more than two possibilities that need to be considered. One
way in which this is done is by **successive else-ifs**. The condition of the first if-
statement eliminates one case, leaving the rest to the else-part. The else-part in its
turn introduces another if-statement which selects out another condition and
leaves the rest to its else-part, and so on. This is illustrated nicely in an example
that prints out a class of pass for various ranges of marks, thus:

```
if marks >= 75 then writeln('First') else
if marks >= 70 then writeln('Upper second') else
if marks >= 60 then writeln('Lower second') else
```

```
if marks >= 50 then writeln('Third') else
                    writeln('Fail');
```

Notice a few points about this statement:

- The conditions are carefully ordered, so that each eliminates a certain range of marks. Thus, the line that writes out a third class for anything over 50 will only be reached when it has already been established that the mark is under 60.

- The last class, fail, is given for all the rest of the marks, and does not need a condition.

- Layout of successive if-statements is important, and should try to reflect the pattern of conditions as much as possible.

A secondary consideration is that the most frequently occurring conditions should be checked first. If it is more likely that people will fail, then it will be marginally more efficient to arrange the order of the conditions thus:

```
if mark < 50 then writeln('Fail') else
if mark < 60 then writeln('Third') else
if mark < 70 then writeln('Lower second') else
if mark < 75 then writeln('Upper second') else
                    writeln('First');
```

EXAMPLE 5.2 The highest number

Problem   Find the largest in a sequence of numbers.

Solution   A program can read in the numbers one at a time, remembering the highest so far, and updating this if necessary. We note that negative numbers should be catered for as well.

Algorithm   This is a very interesting algorithm, because it is based on induction. We start by assuming that we have found the highest of *n* numbers. Then the *n*+1th number is read. To find the highest of the *n*+1 numbers, all that needs to be done is to compare the new number to the highest so far, and if it is higher, to replace the highest. This process can then be repeated for as long as required.

The question is, how does the process start? Well, the highest number of a sequence that is one long must be just that number. So we start by reading in one number, make it the highest and proceed from there. The algorithm is:

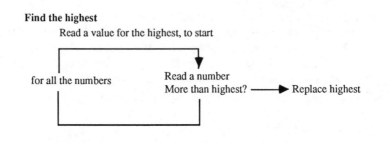

Find the highest
Read a value for the highest, to start

for all the numbers
Read a number
More than highest? ──────▶ Replace highest

Program

```
PROGRAM Highestvalue (input,output);
   VAR
      highest,
      number : integer;
      i, n    : 0..maxint;
   BEGIN
      writeln('*****  Finding the highest number *****');
      write('How many numbers (1 or more)? ');
      readln (n);
      writeln('Type them in');
      read(highest);
      for i := 2 to n do begin
         read(number);
         if number > highest then highest := number;
      end;
      writeln;  writeln('That''s enough, thanks');
      writeln('The highest number was ', highest);
   END.
```

Testing   It is a good idea to test such an algorithm with the first number being the highest, then with the last, and then with one in the middle. Another test would be to have all the numbers except one equal. This is left up to the reader.

5.2   The case-statement

The if-statement is a two-way selection statement based on conditions. However, if there are several simple tests for given values, successive else-if statements can become unwieldy. Pascal provides for so-called **keyed selection** with the case-statement. The form of the case-statement is:

Case-statement

```
CASE key-expression  of
   key-values : statement;
   key-values : statement;
      . . .
   key-values : statement;
END;   {CASE}
```

The case-statement considers the value of the key-expression and then endeavours to find a match among the lists of key-values. If a match is found, then the corresponding statement is executed, after which control passes to the end of the case-statement. If a match is not found, an error should occur. (Some Pascal systems do not give an error, but they should.)

The key-expressions must produce a value which is an integer, character or enumerated type (as defined in Chapter 10). It may not be real. The key-values are lists of constants of the same type as the key-expression, and there may be one or more key-values for a given statement. The key-values do not have to be in any order but may occur only once.

As an example, consider the little jingle which gives the number of days in a month:

> Thirty days hath September, April, June and November.
> All the rest have thirty-one, excepting February alone,
> Which has but twenty-eight days clear,
> And twenty-nine in each leap year.

If we assume that the following declarations and read statement have been made:

```
VAR
   month : 1..12;
   days  : 1..31;

BEGIN
   write('What month (1..12)? ');
   readln (month);
```

then a case-statement can be used to look at the month and set `days` to the appropriate value as follows (ignoring leap years):

```
CASE month of
   9, 4, 6, 11              : days := 30;
   1, 3, 5, 7, 8, 10, 12 : days := 31;
   2                        : days := 28;
END; {CASE}
```

As always, the statement mentioned in the form can be a compound statement and include several statements. This is needed to establish the correct day for February, taking account of leap years. Instead of doing a calculation of the year (divisible by 4 and so on), we simply ask whether the year is leap or not. (In the next chapter we consider how best to do the calculation.) With the extra declaration:

```
VAR
   ans : char;
```

the case-statement now becomes:

```
CASE month of
   9, 4, 6, 11              : days := 30;
   1, 3, 5, 7, 8, 10, 12 : days := 31;
   2  : begin
           write('Is it a leap year?'); readln(ans);
           if ans = 'Y'
           then days := 29
           else days := 28;
        end;
END; {CASE}
```

Multiple key values

In the previous example, the key was a single variable, and it mapped directly on to the values. Sometimes, there are many values for each statement, and there is a simple way of adjusting them so that there is only one per statement. For example, suppose that given an examination mark, it is required to set a symbol depending on the multiple of ten, with anything over 80 being A, over 70 being B, and so on down to anything under 40 being F. The case-statement to achieve such a mapping is:

```
VAR
   mark   : 0..100;
   symbol : 'A'..'F';

CASE trunc(mark / 10) of
   10, 9, 8    : symbol := 'A';
   7           : symbol := 'B';
   6           : symbol := 'C';
   5           : symbol := 'D';
   4           : symbol := 'E';
   3, 2, 1, 0  : symbol := 'F';
END; {CASE}
```

This is the clearest and most efficient way of solving this problem, but it is not the only way. The same effect could be achieved using successive else-ifs and some calculations on characters as described in Section 6.4. However, it is usually easier to see what is going on in a table as opposed to a calculation, so case-statements should be used in preference to if-statements where possible.

When not to use case-statements

The clarity of the case-statement makes it a natural choice for many types of selections. However, it cannot be used in situations where the selection is based on conditions. For example, the following is not valid Pascal:

```
CASE number of
   < 0    : Addtonegatives;
   = 0    : Donothing;
   > 0    : Addtopositives;
END; {CASE}
```

The keys must be actual values. It is also not possible to have ranges of values, so the next attempt is also invalid:

```
CASE number of
   -maxint..-1 : Addtonegatives;
   0           : Donothing;
   1..maxint   : Addtopositives;
END; {CASE}
```

A suitable approach here would employ successive else-ifs, as discussed in the previous section.

Menu handlers

Interactive programs generally have several paths through them, and the user is invited to choose a path from a menu. A common way of expressing a menu is to give each option a letter or number, and invite the user to type in the required choice. This is explored in the next example.

EXAMPLE 5.3   Menu handler for controlling a database _____

Problem   A database is being set up with the facilities to:

- add a new record,
- remove an existing record,
- find a record and display all its details,
- extract records with certain key values,
- sort extracted records,
- print them.

We have been detailed to write the procedure which interfaces with the user and passes control to a specific procedure which will perform the action required.

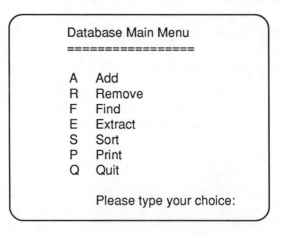

```
            Database Main Menu
            ==================

            A    Add
            R    Remove
            F    Find
            E    Extract
            S    Sort
            P    Print
            Q    Quit

                 Please type your choice:
```

Solution   We should start off by doing a screen layout. The example above is a fairly good first attempt. There are many different styles of menus. Some favour numbers for choices, others letters in sequence. However, an association between the commands and the actions helps the user, and is generally thought to present a good interface. (We were fortunate in this case that the actions all had distinct first letters.)

Algorithm   The natural choice for a control construct is the case-statement. We assume the existence of a procedure to print the menu and to get in the request character. (How this is done is discussed in Problem 6.9.)

Program

```
    PROCEDURE CommandHandler;
        VAR command : char;
        BEGIN
          REPEAT
            PrintMenu;    {Not shown here}
            GetCommand;
            CASE command OF
                'A' : Add;
                'R' : Remove;
                'F' : Find;
                'E' : Extract;
                'S' : Sort;
                'P' : Print;
                'Q' : ;
            END; {case}
          UNTIL command = 'Q';
        END; {CommandHandler}
```

Once a Q is typed, the command module exits, returning control to the program that called it.

5.3   Conditional loops with while and repeat

This text started off by introducing loops in order to emphasize the power of programming in handling repetitive tasks in a simple way. The loops that have been used up to now have all had a common property – their duration was explicit. By looking at the starting and finishing values of the for-statement, the number of times the loop would execute could be calculated. However, not all solutions can be formulated in such precise terms. For example, when reading data, it is not always possible to know in advance how much data there will be, or when the person supplying the data will wish to stop. Thus, we need the concept of a **conditional loop** – one that will stop according to some conditions. Specifically, these conditions need not necessarily be defined in terms of a fixed number of iterations.

The form of conditional loops

Conditional loops are phrased in terms of while or repeat statements. A general form of a loop using the while statement is:

```
While statement

    Initialize the conditions
    WHILE conditions DO BEGIN
       Statements to perform the loop
          and change the conditions
    END;
```

After statements to initialize variables involved in the conditions, the loop itself starts by checking the conditions. If they evaluate to true, the body of the while-statement is entered and executed. When the END is reached, control goes around again to the WHILE and the conditions are checked again. This process is repeated until the test of the conditions evaluates to false, at which point the looping stops, and control is passed to the statement following the END.

The general form of the repeat statement is similar, as shown below. The repeat loop starts off by going through its body at least once before checking the conditions. This can sometimes be a desirable property, but in general the while-statement is more useful.

Repeat statement

```
Initialize the conditions
REPEAT
    Statements to perform the loop
       and change the conditions
    UNTIL conditions;
```

Notice that the repeat statement is the only one in Pascal that does not need a BEGIN-END around a group of statements. Putting them in would not invalidate the statement, but it would look peculiar to experienced Pascal programmers, and is therefore not a good idea.

The two very important points about conditional loops are that:

- the conditions must be initialized;
- the conditions must change during the loop.

If the conditions are not initialized, then the loop will be working on incorrect or even undefined information. If they are not altered during the loop, then there will be no chance of them changing and causing the loop to end.

Simpler forms

The general form of a while loop can be simplified in two ways. If only one statement forms the body of the loop, then the BEGIN-END can (but doesn't have to) be omitted. It is unusual for both processing and changing to be possible in a single statement, but we shall see examples of it later. Most conditional loops will consist of several statements and will need the BEGIN-END.

The other simplification is more common, in that only a single condition may apply to the loop, not several as implied in the general form. A condition is expressed as a boolean expression and this may be as simple as a single variable. Very often the conditions start with not, as we shall see.

Before going on to a problem, consider some small illustrative examples of conditional loops, bearing in mind the importance of formulating them correctly. In order to convey the sense of the looping process, some of the examples make use of procedures, which do as their names suggest.

EXAMPLE 5.4 HCF

Problem   We wish to find the highest common factor (HCF) of two numbers.

Solution   One possible solution would be to find all the factors of each number and then compare both lists for the highest one. Fortunately, there is a quicker way!

Suppose *a* and *b* are the numbers, *a* is larger than *b* and their HCF is *f* Then *a − b* and *b* will also have an HCF of *f*. If we use this fact, repeatedly replacing the larger of the two numbers by their difference, until the two numbers are the same, then this figure will be the HCF, even if it is 1.

Algorithm   The above discussion can be be expressed in the following algorithm:

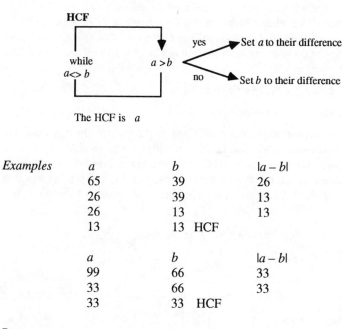

HCF

while
a<> b   a > b

yes   ▸ Set *a* to their difference

no   ▸ Set *b* to their difference

The HCF is *a*

Examples

a	b	|a − b|
65	39	26
26	39	13
26	13	13
13	13 HCF	

a	b	|a − b|
99	66	33
33	66	33
33	33 HCF	

Program

```
PROGRAM HCF (input, output);
   VAR
      a, b : 1..maxint;
   BEGIN
      writeln('****** Finding the HCF ******');
      write('What are the two numbers? ');
      readln(a, b);
      WHILE a <> b do
         if a > b then a := a - b
                  else b := b - a;
      writeln('The HCF is ', a);
   END.
```

Developing a conditional loop

The first example simulates trying to find a pair from a drawerful of mixed coloured socks.

```
PickaSock;
PickAnotherSock;
WHILE not aPair DO BEGIN
   DiscardaSock;
   PickAnotherSock;
END;
```

The loop is initialized by having two socks in hand: this is essential so that the check for a pair can be correctly performed. The loop is correctly formulated in that the condition will change each time round, as a new sock is selected. There are, however, two crucial flaws in the loop.

Suppose a pair is never found. The condition is not met so the loop continues, but the operation `PickAnotherSock` will eventually fail, and the whole operation will crash. The other problem is similar – suppose there were no socks in the drawer to start with. In this case, neither of the initializing statements can be performed, and the program as it stands will not be able to execute. These two situations can be summed up as:

- guard against not being able to begin;
- guard against never ending.

The remedy is to provide additional conditions as the guards. In this case, we need to know if sufficient socks (that is, at least two) exist to be able to test for a pair, and then we need to know when the drawer becomes empty. Both conditions are based on the number of socks in the drawer, and we assume that this figure can be provided in some way. The corrected version of the loop then becomes:

```
IF NumberofSocksinDrawer >= 2 then begin
   PickaSock;
   PickAnotherSock;
END;

WHILE (NumberofSocksinDrawer > 0) and not aPair  DO BEGIN
   DiscardaSock;
   PickAnotherSock;
END;

{At this point, a pair may or may not have been found}
```

There is one final consideration with any conditional loop. If there is more than one part to the condition governing the loop, it may be necessary to know at the end which part caused the loop to stop. In the example, it seems sensible to be able to decide whether the search was successful or not. This is called a **follow-up action**, and is performed by re-checking some of the conditions, as in:

```
IF aPair then writeln('Got a pair of socks')
        else writeln('Bad luck, no pair found.');
```

Notice that when conditions are connected (as they often are), one must be careful as to which is tested. In this case, it would not have been correct to test for empty as in:

```
IF empty then writeln ('Bad luck, no pair found.')
         else writeln ('Got a pair of socks');
```

since the pair could have been found on the very last time round the loop. The drawer would also be empty, but that is irrelevant for this purpose.

Exercise   Write the necessary if-then-else statements to report on whether a pair was found or not, whether the drawer was empty initially, or whether it became empty during the search.

5.4   Conditional loops and input data

The next example deals with input data: we wish to read numbers until a certain target number is found, and then stop. The loop is:

```
read(target);
read(number);
WHILE number <> target do
   read(number);
```

Here we have a case of a single statement in the loop body. Reading is special in that it involves processing data, and it also changes the value of variables. Thus, a read performs the dual function of the body of a loop and changing the conditions.

Now consider the two guards mentioned above: the loop may not be able to start if no data exists, and it may never end if the target does not appear. Both of these relate to an **end of data** condition, which we shall assume for the moment is maintained in a boolean function called endofdata. Assuming that at least the target can be read, then the loop is rephrased as:

```
read(target);
if not endofdata then read(number);
WHILE not endofdata and (target <> number) do
      read(number);
```

The lesson here is that read statements should always be protected, whether by conditions in if-statements or in while-statements. If knowing the reason for stopping is important, then the following statement would be reasonable:

```
IF number=target then writeln('Found ',target:1)
                 else writeln(target:1, ' is not there.');
```

Reasonable, but not strictly correct: if there was no data at all, then nothing is ever read in to number, and so this question cannot be asked. This indicates that the case of no data must be handled and got rid of quite separately from the normal case. The correct statements to do this are given next.

Trailer values

The condition for end of data could be formulated in several ways. One way would be to use the built-in functions, which are discussed in Section 7.2. Another way is to have a **terminator value** which is supplied by the user as the last item. To make things flexible, the trailer for that particular run of the program could also be read in. Thus, the loop to search for a target number and end correctly could be formulated as:

```
read(trailer);
read(target);
read(number);
WHILE (number <> trailer) and (number <> target) do
      read(number);
if number = target then writeln('Found ',  target:1)
                    else writeln(target:1, ' not there);
```

Typical data for such a loop would be:

```
0   5
1   2   7   4   5   9   0
```

The trailer is 0 and the target 5, so the loop will read values until the 5 is reached, and then stop. Since the target was found, the message Found 5 will be printed. Since there are values left in the data, it may be helpful to skip over them. The if-part of the loop could be extended to include a loop, thus:

```
if number = target
   then begin
      writeln('Found ',  target:1);
      repeat
         read(number);
      until number = trailer;
   end
   else writeln(target:1, 'not there.');
```

Nested conditional loops

As with counting-loops, conditional loops can be nested, and both kinds of loops can be nested with each other as the application requires.

EXAMPLE 5.5   Descending sequences _____

Problem   An engineering apparatus is controlled by numbers that may change, but must always be in descending order. As soon as the sequence is no longer descending, the machine stops. How would this aspect of its operation be programmed?

Solution   We assume that the numbers will be read into a program, and that for the purposes of the investigation they can then be ignored. What is important is to get the algorithm for checking on the sequence correct.

Algorithm   To check that a number is in sequence, we have to have both it and the previous number in hand. Each time round the loop, we replace the previous number with the one read in. As far as starting off goes, we cannot make an assumption as to the value of the first number, so the remembered number cannot be preset to a special value. Instead, the first two numbers are read in separately, and then the while-loop starts, checking that even these are in sequence.

Program   The relevant portions of the program would be:

```
VAR
   N, previous : integer;

   read(previous);
   read(N);
   while N < previous do begin
      previous := N;
      read(N);
   end;
```

Extension   Since the program is feasible, the maker of the apparatus has asked that it be written, but with the following additional conditions:

- the first number must be positive;

- the numbers must not go below 0.

For each number, he asks that we print out that many dots on the same line.

Algorithm   The condition on the while-statement will need two parts now: to check the new number against 0 and to check it against previous. In addition, an if-statement is needed at the beginning to check that the very first number is positive. Printing the dots is best done in a separate procedure. Since the reacting will be done with previous in the first case, and then with n, we give the procedure a parameter to make this easy to do.

Program

```
PROGRAM Controller (input, output);
   VAR
      previous : 0..maxint;
      N        : integer;

   PROCEDURE React (dotcount : integer);
      VAR dot : 1..maxint;
         BEGIN
            for dot := 1 to dotcount do write('.');
            writeln;
         END; {React}

   BEGIN
      writeln('***** Controlling the apparatus *****');
      writeln('Type in the numbers');
      read(previous, N);
      if previous <= 0
      then writeln('The machine cannot work on that.')
      else begin
         React (previous);
         WHILE (N >= 0 ) and (N < previous) do begin
```

```
            React (N);
            previous := N;
            read (N);
         END;
         writeln;
      end;
      writeln ('Machine shut down okay.');
   END.
```

Testing　Sample input and output for the program would be:

```
***** Controlling the apparatus *****
Type in the numbers
15 ...............
12 ...........
9  ........
7  .......
3 ...
-1
Machine shut down okay.
```

The testing should include the case where the data starts off negative.

5.5 Case study – RSP game

There is a popular two-person game in which each player makes a choice of Rock, Scissors or Paper, and the winner depends on the following rules:

Rock beats scissors (it can smash them);

Scissors beats paper (they can cut it);

Paper beats rock (it can wrap it).

If the choices are the same, then it is a draw.

We would like to program the computer to play this game against a human. Each will make a choice and the computer will work out who won.

Solution

Programming any two-person game involves seven steps:

1. Give instructions (or omit them if requested to do so);

2. Initialize the game, if necessary;

3. Set up a loop to play the game repeatedly until told to stop;

4. Generate the computer's choice;

5. Get the user's choice;

6. Decide who has won;

7. Play again, or if no more, sign off.

We shall look at each step in turn.

Step 1: instructions

Computer games should always give instructions for new users. These should include not only details on the rules, but also how to enter replies. Two issues which should always be addressed here are whether replies need to be followed by return, and whether capital letters are acceptable as well as smalls.

We shall require the user to type in R, S or P, followed by return. When a question is being asked, we shall expect a Y or N. We shall not permit lower-case letters.

Step 2 : initialize

We need to beg the question here as to how the computer is to make its choice. Ideally, we want a random choice, and therefore need to simulate random numbers. This is done by using a formula such as the following:

```
seed := ln(seed*27.182813 + 31.415917);
seed := seed - trunc(seed);
mychoice := trunc(seed*3) + 1;
```

The last line of the process ensures that the numbers generated are 1, 2 or 3. The seed is any number to start the process off, and so we can ask the user to enter one.

Step 3: set up a loop

Here we have a repeat-until model. We play the game once, and then ask the user if another game is required.

Step 4: generate the computer's choice

We have already seen that this will be done by random numbers. We must realize then, that the computer will be submitting 1, 2 or 3 and the user will be submitting R, S or P. In fact, this will not cause problems.

Step 5: getting the user's choice

Here we have to program defensively. We must check that the character entered is indeed one of the permissible ones. If it isn't, we should give a message and try again. Once again, a repeat-loop is in order. The basic sequence is:

```
repeat
   write('Your choice of R S or P? ');
   readln(yourchoice);
until choice in ['R', 'S'', 'P'];
```

This sequence will force the player to use capital letters. Notice that the initial message serves as an error message as well.

Step 6: decide who has won

This is the most intricate part, algorithmically. We have three choices for the computer, and each of these has three outcomes, depending on the player's choice. This could mean a selection statement with 9 arms! Fortunately, there is a better way, using a procedure with parameters.

Let us consider the first case of the computer having a rock. Then, depending on the player's choice, the computer judges the result as:

scissors   – win
paper   – lose
rock   – draw.

The same process is repeated for the computer having a scissors, except that the list of player's choices is in a different order. Clearly, a procedure will be appropriate here, and the result is shown in the program below.

Step 7: sign off

We can have a very simple sign off, such as thanking the user, or we can print out statistics on how many games were won either way.

Program

The program follows the strategy outlined above, and makes good use of all the control instructions introduced in this chapter, except for the while-loop. Although recommended by many people as the ultimate loop structure, the while-loop is not appropriate in circumstances where interactive input has to be checked, as in this case study.

```
PROGRAM RSP (input, output);
   VAR
      mychoice   : 1..3;
      yourchoice : char;
      ans        : char;
      seed       : real;

   PROCEDURE Report(Iwin, youwin, draw : char);
      BEGIN
         writeln(draw);   {the character for my choice}
         if yourchoice = Iwin then writeln('I win') else
         if yourchoice = youwin then writeln('You win') else
         writeln('It''s a draw');
      END;

   PROCEDURE GiveInstructions;
      BEGIN
      END;

   PROCEDURE Play;
      VAR ans : char;
      PROCEDURE MakeMyChoice;
         BEGIN
            seed := ln(seed*27.182813 + 31.415917);
```

```
            seed := seed - trunc(seed);
            mychoice := trunc(seed*3) + 1;
        END; {MakemyChoice}

    BEGIN
        repeat
            MakeMyChoice;
            write('Your choice of R S or P? ');
            readln(yourchoice);
            write('My choice   ');
            case mychoice of
                1 : {Rock} Report ('S', 'P', 'R');
                2 : {Scissors} Report ('P','R','S');
                3 : {Paper} Report ('R', 'S', 'P');
            end;
            write('Shall we play again? ');
            readln(ans);
        until ans = 'N';
    END; {Play}

    BEGIN
        writeln('Let''s play RSP!');
        writeln('Do you want instructions?');
        readln(ans);
        if ans = 'Y' then GiveInstructions;
        write('To show I''m not cheating, you start me off',
            ' by giving me a number: ');
        readln(seed);
        Play;
        writeln('Thanks for playing!');
    END.
```

Testing

A typical run could go something like this:

```
Let's play RSP!
Do you want instructions? n
To show I'm not cheating, you start me off by giving me a
number: 56
Your choice? P
My choice R
You win
Shall we play again? Y
Your choice? S
My choice S
It's a draw
Shall we play again? N
Thanks for playing!
```

WHAT WE HAVE LEARNT

Four control constructs were covered in this chapter – if, case, while and repeat. (The fifth control construct in Pascal is the for-statement). We introduced **conditions** *with simple operators such as < and > but left a more detailed discussion of them to the next chapter.*

*We showed how **if-statements** could be used singly or in successive conditions, and considered the uses and abuses of the **case-statement** carefully. We looked at the process of developing **while loops** that would work, and considered **repeat loops** in contrast. Examples that illustrated both forms of **conditional loops** were examined.*

*The special case of using while loops for input data was discussed in detail and the concept of **trailer values** introduced to enable a variable amount of data to be read in.*

The case study investigated the general strategy for playing games with a computer and used the control constructs to good effect to get a game that would (probably) not crash.

Programming processes used in this chapter are:

1. *Establishing multiple conditions in the correct order.*
2. *Solving by induction.*
3. *Mapping key-values onto smaller ranges.*
4. *Guarding loops against never beginning or never ending.*
5. *Trailer values for input data.*
6. *Generating random numbers.*
7. *Strategy for managing a game.*

QUIZ

1. Why do you think a particular key-value cannot appear more than once in a case-statement?

2. What are the two important points to remember when designing a conditional loop?

3. What would be suitable trailer values for the following sets of data:

    • ages of people,

    • air temperatures,

    • years?

4. Write out suitable instructions for the RSP game in the case study.

5. The following loop finds the highest numbner. Rewrite it to find both the highest and the lowest number.

```
read(highest);
for i := 2 to n do begin
   read(number);
   if number > highest then highest := number;
end;
```

6. The following set of statements is very inefficient. Why is this so? Rewrite it more efficiently.

```
if pre = 'm' then write('milli');
if pre = 'c' then write('centi');
if pre = 'K' then write('kilo');
```

7. The following piece of program is meant to swap the values in *x* and *y* if it is necessary, so that *x* lands up with the lower one. What will actually happen? Correct the program.

```
if x > y then
   temp := x;
   x := y;
   y := temp;
```

8. The following loop reads and totals a temperature value every second. What is wrong with it?

```
for sec := 1 to 60 do begin
   write(sec);  read(temp);
   total := total + temp;
end;
```

9. What should happen when a case statement is entered with a key value that is not one of those listed?

10. Suppose we have exchange rates quoted between the Zanyland dolly and the franc, mark, pound and dollar. These are declared as constants. Write a case statement to set up an operational exchange rate, if one of the four currency symbols is entered, i.e. F(franc), M (mark), £ (pound) and $ (dollar).

PROBLEMS

5.1 **Large class symbols.** The classes of pass at Zanyland College have names and abbreviations that correspond as follows:

    I   First

    II–1   Upper second

    II–2   Lower second

    III   Third

    F   Fail

Assume that there are five procedures called `eye`, `one`, `two`, `dash` and `eff`, which respectively print out the symbols I, 1, 2, – and F in large format as described in problem 3.1. Now write a successive else-if sequence which uses these procedures to print out in large format the symbol for a given mark.

5.2 **Rainfall figures.** The rainfall figures in mm are available for each day of the past four weeks. We want to know the total rainfall for each week, the wettest day and the driest week.

Write a program which will read in several sets of 28 rainfall figures and print out the three bits of information required. Sample data and results would be:

```
Sample data       Sample results
3 0 0 7 8 21 0    39mm
0 1 1 0 0 0 4     6mm
9 6 7 0 0 0 0     22mm
0 0 0 0 0 0 1     1mm
The wettest day was day 6.
The driest week was week 4.
```

5.3   **Golf scores.** The Zanyland Golf Course has nine holes. At each hole, a player is expected to be able to sink the ball in the hole in 1 to 5 shots. This gives a course average or par of 30. A player's score for the course is the sum of the numbers of shots for each hole.

Depending on his past performance, a player is granted a handicap which is subtracted from his score to give his actual result for a game. Players are also interested in knowing whether they have scored under par or not. When players play together, the winner is the one with the lowest score. If the scoring of a golf game were computerized, sample input and output might be:

```
Player     Handicap    Shots per hole          Total   Result  Under Par?
1          6           1 3 6 2 1 4 3 2 4        26      20      yes
2          3           2 2 2 2 4 4 4 2 2        24      21      yes
3          2           4 5 4 3 4 1 3 5 4        33      31      no
The winner is player 1 with a handicapped result of 20
```

Write a program which

- reads in the shots per hole for several players,
- calculates each total score, handicapped score and par decision,
- determines the winning player and the winning score.

5.4   **Sensitive drugs.** A sensitive drug cannot sustain a change in temperature of more that 30°C in a 24-hour period. The temperatures are monitored and recorded every 2 hours. Write a program the laboratory technician can run once a day to determine whether or not to throw the drug away.

5.5   **Parking meters .** The Zanyland Traffic Department wants to decide whether or not to mount a campaign against illegal parking. A number of traffic inspectors are sent to different zones in the city where parking time is restricted. The different zones have different time restrictions. Each of the traffic officers has to monitor any ten cars in their zone and record the actual time the vehicle was parked in the time restricted zone. If 50% or more of the cars were parked for a longer period than allowed, the traffic department will decide to launch a massive campaign.

Write a program which

- reads in the number of zones,
- reads the time limit and actual parking-time for ten vehicles for each of the zones,
- determines the number of cars exceeding the time limit in each of the zones,
- decides whether a campaign should be mounted or not,
- identifies the zone where the situation is the worst.

Sample input and output might be:

```
Please enter the number of zones: 3
Area      Limit                     Parking times                     Over limit
1         60          20   40   70   35   45   78   34   56   73    5   3
2         45          62   47   68   40   53   62  120    8   15   72   7
3         30          66   32   41   89    7   25   29   33   54   17   6
A campaign must be mounted.
Concentrate on area 2
```

5.6   **Engineering apparatus**. A certain engineering apparatus is controlled by the input of successive numbers. If there is a run of the same number, the apparatus can optimize its performance. Hence we would like to arrange the data so as to indicate that a run is coming. Write a program which reads a sequence of numbers and prints out each run of numbers in the form *(n*m)* where *m* is the number to be repeated *n* times. These instructions are printed in brackets on a new line, to indicate that they are going to the apparatus. Note that a run could just consist of a single number. The numbers are terminated by a zero, which halts the apparatus. Sample input and output would be:

```
Sample input and output
20 20 20 20 20 20 20 20 20 20 50
(10*20)
50 50 50 50 60
(5*50)
60 60 60 60 20
(5*60)
30
(1*20)
30 30 30 90
(4*30)
0
(1*90)
(0)
```

5.7   **Rabbits!** A scientist needs to determine when she will run out of space to house her rabbits. She starts with two rabbits and it is known that a pair of adult rabbits (that is, those more than three months old) produce on average two rabbits every three months. The scientist has space to house 500 rabbits. Write a program which will determine how many months it will be before she runs out of space. Adapt the program to print out a table of the rabbit populations (adult, non-adult and total) every three months for 5 years.

5.8   **Fibonacci again**. Problem 4.3 involved printing out the Fibonacci sequence. Alter the program so that only every third value is printed out. What do you notice about these values?

6 A Closer Look at Types

6.1 Types

Variables, constants, expressions and functions all have **types** in Pascal, and the type governs exactly how they can be used.

Predefined types

Pascal has five **predefined** types which are:

- integer,
- boolean,
- character,
- real,
- text.

Every type has five properties, which completely define the type's values, how the values are represented and what operations can be done on them. These properties are:

- range of values,
- notation for constants,
- input and output capabilities,
- operators,
- predefined functions.

Although we have already seen three of the types – integer, real and character – and used them in programs, we now going into their properties fully. We also consider booleans, and look at text in the next chapter.

User-defined types

Pascal also enables us to construct our own types, often called **user-defined** types, by means of one of the following methods:

- **enumerating** a list of values,
- restricting values to a **subrange**,
- collecting several items of different types into a **record**,
- collecting several items of the same type to form an **array**,
- forming a **set** of items of a certain type,
- collecting items of the same type into a **sequential file**,
- **pointing** to a dynamically created variable.

When we create new types, we give them names, and can then use these names in our programs as easily as we use integer or any of the other predefined type names. These user-defined types are discussed in Chapters 9, 10, 13 and 14.

6.2 Integers

Integers are used for counting – one of the computer's most common tasks. The integer type in Pascal is applicable to all those items that are inherently whole numbers such as a year, number of children, and counters of all sorts. What follows is a full discussion of the properties of the type.

Integer values

In mathematical terms, the integer numbers extend infinitely on either side of zero; on a computer, they are bounded by the storage allocated to hold them. Typically, this will restrict the range to:

$$-2\,147\,483\,648 \quad \text{to} \quad +2\,147\,483\,647$$

On some older computers, the space set aside for integers gives a very much smaller range of:

$$-32\,768 \quad \text{to} \quad +32\,767$$

We should not assume that integers can be very large. It may well be that when programming on such a machine, larger numbers are needed, in which case a solution may be to switch to real numbers.

Whatever the range that is available, Pascal provides a predefined constant called maxint which gives the value of the largest integer. Thus, on any machine, one can discover the range by simply printing out maxint, as in:

```
writeln('Maxint is ', maxint);
```

Literals are the symbols used to express the values of a given type. For integers, the literals are formed from digits optionally preceded by a sign of plus or minus. Pascal is, however, strict about how numbers are written, and in particular, there cannot be spaces or commas in them to separate the thousands. The following are all valid Pascal integers:

```
1000000        -16567        80
```

whereas the following are not:

```
1,000,000     -16 567     80c
```

Integer operators

Integer literals, constants, variables and functions can be formed into integer expressions using any of the three operators + (plus), – (minus) and * (multiply). There are also two more that permit integer division, giving the quotient and remainder respectively. These are:

x div y   divide x by y and discard the remainder

x mod y   remainder after x is divided by y

Mod is not defined if y is negative and, of course, both mod and div are undefined if y is zero. Some examples will clarify this.

```
17 div 6  = 2          17 mod 6  = 5
 6 div 17 = 0           6 mod 17 =6
18 div 6  = 3          18 mod 6  = 0
-13 div 2 = -6         13 mod -3 = undefined
```

Mod and div are frequently used to break an integer up into its digits. If we know that a number has three digits, then the leftmost digit can be extracted by taking n div 100 (that is, how many hundreds are there?), and the rightmost digit is found with n mod 10 (that is, What remains after dividing by 10?). In Pascal, this would be:

```
VAR
   n : 000..999;
   units, hundreds : 0..9;
```

```
units := n mod 10;
tens := (n div 10) mod 10;
hundreds := n div 100;
```

The relational operators such as = and < (introduced in the previous chapter) can also be used between integers.

Integer functions

There are four predefined functions which operate on integers and return integers as their values. They are:

abs(n)	absolute value of n
sqr(n)	square of n i.e. n * n
succ(n)	successor of n i.e. n + 1
pred(n)	predecessor of n i.e. n − 1

Although only the +, − and * are defined between integers to produce integer results, a division operator / can be used between integers and it will produce a real result. There are also the two useful conversion functions, as we saw in Chapter 2:

trunc(x)	smallest integer less than x
round(x)	nearest integer to x

These two functions take a real expression and produce an integer. Trunc cuts off (or truncates) the fractional part of the number, and returns the integer part. Round will round up or down to the nearest integer. Thus, we have:

```
trunc (6.3) = 6        round (6.3) = 6
trunc (6.8) = 6        round (6.8) = 7
```

Integer input and output

Integer values can be read and written using the usual four input/output statements, that is, read, readln, write and writeln. We have already covered the details of reading and writing numbers in previous sections, so here we just summarize the points made:

1.   For input, the number supplied as data must conform to the notation for literals and therefore may not contain commas, full stops or spaces.

2.   The read and readln statements will skip any leading spaces, including blank lines, before the integer begins. However, they will not skip over any other characters.

3.   Standard Pascal permits any non-digit to end a number but this flexibility is not usual in other languages and therefore not all Pascal systems implement it. It is best to restrict data design to numbers that are always terminated by spaces or ends-of-line.

4.   An integer is written right-justified in a fixed space of about 12 characters

unless a field width is given.

5.   If the field width is not large enough, it is expanded. This fact is used to get left-justified numbers by using a field width of :1.

6.   The field width may be any integer expression.

EXAMPLE 6.1   Fleet timetables

Problem   Zanyland Deliveries Inc. has acquired a new fleet of vehicles which are able to travel 15% faster than the old vehicles (while still staying within the speed limit). They would like to know how this will affect journeys.

Solution   Times are represented in a 24 hour clock, such as 0930 or 1755. We need to find out how an arrival time will change, based on the reduction in the total journey time. Therefore, we need to be able to subtract times to find the journey time and multiply the result by 0.85, representing a 15% reduction. The question is how to do arithmetic on times.

Algorithm   Times consist of two parts – hours and minutes. In order to do subtraction and multiplication on times, we have to convert them to minutes first, perform the calculation, then convert back. Assuming we can do this, the overall algorithm is:

> **New fleet**
> > Read in the departure and arrival times
> > Calculate journey time
> > Reduce journey time by 15%
> > Add to the departure time to get the new arrival time
> > Print out new journey time and arrival time.

Notice that we don't convert the departure times, only the arrivals!
    The first conversion involves splitting an integer into two parts, which we can do with the mod and div operators. The algorithm is:

Convert to minutes	Example 0715
Find hours from time div 100	7
Find minutes from time mod 100	15
Set minutes to hours * 60 + minutes	435

Converting back is similar. The algorithm is:

Convert to hours and minutes	Example 435
Set hours to minutes div 60	7
Set minutes minutes mod 60	15
Set time to hours*100+minutes	715

Program   The program to handle one journey is quite simple:

```
PROGRAM NewFleet (input, output);

   CONST
      reduction = 0.85;
   VAR
      depart,
      arrive,
      newarrive : 0000..2359; {24 hour clock times}
      departM,
      arriveM,
      journeytime,
      newjourneytime,
      newarriveM : 0..86400; {minutes in a day}

   BEGIN
      write('What are the current departure ',
            'and arrival times? ');
      readln(depart, arrive);
      departM := (depart div 100)*60 + depart mod 100;
      arriveM := (arrive div 100)*60 + arrive mod 100;
      journeytime := arriveM - departM;
      newjourneytime := round(journeytime*reduction);
      newarriveM := departM + newjourneytime;
      newarrive := (newarriveM div 60)*100
                      + newarriveM mod 60;
      writeln('Old journey time is ',
               journeytime:1,' mins ');
      writeln('New journey time is ',
               newjourneytime:1,' mins ');
      writeln('New arrival time is ',newarrive:1);
      readln;
   END.
```

Notice that we use eight different variables to keep all the values relevant at any one time. They are also given names which indicate their meaning well.

Testing   A couple of tests are:

```
What are the current departure and arrival times? 0600 0650
Old journey time is 50 mins
New journey time is 43 mins
New arrival time is 643

What are the current departure and arrival times? 0000 1200
Old journey time is 720 mins
New journey time is 612 mins
New arrival time is 1012
```

6.3 Booleans

Conditions govern the decisions made in programs as to alternative paths to follow. A condition yields a value **true** or **false**. Another name for a condition is a **boolean expression** and the result of such an expression can be stored in a **boolean variable**. Booleans are named after the nineteenth century mathematician George Boole.

For example, given the declarations:

```
VAR
   minor, pensioner : boolean;
   age              : 0..140;
```

we can store various facts about the age of someone as:

```
minor := age < 18;
pensioner := age >=65;
```

and then use these later to make decisions such as:

```
if minor then writeln('No driver''s licence for you!');
if pensioner then writeln('You need not pay on the bus.');
```

It could be argued that the boolean variables are unnecessary because the statements:

```
if age < 18 then writeln('No driver''s licence for you!');
if age >= 65 then writeln('You need not pay on the bus.');
```

will achieve the same effect. However, this would not be the case if the value of age had been changed before the if-statement executed. Thus, boolean variables, like any variables, are really useful when the value of a condition must be remembered after other things have happened. This is illustrated in the following example.

EXAMPLE 6.2   Counterfeit cheques

Problem   Counterfeit cheques are in circulation and the banks have discovered that they all have the same distinctive properties. In the 10-digit cheque number, if there are:

- three or more zeros in succession,

- and/or four or more non-zeros in succession,

then the cheque could be counterfeit. We would like the computer to assist in warning of a possible counterfeit.

Solution   When the cheques are handled by the banks' computers, the first thing that is read is the number. For the purposes of this example, we could write a program to read in cheque numbers and to analyse them for the above properties. The analysis could detect the occurrence of either of the runs described above and if either is found then the cheque can be marked as suspect.

Algorithm   The algorithm for analysing a number involves reading it in, digit by digit, and counting the number of zeros and non-zeros. However, these have to occur in runs, so once a run is 'broken', the relevant count will be reset. It will therefore be necessary to remember that a critical count was reached at some stage: this is best done with a boolean variable. The algorithm looks like this:

Read a digit

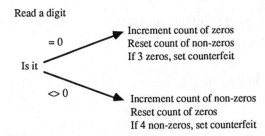

Is it

= 0 → Increment count of zeros
Reset count of non-zeros
If 3 zeros, set counterfeit

<> 0 → Increment count of non-zeros
Reset count of zeros
If 4 non-zeros, set counterfeit

Program The program follows the algorithm closely, making use of procedures for clarity. The digits of the cheque have to be entered with spaces following, so that they can be read as integers using the read statement.

```
PROGRAM CheckaCheque (input, output);
   {For the occurrence of >= 3 zeros
     or >= 4 non-zeros in a row}

   CONST
      NoofDigits = 10;
   VAR
      counterfeit       : boolean;
      CountofZeros,
      CountofNonZeros : 0 ..10;
      digit             : 0..9;
      i, n              : 1..10000;   {maximum in a batch}

   PROCEDURE RecordZero;
      {Uses and updates globals : CountofZeros,
                                  CountofNonzeros
                                  Counterfeit}
      BEGIN
         CountofZeros := CountofZeros + 1;
         CountofNonzeros := 0;
         if CountofZeros = 3 then counterfeit := true;
      END; {RecordZero}

   PROCEDURE RecordNonzero;
      {Uses and updates globals  : CountofZeros,
                                   CountofNonzeros
                                   Counterfeit}
      BEGIN
         CountofNonzeros := CountofNonzeros + 1;
         CountofZeros := 0;
         if CountofNonzeros = 4 then counterfeit := true;
      END; {RecordNonzero}

   BEGIN
      writeln('****** Checking for counterfeits ******');
      writeln('Enter a cheque number with digits ',
              'separated by a space');
      counterfeit := false;
      CountofZeros := 0;
      CountofNonzeros := 0;
      FOR i := 1 to NoofDigits do begin
         read (digit);
         if digit = 0 then RecordZero
                      else RecordNonzero;
```

```
        END;
        if counterfeit then write ('        COUNTERFEIT')
                        else write ('        OK');
        writeln;
    END.
```

Testing   Cheque numbers should be chosen so as to test the special cases. For
example, a sample input and output might be:

```
****** Checking for counterfeits ******
Enter a cheque number with digits separated by a space
0 0 0 3 3 0 0 4 4 0  COUNTERFEIT

****** Checking for counterfeits ******
Enter a cheque number with digits separated by a space
0 0 3 3 3 0 0 3 3 3  OK


****** Checking for counterfeits ******
Enter a cheque number with digits separated by a space
0 0 3 3 3 0 3 0 0 0  COUNTERFEIT


****** Checking for counterfeits ******
Enter a cheque number with digits separated by a space
4 4 4 4 0 0 5 5 0 0  COUNTERFEIT
```

Once again, we used the cursor control routines to get the answers on the same
line as the input.

Boolean values

There are only two boolean values – false and true – and they are known by these
identifiers. This is in contrast to integers, which have a numeric notation, and to
characters and strings, which also have a special notation, as we shall see
later. The fact that boolean literals are identifiers means that care must be taken
not to redefine them. If we had a declaration such as:

```
VAR true : integer;
```

implying that we were going to count or compute something in the variable called
true, then this would hide the boolean meaning of the identifier true, and we
would not be able to use it.

Boolean operators

There are three boolean operators namely and, or and not which can be
explained by means of tables. For the expression x and y to be true, both x and
y must be true; for the expression x or y to be true, either x or y or both can be
true. There is also a precedence between the operators, in that in the absence of
parentheses, not and and will always be evaluated before or.

not		**and**	false	true		**or**	false	true
false	true	false	false	false		false	false	true
true	false	true	false	true		true	true	true

Referring back to the earlier example with the minor and pensioner conditions, suppose the variable `employed` contains the information whether the person is working or not. Then further facts can be deduced as follows:

```
youngworker := minor and employed;
voter := not minor;
taxpayer := voter or employed;
```

Boolean operators can be combined to express more complex conditions. For example, if both minors and pensioners can go free on the buses provided they are not working, then we have:

```
freebus := (pensioner or minor) and not employed;
```

Boolean operators are very useful in conjunction with the relational operators in establishing detailed conditions. For example, to test whether a number falls between two limits, `min` and `max`, we can say:

```
if (number >= min) and (number <= max) then . . .
```

In Pascal, the precedence between the relational operators and the boolean ones is such that the boolean operators will always be executed first (that is, they have higher precedence). This is why the parentheses are needed in the above example. If they are omitted, the compiler would first try to group `min` and `number,` which is not what was intended.

Another example is an expression for deciding whether school should be cancelled because it is too cold or too hot, that is:

```
gohome := (temperature > 40) or (temperature < 0);
```

It is necessary to mention the variable being tested for each test, that is, it is incorrect to say:

temperature > 40 or < 0

It is worth noting that expressions with `and` operators can be converted into equivalent expressions using `not` and `or` operators, such as:

```
not a and not b    =>     not (a or b)
not a or not b     =>     not (a and b)
```

In programming, it is best to choose one style or the other and stick to it, so as not to get confused. Note finally that when using `not`, the brackets are important, in that

```
not a or b
```

is very different to

```
not(a or b).
```

A boolean can be used as the loop variable in a for-statement, though of course the loop will never be more than two iterations long.

Boolean functions

There is one useful function which takes an integer and returns a boolean value, that is:

odd(n)   returns true if n is odd, false if it is even

An example of the use of this function would be in deciding whether one is allowed to water the garden, which in times of drought may only be permitted for even-numbered houses on even days (Monday is 1), and odd-numbered houses on odd days, or on Sunday (the seventh day). Given the declarations:

```
VAR
    housenumber : 1..500;
    day         : 1..7;    {Monday is 1}
```

and appropriate values in the variables, we could say:

```
AllowedtoWater :=
    (odd(housenumber) and odd(day)) or
    (not odd(housenumber) and not odd(day)) or (day = 7);
```

If instructions could be left that watering was to be done whenever possible, then an if-statement would be appropriate, as in:

```
if (odd(housenumber) and odd(day)) or
    (not odd(housenumber) and not odd(day)) or (day = 7)
then WatertheGarden;
```

In addition to the odd function, ord, succ and pred can be applied to boolean values, but their use is fairly limited. Two other functions return boolean values. These are eoln and eof, which are discussed in the next chapter along with text files.

Boolean input and output

Boolean values cannot be read but they can be written, producing the values TRUE and FALSE. The space taken on output is 4 and 5 characters respectively, but can be increased by using a width indicator.

EXAMPLE 6.3   Truth tables _____

Problem   We would like to print out the truth tables for and, or and xor, where xor is defined as:

```
x or y and not (x and y)
```

Solution   Unlike previous examples, this one is actually easier when the tables are next to each other. We use for-loops and produce them!

Algorithm   The top heading is printed. Then we loop through the two boolean values and write out the value of the required operator combinations for each.

Program   The program is:

```
PROGRAM Truthtables (input, output);
   VAR b, c : boolean;
   BEGIN
      rewrite('truth.out');
      writeln('****** Truth tables ******');
      writeln;
      writeln('and   | false  true      or   |','
              ' false  true      xor  | false true');
      writeln('====================   ',
              '====================   ===================');
      FOR b := false to true do begin
         write(b:6);
         FOR c := false to true do write(b and c:7);
         write(b:10);
         FOR c := false to true do write(b or c:7);
         write(b:10);
         for c := false to true do
              write(b or c) and not (b and c):7);
         writeln;
      end;
   END.
```

Testing   The program only has one test path:

```
****** Truth tables ******
```

and	false	true		or	false	true		xor	false	true
====================				====================				====================		
FALSE	FALSE	FALSE		FALSE	FALSE	TRUE		FALSE	FALSE	TRUE
TRUE	FALSE	TRUE		TRUE	TRUE	TRUE		TRUE	TRUE	FALSE

6.4 Characters

Character values

There are usually 256 different character symbols that one can use in a program. These include the letters, digits, punctuation symbols, arithmetic operators and various other special control characters. The latter cause things to happen, such as feeding a page of paper or ringing a bell. The particular range of values depends on the underlying character set of the computer, which is most often the ASCII set. (ASCII stands for American Standard Codes for Information Interchange.) This set includes:

```
A B C D ...
a b c d ...
0 1 2 3 ...
. , ; : ? ! % ( ) + – = / * @ $ ...
```

The full list of characters in the ASCII set is given in the next example: if your system uses some other set (such as EBCDIC), consult the manual for your particular computer.

A character literal is written within single quotes (or apostrophes), for example, 'A' or '+'. A quote itself is written twice, within its own quotes, that is, ''''.

Character input and output is straightforward. Characters can appear in read and write statements, interspersed with numbers and strings. If ch and sign are character variables and amount is an integer, then we can have statements such as:

```
read(ch);
writeln('The balance is ', sign, amount:1);
```

which would produce the output:

```
The balance is -300
```

The length of a character is one. If a field width is specified in the write statement, the character will be right-justified in the appropriate number of spaces. For example, we might have the statement and output:

```
writeln ('Jones', 'A':10);

Jones~ ~ ~ ~ ~ ~ ~ ~ ~ A
```

Character operators and functions

The six relational operators are defined for characters, that is:

```
 =    <>    <    >    <=    >=
```

There is no inbuilt ordering between letters and digits. The ordering achieved by the relational operators is based on the underlying character set, and may well differ from computer to computer. Therefore, we cannot rely on any group of characters, say the letters, always coming before, say, the digits. However, we can assume that the letters themselves are in the correct alphabetical order and that the digits 0 to 9 are also in sequence.

A loop variable of a for-statement can be of type character, as can the key of a case-statement (see Section 5.2). For example, consider the excerpt:

```
{Printing all characters between two that are given}
read(first, last);
if first < last
then
    for ch := first to last do write(ch)
else
```

```
for ch := last to first do write(ch);
```

Given OK as data, it will write out **KLMNO**.

There is also a special operator for set membership, in, which can be put to good use with characters. It is discussed at the end of the section.

There are four predefined functions for characters, namely:

succ(ch)	the next character after ch (compare +1 for integers)
pred(ch)	the character before ch (compare −1 for integers)
ord(ch)	the ordinal value of ch in the underlying character set
chr(n)	the character whose ordinal value is n.

There are natural error conditions associated with these functions. If there are 256 possible characters with ordinal values from 0 to 255, then pred(0) and succ(255) are undefined, as is the chr of any number outside this range.

As an example of the use of ord, consider how to convert a capital letter to a small one. Subtracting the ordinal value of the first capital letter − 'A' − from the given character's ordinal value, gives us an ordinal value for that character starting at 0. Then, if we add the ordinal value of the first lower-case 'a', and convert the value back to a character, it will be in the range of the lower-case letters. The full Pascal formula is:

```
smallch := chr(ord(ch) - ord('A') + ord('a'));
```

We can test this out on the ASCII set where ord('A') is 65 and ord('a') is 97. Then given ch is 'S', we have:

```
smallch   = chr(83 - 65 + 97)   = chr(115)   = 's'
```

The important point to note is that we do not have to know the ordinal values of 'A' and 'a' in order to do the conversion, nor do we need to know whether the capitals come before the smalls in the character set. The above formula is completely general. This conversion formula fits nicely into a function, which is covered later in Section 8.1. For now, we shall just use it in a statement:

```
if ch in ['A'..'Z'] then
   ch := chr(ord(ch) - ord('A') + ord('a'));
```

Notice that it is important to check whether the character is a capital before converting it.

When we looked at the example of converting marks to symbols in Section 5.2, we gave the case-statement solution, that is:

```
VAR
   mark   : 0..100;
   symbol : 'A'..'F';

CASE mark div 10 of
   10, 9, 8   : symbol := 'A';
   7          : symbol := 'B';
   6          : symbol := 'C';
   5          : symbol := 'D';
   4          : symbol := 'E';
```

```
      3, 2, 1, 0 : symbol := 'F';
END; {CASE}
```

An alternative would be to use successive if-then-else statements, using a calculation on the mark to produce the correct symbol.

```
if mark >= 80 then symbol := 'A' else
if mark <= 30 then symbol := 'F' else
symbol := chr(mark-40+ord('E'));
```

EXAMPLE 6.4   Printing the character set _____

Problem   What is the character set we are using?

Solution   The ord and chr functions can be used to discover the ordering of the characters on a computer. Assuming that there are 128 characters, the following program will print them out, together with their ordinal values.

```
PROGRAM CharacterSet (output);
   VAR i : 0..255;
   BEGIN
      for i := 0 to 255 do write(i:4, chr(i):2);
   END.
```

Running this program, one notices that funny things happen on the screen at first – this is because special characters such as DEL, LF, and so on, are being printed. To omit these characters, the loop can start at 32 or so. Moreover, we can carefully arrange the characters and their values in columns.

Program   We can write each pair in 7 characters, thus having 10 per line. A better program is:

```
PROGRAM CharacterSet (output);
   VAR i : 0..255;
      col : 1.. ;

   BEGIN
      for i := 32 to 255 do begin
         write(i:5, chr(i):2);
         if i mod 10 = 0 then writeln;
      end;
   END.
```

Testing   On a computer using the ASCII code, the output should be like this:

32	33 !	34 "	35 #	36 $	37 %	38 &	39 '	40 (	
41)	42 *	43 +	44 ,	45 -	46 .	47 /	48 0	49 1	50 2
51 3	52 4	53 5	54 6	55 7	56 8	57 9	58 :	59 ;	60 <
61 =	62 >	63 ?	64 @	65 A	66 B	67 C	68 D	69 E	70 F
71 G	72 H	73 I	74 J	75 K	76 L	77 M	78 N	79 O	80 P
81 Q	82 R	83 S	84 T	85 U	86 V	87 W	88 X	89 Y	90 Z
91 [	92 \	93]	94 ^	95 _	96 `	97 a	98 b	99 c	100 d
101 e	102 f	103 g	104 h	105 i	106 j	107 k	108 l	109 m	110 n
111 o	112 p	113 q	114 r	115 s	116 t	117 u	118 v	119 w	120 x

121 y	122 z	123 {	124 |	125 }	126 ~	127	128 Ä	129 Å	130 Ç
131 É	132 Ñ	133 Ö	134 Ü	135 á	136 à	137 â	138 ä	139 ã	140 å
141 ç	142 é	143 è	144 ê	145 ë	146 í	147 ì	148 î	149 ï	150 ñ
151 ó	152 ò	153 ô	154 ö	155 õ	156 ú	157 ù	158 û	159 ü	160 †
161 °	162 ¢	163 £	164 §	165 •	166 ¶	167 ß	168 ®	169 ©	170 ™
171 ´	172 ¨	173 ≠	174 Æ	175 Ø	176 ∞	177 ±	178 ≤	179 ≥	180 ¥
181 µ	182 ∂	183 Σ	184 ∏	185 π	186 ∫	187 ª	188 º	189 Ω	190 æ
191 ø	192 ¿	193 ¡	194 ¬	195 √	196 ƒ	197 ≈	198 ∆	199 «	200 »
201 …	202	203 À	204 Ã	205 Õ	206 Œ	207 œ	208 –	209 —	210 "
211 "	212 '	213 '	214 +	215 ◊	216 ÿ	217 Ÿ	218 ⁄	219 ¤	220 ‹
221 ›	222 fi	223 fl	224 ‡	225 ·	226 ‚	227 „	228 ‰	229 Â	230 Ê
231 Á	232 Ë	233 È	234 Í	235 Î	236 Ï	237 Ì	238 Ó	239 Ô	240
241 Ò	242 Ú	243 Û	244 Ù	245 ı	246 ^	247 ~	248 ¯	249 ˘	250 ˙
251 ˚	252 ¸	253 ˝	254 ˛	255 ˇ					

The in-operator

Characters form natural subsets. For example, there is the set of digits, the set of capital letters, the set of vowels, and so on. In Pascal, we can construct sets of characters and use the `in` operator to check whether a value is in a given set.

A set is constructed from a list of items and ranges of items, enclosed in square brackets. The ranges are expressed as starting value and ending value either side of double dots. For example, typical sets are:

```
['A', 'E', 'I', 'O', 'U', 'a', 'e', 'i', 'o', 'u']
['0'..'9']
['+', '-', '0'..'9', '.', 'E']
```

There is more about sets in Chapter 10, but note here that we can also construct sets of integers, and that the elements of a set must all be of the same type. Thus, we cannot mix character literals and integer literals in the same set.

To use the in-operator for expression e and set s, we have:

```
e in s
```

When checking for something not in a set, we have to use the somewhat clumsy notation:

```
not (e in s)
```

In Example 5.3 we considered a menu system, where commands were typed in and processed by the procedure `GetCommand`. One of the functions of `GetCommand` would be to check that the characters typed in were valid commands. If not, the request could be repeated. The loop would look like this:

```
REPEAT
  write(Please type in your choice: );
  readln(command);
  if ch in ['A'..'Z'] then
    ch := chr(ord(ch) - ord('A') + ord('a'));
UNTIL command in ['A','R','F','E','S','P','Q'];
```

EXAMPLE 6.5   Validating course codes _____

Problem   Course codes at Zanyland University have a precise form: 4 capital letters followed immediately by 3 digits and terminated by a space. As a first step in validating that student registrations have been typed correctly into the computer database, we want a procedure that checks the above rule.

Solution   The procedure can be written to perform the check, and put with a small program that can read possible course codes and validate them.

Algorithm   The algorithm is straightforward. We have to check a sequence of eight characters where the first four must be capital letters, the next three must be digits and the eighth must be a space. If an error occurs at any stage, we want to note the fact, but carry on checking to see how many errors there are. So we declare an integer variable error, initially set to zero, and every time a rule is broken, we increase its value by one. After all the characters have been read, the course code is correct provided that error is still zero.

Program

```
PROGRAM ValidateCourseCode(input,output);
    VAR
       error : 0..99;

  PROCEDURE check;
    {Returns global variable : error}
    CONST
       space = ' ';
    VAR
       i : 1 ..4;
       ch : char;
    BEGIN
       error := 0;
       FOR i := 1 to 4 do begin
          read(ch);
          IF not (ch in ['A'..'Z'])
             then error := error + 1;
       END;
       FOR i := 1 to 3 do begin
          read(ch);
          IF not (ch in ['0'..'9'])
             then error := error + 1;
       END;
       read(ch);
       IF ch <> space
          then error := error + 1;
       END; {check}


  BEGIN
     writeln('*******Course Code validation********');
     writeln;
     writeln ('Type a possible course code, '
              'followed by a space and return.');
     error := 0;
     Check;
     readln;
```

```
      IF error = 0
         then writeln('Course code correct')
         else writeln('Course code incorrect: ',
                       error:2,' error(s)');
   END.
```

Testing   A typical run might be:

```
******* Course code validation *******
Type a possible course code, followed by a space and return.
CM104
Course code incorrect: 1 error(s)
```

6.5   Reals

Real numbers are those that may have fractional parts, and are used for quantities where this is appropriate, such as prices, weights and measures, and mathematical results. A real number does not have to have a fractional part, though, and the values of all the integer numbers are contained in the set of reals. We now discuss all the properties of the type real.

Real values

There are two ways of writing real numbers. Fixed point is the usual way, with a decimal point (not comma) being used. Examples of fixed point reals are:

```
   3.141593      0.18      5.0      0.000004      10000000
```

The second real form is one that splits the number into a **mantissa** and an **exponent**. This is known as **floating point** form. The purpose of the floating point is to be able to represent very large or very small numbers without having all the zeros. The exponent indicates a power of 10 by which the mantissa must be modified. Since the power can be positive or negative, and there is no rule about how the split must be made, there can be many ways of representing a single number in floating point form. For example, consider the number forty million. In fixed point form it is 40000000.0, which is rather hard to read. In floating point form it can be written as 4E7 or 40E6. Similarly, for a very small fraction such as 0.000001, the floating point form could be 0.1E–5 or 1.0E–6.

When dealing with physical values measured in kilometres or nanoseconds or megabytes for example, keeping exponents to multiples of three helps to reflect the prefix conventions of metric units. Thus, we would have:

5085 kilometres	5.085E6 metres
7 nanoseconds	7.0E–9 seconds
10 megawatts	10E6 watts

Range of values

The range of values of a real number is very much larger than that of an integer. Since there are two parts to a real number – the fraction and exponent – the range is expressed in terms of the number of significant digits that can be accommodated and the highest value of the exponent. As with the integers, the range depends on the number of bits allocated to each part. Typically, reals will be stored in 64 bits, giving the following range:

- 16 digits of accuracy

- exponent from –38 to +38

If only 32 bits are used, then the exponent stays the same, but the number of significant digits in the fraction drops to a mere six. The effect of the limit on significant digits is that the following two numbers, if read in, would both be stored as the same value:

```
12345678.12345678
12345678.1234567812345
```

Further implications of floating point on computation are discussed below.

Because they cannot be exactly expressed in decimal notation, real variables cannot have lower and upper bounds that can be checked by the compiler, as is the case with integers. However, such information is useful to readers of the program and it is good practice to indicate the expected accuracy and range of each variable as a comment. Examples of real constant and variable declarations are:

```
CONST
   VAT = 0.15;    {15%}

VAR
   second      : real;    {0.00..59.99}
   percentage  : real;    {0.0..100.0}
   share       : real;    {0.00..0.99}
   cost        : real;    {0..100E6}
   temperature : real;    {- 40..50}
   x, y, z      : real;    {-1.000000E-15..1.000000E15}
```

Real operators and functions

There are four operators for reals: $+ - * /$. The slash symbol is used for division. It is not applicable to integers in the sense that it does not produce an integer result. However, if / is applied to integers, Pascal will perform the division and produce a real result.

There are ten standard functions that operate on real numbers. They can be divided into the five mathematical functions:

abs(x)	$\lvert x \rvert$	absolute value
sqr(x)	x^2	square
sqrt(x)	$\sqrt{x}$	square root
ln(x)	$\log_e x$	natural logarithm

`exp(x)`	e^x	natural anti-logarithm

the three trigonometric functions, for angles in radians (not degrees):

`sin(x)`	$\sin x$	sine in radians
`cos(x)`	$\cos x$	cosine in radians
`arctan(x)`	$\tan^{-1} x$	inverse tangent

and the two conversion functions:

`trunc(x)`	smallest integer less than x
`round(x)`	nearest integer to x

These last two functions were discussed in the section on integers.

Real numbers are used mainly for mathematical calculations and, because programs are written a line at a time, the formulae sometimes look quite different to the usual mathematical layout. The main difference is in the use of / for division, rather than a line underneath the numerator, and in the use of functions for square root and so on. These points are illustrated in the following examples of real expressions, with their mathematical equivalents:

`sqr(x) * sin(sqr(x))`	$x^2 \sin x^2$
`sqrt(sqr(b) - 4 * a * c)`	$\sqrt{b^2 - 4ac}$
`a / (b * c)`	$\dfrac{a}{bc}$
`5 / 9 * (F - 32)`	$\dfrac{5}{9}(F - 32)$

Parentheses are often needed in order to ensure the correct precedence. The operators / and * have the same precedence and are evaluated left to right, so that:

`a / b * c`	is	$\dfrac{ac}{b}$	not	$\dfrac{a}{bc}$

Pascal does not have a built-in operator for raising something to a power. Exponentiation is achieved by using the `ln` and `exp` functions as follows:

$$x^y \;=\; e^{y\ln(x)} \;=\; \texttt{exp(y * ln(x))}$$

However, if y is a small known integer, then it may be easier to simply use multiplication, as in:

$$x^4 \;=\; \texttt{x * x * x * x}$$

Note that it is not permissible to raise a negative number to a fractional power using `exp` and `ln` directly.

Real input and output

Real numbers of either form can be read in using read and readln, with the same convention as for integers, that the number should end with a space or the end of a line. Real numbers can be written out in write and writeln statements, but in the absence of any formatting, they are written in floating point. Most of the time, though, numbers will be required to be output in fixed point, in which case, two field widths must be given for:

- the complete number,
- the decimal places.

If the number as stored in the computer has more decimal places than specified for printing, then it is rounded. The complete number is right-justified in the field given for it. If the integer part of the number needs more space than is given, then the number reverts to floating point form. The column for the sign can be used by the number itself if the number is positive. Finally, if the width for the decimals is missing or zero, floating point is used. These rules are illustrated in the following few examples, where ~ indicates a printed space:

```
CONST
    x  = -1024.83;
    pi = 0.3141593;

writeln (pi:5:3);              3.142
writeln (pi:10:7);             ~3.1415930
writeln (pi:12:1);             ~~~~~~~~~~3.1
writeln (pi:7);                3.142E0
writeln (x:8:2);               -1024.83
writeln (x:6:2);               -1.02E3
```

EXAMPLE 6.6   Compound interest

Problem   ZanBank have decided to offer their customers compound interest on special accounts. The interest is calculated at the end of each year, based on the initial principal and the prevailing rate. How will the money grow?

Solution   The formula for compound interest is:

$$P_n = P \left(1 + \frac{R}{100}\right)^Y$$

where Y is the number of years the money is left in. We can use the Simple Interest program from Section 3.5 as it stands for the output, and just insert this formula to calculate the interest over each of the periods 5 to 15 years.

Algorithm   Translating the formula into Pascal means using the real functions exp and ln to raise to the power. In other words, we have:

```
PN := P * exp(years*ln(1+rate/100));
```

Testing   Running the program, we should get the following results. It may be interesting to compare them to those for simple interest.

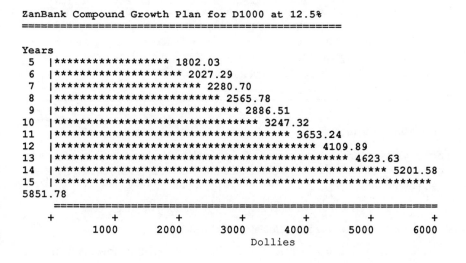

```
ZanBank Compound Growth Plan for D1000 at 12.5%
=======================================================

Years
  5  |***************** 1802.03
  6  |******************* 2027.29
  7  |*********************** 2280.70
  8  |************************* 2565.78
  9  |*************************** 2886.51
 10  |****************************** 3247.32
 11  |*********************************** 3653.24
 12  |**************************************** 4109.89
 13  |********************************************* 4623.63
 14  |**************************************************** 5201.58
 15  |*********************************************************
5851.78
        =================================================================
     +        +        +        +        +        +        +
           1000     2000     3000     4000     5000     6000
                              Dollies
```

Program   The program is:

```
PROGRAM Interest (input, output);
  CONST
    P = 1000; {dollies}
    rate = 12.5; {%}

  PROCEDURE axis;
    {Draws a horizontal axis labelled
    from 0 to 6000 in steps of 1000}
    … as before
    END;

  PROCEDURE histo(years : integer; h : real);
    {Draws a histogram bar for values
    between 1 and 8000, scaled by 100}
    VAR
      star : 1..80;
    BEGIN
      write(years:2,'  |');
      for star := 1 to round(h/100) do
        write('*');
      writeln (h:9:2);
    END;

  PROCEDURE Calculate;
    VAR
      PN : real;
      years : 5..15;

    BEGIN
      for years := 5 to 15 do begin
        PN := P * exp(years*ln(1+rate/100));
        histo(years, PN);
      end;
    END;
```

```
BEGIN
    writeln('ZanBank Compound Growth Plan for D',P:1,
            ' at 12.5%');
    writeln('=====================================================');
    writeln;
    writeln('Years');
    Calculate;
    Axis;
END.
```

Arithmetic limits

Since computer arithmetic is done in fixed-sized words there has to be some way of handling calculations that go outside the range of numbers provided. There are two possibilities:

- an approximate value is used and calculation continues; or

- an error occurs and calculation is abandoned.

The first approach is used when there is a loss of precision in how the number is stored, and the second is used when the number actually goes outside the range. These two cases are now considered.

Loss of precision

The mantissa of a floating point number holds all the digits of precision available. Sometimes an operation may produce a number which has more digits than can be accommodated. Some digits will be lost, and this may affect subsequent calculations and the end result.

To illustrate this effect, assume that there is a little computer with reals stored with:

- 4 digits in the mantissa,

- 1 digit in the exponent.

First, consider the problem of inexact division. The expression 10 / 3 * 3 should produce 10, but in fact may work out as:

```
10 / 3 * 3   =    3.333
                    *3
             =    9.999
```

Precision was irretrievably lost in the division. This is quite a common result and you should see if it happens on your computer. If the answer is printed in floating point form, the inaccuracy should be apparent; if printed in fixed point with a field width for the fraction smaller than the digits provided by the mantissa, then the number may be rounded and appear to be correct. Thus, on the little computer with 4 digits in the mantissa:

```
writeln (10 / 3 * 3,   10 / 3 * 3 :8:1);
```

gives:

```
.999E0                10.0
```

This phenomenon is the same no matter how large the mantissa.

The second problem occurs in large multiplications. If two four-digit numbers are multiplied, the result will have seven or eight digits, but still, on our little computer, only four can be stored. For example:

```
60.08 * 4.134 = 248.3 7072  cannot be represented
              = 248.4
```

Such effects become more noticeable with very large numbers. On this little computer with a 4-digit mantissa, we have:

largest number	0.9999 E 9 or 999 900 000
second largest number	0.9998 E 9 or 999 800 000

In between these, there is nothing, so that any of the 100 000 missing values have to be represented by one of these. For example:

999 934 628 is represented by 999 900 000
999 876 543 is represented by 999 900 000

When multiplying, see what happens:

```
73.56 * 1101 = 80 98 9.56   cannot be represented
             = 80 990
```

Overflow and underflow

These are error conditions where a number itself, rather than just its precision, is too large or too small. They apply to integers and reals.

The largest integer value is given by the constant `maxint`. It is not possible to create or store an integer value larger than this. The computer should catch such attempts and signal an error. More subtly, it is also not permissible to go out of range during a computation, even if the final result is within range. So, for example, the following expression cannot be evaluated:

```
maxint * 2 div 3
```

because twice the value of `maxint` cannot be represented, even as a temporary value. However, if the expression is rewritten in the following way, the evaluation becomes possible:

```
maxint div 3 * 2
```

Just switching to real arithmetic as in:

```
maxint * 2 / 3
```

would not help because most Pascal systems will remain in integer mode as long as possible. Thus, they will still treat the multiplication as an integer operator, and only switch to real when encountering the /. It is, however, always better to use integers if they are applicable, because rounding error problems are avoided. Moreover, real variables cannot be used in several places where integers are acceptable, for example as loop variables in for-statements or as key-expressions in case-statements.

At the other end of the scale, for floating point, we have for our little 4-digit computer:

smallest number   0.1000E–9 or 0.0000000001

Any value less than half of this will be stored as zero. This fact must be remembered when performing computations with very small numbers. Multiplication is especially vulnerable, as shown in this expression:

$a / (b * c)$ where $a = 0.0000004$ or $0.4E{-}6$
                                 $b = 0.00001$ or $0.1E{-}4$
                                 $c = 0.000\ 004$ or $0.4E{-}5$

$b * c$ produces $0.4E{-}10$ which is smaller than the smallest real, and therefore is represented as 0. As a result, the division will fail. As often happens, reordering an expression enables it to be evaluated more accurately. In this case, the equivalent form of $a / b / c$ will work. a / b gives 0.04, and this divided by c gives the answer of 10 000.

Numerical computing

There is an area of computer science – called numerical analysis – which examines how to deal with boundary cases of finite number systems. For ordinary programming, it is sufficient just to be aware of the problems and to be able to recognize the effects when they occur. Remember that difficulties in integer arithmetic will not necessarily go away if the calculation is done in reals. It is always better to use integers if they are applicable, because the precision problems are avoided. Moreover, real variables cannot be used in several places where integers are acceptable, for example as loop variables in for-statements or as key-expressions in case-statements.

WHAT WE HAVE LEARNT

This chapter has ranged over four of Pascal's five predefined types. Although the usage of the types was familiar to us from earlier chapters, we spent time here formally defining the values, operators, functions, procedures and input/output facilities associated with each type.

For integers, we highlighted the use of the mod and div operators. For characters, we printed out the ASCII character set.

*For **booleans**, we looked at how they are used to save the state of a condition, and for **real** numbers we looked at the wealth of functions that are available (and remarked on some that are not).*

*The chapter ended by discussing the importance of being aware of the limitations of **floating point** form in a computer. Programming processes introduced are:*

1. *Converting numbers to different bases using mod and div.*
2. *Regulating flow based on stored conditions.*
3. *Examining new boolean operators.*
4. *Checking character input.*
5. *Watching the size of numbers.*

QUIZ

1. What are the five properties that define a type?

2. How would you write out the value of the smallest integer on your computer?

3. If x has the value 1948, what would be the output of:

```
write (x, x:10, x mod 2,ord(odd(x)));
```

4. Under what conditions are the mod operator and the exp, ln and arctan functions not defined?

5. Rewrite the following as a single assignment statement:

```
if (day = 29) and (month = 2)
  then possiblyleap := true
  else possiblyleap := false;
```

6. The following expression is meant to compute whether x is in the interval 1 to 10 inclusive. What is wrong with the expression? Rewrite it correctly.

    (x >= 1) or (x <= 10)

7. The following loop reads and totals a temperature value every second. What is wrong with it?
```
for sec := 1 to 60 do begin
  write(sec); read(temp);
  total := total + temp;
end;
```

8. The totalling has now to be done every tenth of a second. Could the for-loop be adapted? Rewrite the loop as a while-loop and then as a repeat-loop.

9. Given the following constant declaration and corresponding write statement what would the output be, if the computer being used has 11 decimal digits of precision? What would it be on a computer with 4 digits of precision?

```
CONST  pi = 3.14159265;
writeln(pi : 10:6);
```

10. At the Zanyland Factory, the 24-hour day is divided into three shifts:

     Shift 1   – from 00.00 to 07.59

Shift 2   – from 08.00 to 15.59

Shift 3   – from 16.00 to 23.59

Write an assignment statement which calculates from the time (which is given as a real number) the appropriate shift (which is an integer number).

PROBLEMS

6.1   **Real functions** Write a program to tabulate the values for all the real functions, for values between two given limits. Experiment with the layout and field widths to obtain a reasonable-looking table.

6.2   **Easter**   Easter is a very movable feast, occurring on a day over about six weeks in different years. There is a formula which will work out Easter for the 20th and 21st centuries, namely:

```
a = year mod 19
b = year mod 4
c = year mod 7
d = (19A + 24) mod 30
e = (2b + 4c + 6d +5) mod 7
f = 22 + d + e - 1
if f in [1954, 1981, 2049, 2076] then f = f - 7
Easter is on f th day after 1st March (which may be in April)
```

Write a program that asks for the year and prints out the date of Easter.

6.3   **Birthdays** The probability of two people in a group of n having the same birthday is:

$$p(n) = 1 - \frac{365}{365} \times \frac{364}{365} \times \frac{363}{365} \cdots \frac{365 - n + 1}{365}$$

Write a program to evaluate and print this probability for groups of 2 to 60 people.

6.4   **Car tax**   There is a special tax on cars in Zanyland which is presently at the following rate:

Net price	Rate
< D5000	15%
D5000 – D10000	D1000 (flat rate)
>D10000	10%

Write a program which prints out the net price, tax and gross price for cars, with net prices between D2500 and D12500 in steps of D500.

6.5   **Powers** Raising to a power x^y can be done by a loop, provided y is an integer. Using nested loops with x and y, write a program to print out a table of x to the power y, for y up to 5 and x up to as high as your computer will go in integers. Then convert x to a real number by multiplying by 1.0 and see how high you can go.

6.6   **E-mail ids**. At Zanyland University, users are assigned id names for using the e-mail system, which consist of their first initial and the first seven letters of their surname. Write a program which will take in a name in ordinary form and produce the appropriate user id. For example,

J M Bishop	jbishop
G V Oosthuizen	goosthui
R W Van Den Heever	rvandenh

6.7   **Summing a series**   Write a program which prints out the first 10 terms in the series:

$$\sum \frac{1}{i^2} = 1 + \frac{1}{2^2} + \frac{1}{3^2} + \dots$$

6.8   **Lamps.**   A street is lit by 4 lamps of 1000 W each on lamp posts 20 m high and 50 m apart, that is:

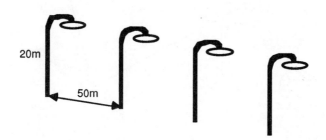

The intensity of illumination, in candelas, produced by a lamp of height h and power C at a point d from the post is given by:

$$L = \frac{C\,h}{(h^2 + d^2)^{1.5}}$$

The level of illumination at any one point can therefore be found by adding up the contributions of each of the four lamps.

Write a program which calculates the intensity of illumination at 10 metre intervals under the lamps. *Hint*: Although specific values have been given for C, h and d, construct the program so that these values are read in, and test your program for various different sets of data.

6.9   **Menus.**   Design a standard procedure which will accept commands and activate operations based on a menu. Use Example 5.3 as a starting point, but verify the commands, and permit upper and lower case as well.

6.10   **Roman calculator.**   The ancient Romans really did use their number system for calculation, but they wrote the numbers in a simpler than usual form. Instead of using IX for 9 or IV for 4, they just wrote out the symbols required, that is, VIIII or IIII. Using this form, write a program to read in two Roman numbers and an operator (+ – or *) and print out the result in Roman numerals. For example, to add 45 and 18, we would have:

```
First number? XXXXV
Operator? +
Second number? XVIII
This is 45 plus 18 and the answer is 63 or LXIII.
```

6.11 **Fences.** A farmer wishes to build a fence around an irregular paddock. He has measured the position of the four corners as (x,y) distances in kilometres relative to his house as follows:

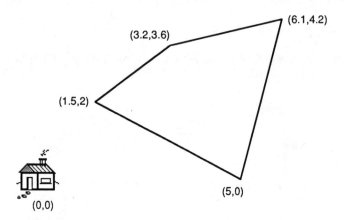

Write a program to print out the perimeter of the paddock, using the formula for the distance between two points as:

$$\sqrt{(x_1 - x_2)^2 + (y_1 - y_2)^2}$$

6.12 **Sine function.** The sine function can be approximated by the series:

$$\sin (x) = x - \frac{x^3}{3!} + \frac{x^5}{5!} - \frac{x^7}{7!} \cdots$$

Write a program which will calculate the value of sin at an angle to be read in, using as many terms as necessary to achieve:

a) an accuracy of 10E-6, and then

b) the same accuracy as the built-in sin function.

Hint: Don't calculate the powers and factorials anew for each term – keep running totals which are updated.

7 Files and Windows

7.1 Processing data
7.2 Text files
7.3 The Screen Manager
7.4 Windows

7.1 Processing data

When we discussed loops in earlier chapters, we mentioned four ways of detecting the end of data:

- build in a count;

- preface with a count;

- end with a signal value;

- use a built-in signal value.

The last method has the decided advantage that the data can be of any length and does not need an additional terminating value. It can be achieved in Pascal by using the end-of-file function.

End-of-file

The data that is typed in from a keyboard, and which is shown simultaneously on the screen, forms a **file**. A file has an end, and on most systems it is possible to indicate this explicitly by typing some special character on the keyboard, such as

ESC or CTRL-Z. (The particular character differs from computer to computer.) When this end-of-file character is typed, an end-of-file flag is set in the Pascal system, and it can be tested by calling the function `eof`.

Pascal defines `eof` as a boolean function which returns true or false depending on the value of the end-of-file flag. Thus if we have a simple loop such as

```
while not eof do
   read(ch);
writeln('All done');
```

data will be accepted from the keyboard, until the end-of-file character is pressed. This will cause the loop to end and the closing message to appear. The end-of-file character itself is not read because `eof` becomes true when the character is pressed, not when it is read.

One important property of data, when viewed as constituting a file, is that it may not be present at all. In other words, the file may be empty. To guard against this eventuality it is better to use while-loops rather than repeat-loops when processing files.

EXAMPLE 7.1   Average word lengths

Problem   Suppose we wish to calculate the average length of words for a large amount of text.

Solution   We can write a program which reads the text, character by character, keeping a count of the number of letters and the number of words. We can define a word as

- starting with a letter or an apostrophe,

- containing letters, apostrophes and hyphens,

- ending with anything that isn't one of those.

Notice that punctuation that occurs within a word *is* counted. To detect the end of the data, we shall use `eof`.

Examples   Word counts for the following phrases illustrate what we are after:

It is hot today, isn't it?	2 2 3 5 5 2	average = 3
end-of-file	11	average = 11
Good – that's OK	4 6 2	average = 4

Algorithm   There are two ways of tackling the algorithm. The first is to regard the sentence as consisting of words and gaps (as it does) and having a loop to successively process these. Reading a word and skipping over a gap are actions that would require loops themselves. We can therefore call this the **nested loops** or **structured** solution. The algorithm is:

Word averages

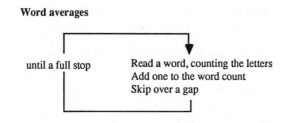

until a full stop   Read a word, counting the letters
                         Add one to the word count
                         Skip over a gap

The second approach is to regard the sentence as a single stream of characters, some of which trigger events such as incrementing a count. The structure of this algorithm is quite different, that is:

Word averages

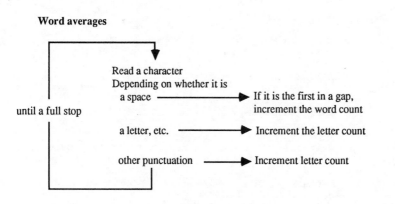

                         Read a character
                         Depending on whether it is
                              a space ──────────────▶ If it is the first in a gap,
until a full stop   increment the word count

                              a letter, etc. ────────▶ Increment the letter count

                              other punctuation ─────▶ Increment letter count

Looking at this algorithm, we can see that it depends on the state of a 'key' – the character just read. This would map into a program based on a case-statement, as described in the next chapter.

Both algorithms have their difficult parts. In the nested loops version, the problem is that in order for one of the loops to stop, it will have to have already read the first character of the next item. For example, the end of a gap is determined by the presence of a non-space. If the word-reading loop is phrased as a read-count sequence, then this letter will be lost from the count. Instead, the loops should follow a read then count-read pattern, so that the read comes at the end of a loop, providing a trigger, but not actually processing the character.

In the state approach, the problem is to distinguish between the first space in a gap (which causes the word count to be incremented) and the other spaces, which must simply be ignored. This is handled by a boolean variable which is set and tested appropriately.

Program We shall proceed with the structured solution, using procedures to good effect to emphasize that we are dealing with words and gaps alternately. Notice that we can avoid having to list all possible punctuation marks, by only referring to the ones in words, and using not to get the others.

We would like to be free to start the text with a gap, and in fact to have no data at all. This is taken care of by setting ch to some gap character such as space, and going straight into the `skipagap` procedure. The while-loop then ensures that nothing happens if in fact no gap or no data exists.

```
PROGRAM CalculateWordAverage (input, output);
   VAR
      ch       : char;
      words,
      letters  : 0..maxint;

   PROCEDURE ProcessaWord;
      {called once a letter or apostrophe has been found}
      BEGIN
         WHILE not eof and
            (ch in ['A'..'Z','a'..'z','-','''']) do begin
            letters := letters +1;
            read(ch);
         END;
      END; {ProcessaWord}

   PROCEDURE skipagap;
      {called once a non-word character has been found}
      BEGIN
         while not eof and
            not (ch in ['A'..'Z','a'..'z','''']) do
            read(ch);
      END; {skipagap}

   BEGIN
      writeln('****** Word averages ******');  writeln;
      writeln('Type in text ending with the eof character');
      words := 0;
      letters := 0;
      ch := ' ';
      skipagap;
      while not eof do begin
         ProcessaWord;
         words := words + 1;
         skipagap;
      end;
      writeln;
      writeln('The number of letters is ', letters:1);
      writeln('The number of words is ', words:1);
      writeln('The average letters per word is ',
                round(letters / words));
   END.
```

Testing   The test data should include all possibilities. Just looking at the program, what would it do if we had text which did not end with a punctuation mark? For example, try:

    J A Jones

When we get into `ProcessaWord` to read Jones, we will read the `'s'`, go round the loop and try to read again. Since this is the end of the file, the loop stops and we exit `ProcessaWord` into the main loop, and hence straight into `skipagap`. Since `eof` is now set, `skipagap` does nothing and we come out of that loop and end gracefully. The ending is not quite as graceful if there are no words at all because then the division at the end will fail. This situation should be checked for.

End-of-file and numbers

End-of-file can also be used with data consisting of numbers, though here we have to be a bit careful. Given a list of numbers such as:

```
81  53  12
97
34  2  704
```

then the special end-of-file character must be pressed immediately after the 4, without any spaces or returns intervening. If this is not done, then after the 704, end-of-file will not be set, and a program may try to read another number – which isn't there.

EXAMPLE 7.2   Summation again

Problem   Suppose we wish to adapt the program that sums a list of numbers (Section 4.4) so that it will not need a count or terminator.

Solution   The end-of-file can be used. In order to record how many numbers were read, a count is kept inside the loop.

Program

```
PROGRAM Summation3 ((input, output);
VAR
    i       : 1..10000; {say}
    total,
    number : integer;   {anything}

BEGIN
    writeln('****** Summing numbers ',
                ' (Version 3 - with eof)******');
    writeln('Type in the numbers ending with eof');
    total := 0;
    i := 0;
    WHILE not eof do begin
        i := i + 1;
        write(i,': ');   read(number);
        total := total + number;
    END;
    writeln;
    writeln('That''s enough, thanks.');
    writeln('The total of the ',i:1,
            ' numbers is ', total);
END.
```

Testing   See what happens if the end-of-file does not come immediately after the last number.

End-of-line

Text is composed of characters, as we have seen, but Pascal goes a step further in recognizing that characters can also be composed into lines. Files that have this structure are given a special type, text. In such files, the end of each line of data has an additional special **end-of-line** marker. Just before the marker is read, an end-of-line flag is set in the system. This flag can be tested using a function called eoln. Thus, we can find out where lines end in the data, and take appropriate action.

Pascal defines eoln as a boolean function which is true if the character which is just about to be read is the end-of-line marker, and false otherwise. Thus, if we wanted to count how many lines there were in a piece of text, we would use statements such as:

```
lines := 0;
WHILE not eof do begin
    read(ch);
    if eoln then lines := lines + 1;
END;
```

When reading numbers, the fact that data comes on different lines can usually be ignored; this is made possible by the usual interpretation of the end-of-line marker as a space. Examples of the use of eoln are kept until the next section, which deals with files.

The buffer variable

Every file has associated with it a buffer variable, which is denoted by the file name and the symbol ↑ (up-arrow). Thus, the buffer variable for the default input file is called input↑. In an input file, the buffer variable is the item which is about to be read, and it can be accessed. This facility enables us to look ahead at the data before committing ourselves.

A typical use of the buffer variable would be to switch between reading numbers and characters, depending on what comes up. An example of such a code would be:

```
if input↑ in ['0'..'9','+','-'] then read(n)
                            else read(ch);
```

The buffer variable is peculiar to Pascal, and is not used in most other programming environments, so it is not used much in this book. However, there is further reference to it in Section 10.3.

7.2 Text files

Up to now, we have used the terminal for all our communication with our programs. As our programs become more sophisticated, and the amount of data they handle and results they produce increases, a single device for all input and output will become inadequate. We need to bring in other devices, such as the printer and disk files. Which device is appropriate at a given time will depend on what the program is doing then, and on the size and meaning of the information.

Input-output streams

A program goes through several **stages** during its running time, and with each we can associate various **input/output streams,** as shown in the diagram.

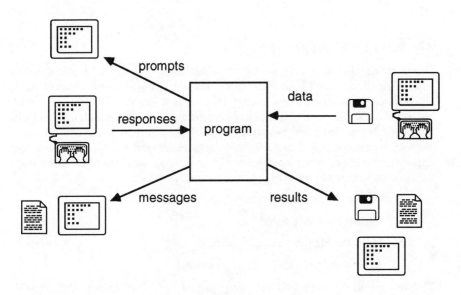

Figure 7.1   Diagram of input/output streams for a typical program.

The common stages and streams are:

1. **Initialization.** During this stage, there is dialogue with the user, consisting of **prompts** and **responses**. These are most typically directed to the screen and accepted from the keyboard of the terminal, respectively.

2. **Processing.** If there is a large amount of **data** to be processed, or if it consists of permanent information, then the most appropriate place for it is a disk file. Similarly, **results** usually need to be perused after a program has run, which means sending them to a printer or to a file again. Also during this phase, errors may occur, or it may be desirable to output comforting status **messages** such as '2000 records processed so far...'. These would go on to the screen, so that the user could be informed immediately, or could go to a printer, to appear intermingled with the results.

3. **Finalization.** It is a very good idea to end any program that processes or produces large amounts of information with a simple **message** indicating how much work was done. Once again, this could go to screen or printer.

The two key issues here, are how to connect a particular device to the program and, in the case of the streams with the option of various devices, how to leave the decision as late as possible – even to runtime. The ability to connect and reconnect devices for various streams relies on the Pascal concept of a **file.** In this section we shall consider files of text; Chapter 10 considers files of other types.

The form of file usage

In Pascal, all information that is read or written using the standard read and write statements is associated with a text file. This fact has been largely hidden from us because we have been using the default files, called input and output. These files are nearly always connected to the default devices, which are most often the keyboard and screen respectively. In order to use other devices such as the printer or the disk, we must declare other files and indicate in the appropriate read and write statements that we want to use these files, rather than the defaults. There are actually several steps in this process:

1. **Declare** a file in the program.

2. **Connect** a device to the file.

3. **Open** the file for reading or writing.

4. **Refer** to it in all input/output statements.

The declaring, opening and referring can all be done in standard Pascal statements which have the following forms. To declare a text file called F, open it, and then use the device via the name of F.

Declaring a text file

```
VAR   F  ; text;
```

Referring to text files

```
    read (F, …);
    write(F, …);
    readln (F, …);
    writeln(F, …);
    eoln (F)
    eof (F)
    page(F);
```

```
┌─────────────────────────────────────────────────────┐
│  Opening a text file                                  │
├─────────────────────────────────────────────────────┤
│   reset (F);        {to open for reading}             │
│   rewrite (F);      {to open for writing}             │
└─────────────────────────────────────────────────────┘
```

It is important always to ensure that the file name has been added to each relevant `read`, `eof` and so on. Omitting them by mistake is a common source of odd errors in programs.

The only essential difference between setting up a file that is designated for reading and one that is designated for writing is in the procedure used to open it: `reset` or `rewrite`. However, there may be an additional requirement for output files. Some systems need to know when you have finished writing to a file so that they can close it; this is not always done automatically when a program ends. Therefore, you may have to call a close procedure, and if you want the file to be closed and saved, then typically the call would be something like:

```
close (F);
```

Connecting up a text file

Unfortunately, the Pascal standard side-steps the issue of connecting devices to files (step 2 above). As a result, each Pascal system provides its own way of connecting files. For example, on a mainframe computer, there would be some Job Control Commands that would set up the required association, such as:

```
FILEDEF OUTPUT DISK MARKS.OUT (RECFM=V)
```

This will connect the Pascal file called `OUTPUT` to the physical file called `MARKS.OUT`. On Unix and Macintosh systems, it is more common to have an extension to the `reset` and `rewrite` procedures, so that the connecting is done from within the Pascal program. The above association would be done by:

```
rewrite (output, 'MARKS.OUT');
```

EXAMPLE 7.3 Averaging marks from a file _____

Problem Suppose we wish to calculate the average mark for students in various classes whose marks and names are stored on disk files.

Solution We can use the `Summation3` program, removing the input prompt statements, adding a statement to calculate the average, and making the changes outlined above in order to use disk files.

Example The following example is of data on a disk file named `compsci2`:

```
73  Jones R
51  Grant A E
65  White B
90  Scarthorpe K
```

Because the name comes after the number, it can be ignored when reading, by making use of `readln`. Recall that `readln` skips everything that remains on a line. Therefore, if we call `readln(mark)` the mark will be read and the name ignored.

Program

```
PROGRAM FileAverages (input, output, marks);

    CONST
      studentmax = 500;
    VAR
      count      : 0..studentmax;
      n, total   : 0..5000;   {100 x studentmax}
      markfile : text;

    BEGIN
      writeln('****** Mark averages ******');
      writeln('The marks file is COMPSCI2');
      reset (markfile,'compsci2');
      total := 0;   count := 0;
      WHILE not eof(markfile) do begin
         readln(markfile, n);   {ignores the name}
         count := count + 1;
         total := total + n;
      END;
      if count = 0
      then writeln('No data in that file')
      else writeln('The average for the ', count:1,
                    ' students is ',round(total / count));
    END.
```

Testing   Let's perform a sample run, using the data above.

```
****** Mark averages ******
The marks file is COMPSCI2
The average for the 4 students is 70
```

EXAMPLE 7.4   Inserting line numbers

Problem   Suppose we wish to list a piece of text, numbering the lines as we go. The first line number need not necessarily be 1.

Solution   Copy the lines of text to their destination stream, adding on the line numbers. The starting number can be read off the terminal in response to a query.

Example   Given a disk file called POEM containing text such as:

```
"Baa, Baa, black sheep
Have you any wool?"
"Yes sir, yes sir,
Three bags full."
```

the numbered version can be written to a disk file called NUMPOEM with numbers starting at, say, 100, that is:

```
100    "Baa, Baa, black sheep
101    Have you any wool?"
102    "Yes sir, yes sir,
103    Three bags full."
```

Algorithm   This is a classic example of a copying program, where the twin concerns are recognizing the end of a line, and checking for the end of a file. The simplest algorithm is as follows:

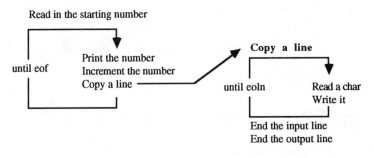

Another consideration in this example is that there are now two places from which input is coming (the terminal for the starting number and the file for the lines), and two to which output must go (the screen for the prompt and the file for the numbered lines). This is handled quite simply by making sure that each read and write statement is directed to the correct place, with the default being the terminal.

It seems convenient to hive off the 'copy a line' part into a procedure, and this will be reflected in the program. Notice that handling the end of an input line can be done with readln – in fact it must be done, or else the next character read will be the end-of-line marker.

Program

```
PROGRAM numberlines (input, output, data, results);

   VAR
      data, results   : text;
      line, firstline : integer;

   PROCEDURE initialize;
      BEGIN
         writeln('****** Numbering lines ******');
         writeln('The data file is POEM');
```

```
                  reset(data,'POEM');
                  writeln('The results file is NUMPOEM');
                  rewrite(results,'NUMPOEM');
                  write('What is the first line number? ');
                  readln(firstline);
                  line := firstline;
              END; {initialize}

          PROCEDURE copyaline;
              VAR ch   : char;
              BEGIN
                  while not eoln(data) do begin
                     read(data,ch);
                     write(results,ch);
                  end;
                  readln(data);  writeln(results);
              END; {copyaline}

          BEGIN
              initialize;
              while not eof(data) do begin
                  write(results, line:4,'  ');
                  line := line + 1;
                  copyaline;
              end;
              writeln(line-firstline:1, ' lines written');
              close (results);
              readln;
          END.
```

Testing   Given the data above, a test run would produce the following at the terminal:

```
****** Numbering lines ******
The data file is POEM
The results file is NUMPOEM
What is the first line number? 100
4 lines written
```

Reusing disk files

A disk file can be read to the end, and then read from the beginning again by the same program. All that needs to be done is to call `reset`, which will put the file back at the start. Similarly, a disk file that has been written by a program, can be read back by it. What is required here is that the file be closed (if the system demands this) and then reset, which will open it for reading.

Several devices can be connected to the same file, one after another. For example, suppose the average mark has to be calculated for several classes, each held on a separate disk file. An additional loop can be placed around the existing `FileAverages` program and on each iteration a new file can be connected and reset.

Of course, one can see that it will be messy to keep all the file names in the program; it would be much better if the names could be read in at the start of the program. To do this, we need strings, which are introduced later in this chapter.

7.3   The screen manager

Pascal was invented in the 1970s before the widespread use of colour graphics screens. Modern dialects of Pascal, such as Turbo Pascal for the PC, have added library packages to Pascal which enable programmers to take full advantage of this hardware and thereby develop more user-friendly and exciting programs.

In this book, we must stick to Standard Pascal, but it is amazing what one can still do to get the best out of screen handling. In this section we shall discuss the screen as an output device in its own right – rather than another direction for text. Then, we introduce a library package written especially for the book which will enable us to achieve effects comparable to that of Turbo Pascal's CRT unit, without any special hardware or software.

Introducing the screen

The screen can be viewed as an (x,y) coordinate system, with the x-axis running across the screen and the y-axis running down.

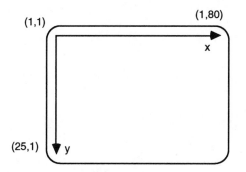

When using the screen as a normal text device, each new line is written after the next, and there is no means for going back up the screen. Let us illustrate this by means of a simple example.

EXAMPLE 7.5   Drawing a graph _____

Problem   Draw a sin graph on the screen, from 0 to 180 degrees.

Solution   It is very easy to print a sin graph going **down** the page, that is with the x-axis going down, and the y-axis across. The known variable, x, can increase linearly and an asterisk be printed at the appropriate place on each successive line. The simplest program to do this is:

```
PROGRAM GraphDown (input, output);
   CONST pi = 3.141592;
   VAR
      d : 0..190;
```

```
        y : real;

BEGIN
  writeln('****** Sin Graph ******');
  writeln;
  d := 0;
  while d <= 180 do begin
     y := sin(d*pi/180)*80;
     if round(y) = 0
        then writeln('*')
        else writeln('*':round(y));
     d := d + 8;
  end;
END.
```

The output for GraphDown is:

```
****** Sin Graph ******

*
        *
                *
                        *
                                *
                                        *
                                                *
                                                        *
                                                                *

                                                                *
                                                        *
                                                *
                                        *
                                *
                        *
                *
        *
*
```

Apart from being displayed sideways, there is also the problem that this part of the graph will zoom off the screen if more is displayed. Scrolling, as it is called, has to be brought under control. The program also assumes that there is only one *y* value for each *x*, which is quite a restriction.

Algorithm   Consider the algorithm:

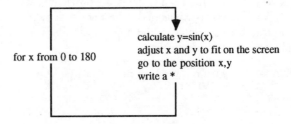

Clear the screen

for x from 0 to 180

calculate y=sin(x)
adjust x and y to fit on the screen
go to the position x,y
write a *

What we want is a means of moving to any *x-y* position on the screen. To do this, we need the ScreenMan library package, developed especially for this book.

Introducing ScreenMan

ScreenMan is a group of types, variables and procedures which together enable us to manage the screen more effectively. In its simplest form, ScreenMan maintains an image of the screen as an 80 x 24 matrix of characters, and allows us to move anywhere in the matrix, write information there, and display the result.

ScreenMan regards the screen as a window, and in many ways treats it like a file. To use ScreenMan, we have to declare the screen as we would a file, and the type we use is **windows**. Thus, we include the declaration:

```
VAR
    screen : windows;
```

Later on, we shall see how we can create more windows on the screen, and swap between them. For now, we assume that we are looking at the whole screen. To tell ScreenMan this, we must call the procedure:

```
whole(screen);
```

This sets up the screen, and clears it for us.

To move to a position on the screen, we use the procedure gotoxy. This takes three parameters; the name of the window – in our case it is just screen – and the coordinates required, which must be in the correct ranges. These are 1–80 for *x* and 1–24 for *y*. So we might say:

```
gotoxy (screen, 40,10);
```

which will get us into the middle of the screen. Remember that the *y* axis goes *downwards*, and so the call:

```
gotoxy (screen, 40,5);
```

will refer to a position higher up the screen, not lower down.

Output with ScreenMan

Having reached a position on the screen, we would obviously like to write something. Because ScreenMan is keeping its own image of the screen, we have to go through ScreenMan procedures when we write.
The first few such procedures are:

```
writech
writeint
writeintln
writestr
writestrln
newline
```

As their names suggest, these will write out a character, string or integer. They will only write out *one* such item, however, unlike the built-in write procedure which can take several parameters. In each case, we have to mention `screen` first. The two procedures with -ln at the end have the added effect of moving down a line on the screen. This can also be done by calling `newline`. `newline` has a parameter which indicates the number of lines to move down – usually one.

Do you remember the `Box` procedure of Section 2.3? If we rewrite it using ScreenMan procedures, and with an identifying parameter as follows:

```
PROCEDURE DisplayBox(id : char);
  BEGIN
      writestrln   (screen, '----------------');
      writestrln   (screen, '|              |');
      writestr     (screen, '|      '
      writech      (screen,id);
      writestrln   (screen, '      |');
      writestrln   (screen, '|              |');
      writestrln   (screen, '----------------');
  END; {DisplayBox}
```

then we can place boxes all over the screen with:

```
whole (screen);
gotoxy (screen,35,10);
DisplayBox('1');
gotoxy (screen,70,15);
DisplayBox('2');
gotoxy (screen,2,5);
DisplayBox('3');
```

which will display the following boxes:

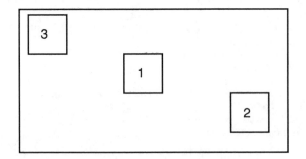

Notice that we deliberately wrote the boxes in any order, to emphasize that the screen is ours to use as we want.

Finally, we introduce a very important procedure. When we write to ScreenMan, it records the information in its image of the screen, but does not actually display it. To cause a display, we call:

```
Show;
```

Including ScreenMan in a program

To acquire ScreenMan facilities in a program, we have to use a text include feature which is available in most Pascal systems. If yours does not have it, then you must physically copy ScreenMan into your program. There are two parts to ScreenMan, and they must be included in two places. These are:

After the keyword CONST	{$I SM1.pas}
Before the first procedure	{$I SM2.pas}

Notice that CONST must appear in your program, even if you have no constants to declare. If your Pascal system permits the declaration parts to be repeated, that is for CONST, VAR, and so on to appear more than once in any program or procedure, then you can use the single version of ScreenMan and simply include

```
{$I SM.pas}
```

anywhere at the start of your program. Now, we can complete the graph example.

EXAMPLE 7.6   Graphs continued _____

Problem   Draw a sin graph neatly across the page.

Solution   Use ScreenMan.

Algorithm   The program that follows now conforms exactly to the algorithm developed earlier. Note that the scaling factors for the actual x and y coordinates are slightly different to those in the previous example, because the x and y axes have different granularities. To summarize:

Axis	Min	Max	for x 0..180	for y 0 ..1
x	1	80	steps of 8, divide by 2.5	multiply by 80
y	1	24	steps of 8	multiply by 22, offset from 24

Table of scaling factors for x and y axes.

It would make sense to abstract away from actual numbers in the program and to create constants which would allow graphs to be displayed over different ranges. This is explored in one of the problems at the end of the chapter.

Program

```
PROGRAM GraphAcross (input,output);

    CONST
      pi =3.141592;
```

```
{$I SM1.pas}

VAR
   d : integer;
   y : real;
   win : windows;

{$I SM2.pas}

BEGIN
   whole(win)
   writestrln(win,'***** Sin graph across *****');
   newline(win,1);
   d := 0;
   while d <= 180 do begin
      y := sin(d * pi / 180) * 22;
      gotoxy (win,round(d / 2.5) +1,24-round(y));
      writech(win,'*');
      d := d + 8;
   end;
   show;
END.
```

Testing   The output from the program is as follows:

```
***** Sin graph across *****
                                    *   *   *
                                 *            *
                             *                  *
                          *                        *
                      *                              *
                   *                                   *
                *                                         *
             *                                              *
          *                                                    *
       *                                                          *
    *                                                               *
 *                                                                    *
*                                                                       *
```

7.4 Windows

A very important feature of modern programming is the ability to create **windows**. A window is a subarea of the screen, defined by minimum and maximum *x* and *y* coordinates. Once a window has been defined, input and output can be directed to that window. If more lines of output are written, then the text in the window scrolls *only in that window* and not on the whole screen. We shall demonstrate two of the main uses of windows:

- positioning shapes and text at different places on the screen, without changing the original procedures;
- using different portions of the screen for different aspects of the output and interface with the user.

To define a ScreenMan window, we call the `Window` procedure with the name of the window and its top-left and bottom-right coordinates. We also supply a string which is the name by which that window can be known later on for input purposes. This parameter can be left blank for now. For example, a 5×5 window in the middle of the screen would be:

```
VAR
   win : windows;

window (win, 38,10,43,15,' ');
```

Notice that we have declared a new variable called `win`, which we give to ScreenMan to record the window's position. Once we have finished with a window, we can reuse the window variable in exactly the same way as we can reuse a file variable. This is illustrated in the next example.

EXAMPLE 7.7   A page of labels _____

Problem   Recall the label printing Examples 2.4 and 3.2. Will ScreenMan make printing labels across the page any easier?

Solution   Certainly! Instead of having to unravel the lines of each box to print them out row by row, we can design the program in the intuitive fashion.

Program

```
PROGRAM PageofLabels (input, output);
   CONST
   {$I SM1.pas}

   VAR
      i : 1..4;
      screen : windows;

   {$I SM2.pas}

PROCEDURE DisplayBox;
   BEGIN
      writestrln   (win,'--------------');
      writestrln   (win,'|            |');
      writestrln   (win,'|            |');
      writestrln   (win,'|            |');
      writestrln   (win,'--------------');
   END; {DisplayBox}
```

```
BEGIN
    whole(screen);
    for i := 0 to 3 do begin
        window(win, i*15+1, 4,i*15+10,10,' ');
        DisplayBox;
    end;
    show;
END.
```

Testing   Running the program will produce the following on the screen:

The loop can then be repeated in order to get a whole page of labels.

Multiple windows

As with files, we can also have multiple windows open at any one time, and alternate between them. In fact, once the windows are open, we can use them at any time, just by mentioning the window name in the special write procedures of ScreenMan.

EXAMPLE 7.8   Racing stars

Problem   Write a program to illustrate output going to more than one window.

Solution   A simple example would be to declare two windows on the screen, and then to send a character to one or the other, chosen at random.

Algorithm   The algorithm consists of looping through the following sequence:

> Generate a random number 1 or 2
> Depending on the number, write a character
>   in window 1 or window 2.

In order to generate a random number we use the formula:

$$s = \text{frac}(s\,a + b) \times n + 1$$

where s is regarded as a seed for the random generating process, and n is the limit of the numbers required. a and b are real constants.

Program

```
PROGRAM Racing (input, output);
  CONST
  {$I SM1.pas}
  VAR
    screen, left, right : windows;
    i : 1..200;
    r : 1..2;
    seed : real;

  {$I SM2.pas}

BEGIN
  whole(screen);
  gotoxy(screen,20,1);
  writestrln(screen,'***** Racing stars *****');
  window(left,2,3,20,12,' ');
  window(right,42,5,62,15,' ');
  seed := 1.23456789;
  for i := 1 to 200 do begin
    seed := seed * 27.182813 + 31.415917;
    seed := seed - trunc(seed);
    r := trunc(seed*2)+1;
    case r of
      1 : writech(left,'*');
      2 : writech(right,'+');
    end;
  end;
  show;
END.
```

Testing   Testing the program, we might get the output that follows.

Snapshots

It is often extremely useful to be able to take snapshots of the screen to use in a report or to take home for debugging. Many computer systems allow the screen to be 'dumped' to the printer, but some do not. ScreenMan provides this facility in a portable way.

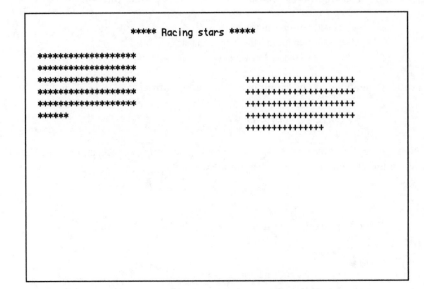

Calling the procedure `SnapShot` produces an exact copy of the screen in a file called *snapₙ*, where *n* starts at 1 and increases with each snapshot required by a particular program. For example, by calling

```
SnapShot;
```

the above output would be copied to a file **snap01**. The file can then be printed.

Input with ScreenMan

Before leaving ScreenMan, we must consider how to read in values. Once again, we must use special ScreenMan procedures, some of which are:

```
readch
readint
readstr
```

As before, each of these takes the window name as its first parameter and the variable that is to receive the value as the second parameter.

When a ScreenMan read procedure is called, the current screen image is displayed and a prompt is put on the last line of the screen. The value required must be typed in here. When next the screen is displayed, this value will appear in the screen at the required point to make for sensible dialogue. Thus if we write

```
writestr(screen, 'How old are you? ');
readint(age);
show;
```

then the screen will contain

How old are you? 23

This manner of inputting is very similar to that used by full-screen terminals connected to mainframe computers.

Because the read procedures do a quick show of the screen, it is usually unnecessary to call show explicitly in an interactive programme. Some experience will be needed to get the right balance of writes, reads, and shows, but the following example can be used as a guide.

Since input could be requested from one of several active windows, the final parameter to the window procedure is used to augment the prompt. If we set up a window thus:

```
window (inwin, 1, 39, 1, 10, 'Data');
```

Then the prompt will be:

Data>

EXAMPLE 7.9 Summation with snappy dialogue

Problem Improve the summation program to use different windows for different purposes, for example one for dialogue and one for the data.

Solution Use ScreenMan. We divide the screen horizontally at line 19, and draw a line there. Then the bottom five lines are used for dialogue, which can scroll, and the rest of the screen is used for data input.

Program

```
PROGRAM Summation4 (input, output);

    CONST
       max = 10000;
       split = 19;
    {$I SM1.pas}

    VAR
       i            : 1..80;
       sets, s      : 0..10;
       count        : 1..100;
       total        : integer;
       screen,
       data,
       dialogue     : windows;

    {$I SM2.pas}

    PROCEDURE sum;
        VAR
           number : integer;
           i : 1..max;
        BEGIN
           total := 0;
           clear(data);
           FOR i := 1 to count do begin
```

```
                    writestr(data,'    ');
                    writeint(data, i);
                    writestr(data,': ');
                    readint(data,number);
                    total := total + number;
                 end;
             END; {sum}

          BEGIN
             whole(screen);
             gotoxy(screen,1,split);
             for i := 1 to 75 do writech(screen,'-');
             window (data,1,1,80,split-1,'Data');
             window (dialogue,1,split+1,80,linemax-1,
                    'Dialogue');

             writestrln(dialogue,'****** Summing numbers ',
                    'with snappy dialogue ******');
             writestr (dialogue,'How many sets of numbers (1..20)? ');
             readint(dialogue,sets);

             for s := 1 to sets do begin
                writestr (dialogue,'How many numbers for set ');
                writeint(dialogue,s); writestr(dialogue,' ? ');
                readint(dialogue,count);
                writestr(dialogue,'Type in the numbers (any size)');
                snapshot;
                newline(dialogue,1);
                sum;
                writestrln(data,'That''s enough, thanks.');
                writestr(dialogue,'The total for the numbers ',
                    'in this set is ');
                writeintln(dialogue, total);
                snapshot;
             end;
             show;
          END.
```

Testing We have used SnapShot to show the state of the screen at two different points. The first snapshot was taken just after the initial dialogue and the request to enter data and would be stored in the file snap01.

The second snapshot was taken after the data had been entered and the results printed out in the dialogue window. Notice that scrolling has occurred in the dialogue window.

Objects

Object-oriented programming is a very important paradigm these days. Pascal was invented at least fifteen years before object-oriented programming and systems (called 'oops') became popular. Therefore, Pascal does not, in its standard form, have any features for supporting oops directly. Nevertheless, Pascal is a powerful enough language that one can adapt it to define and use objects.

```
    ------------------------------------------------------------------
    ****** Summing numbers with snappy dialogue ******
    How many sets of numbers (1..20)? 1
    How many numbers for set 1 ? 4
    Type in the numbers (any size)
```

```
      1: 56
      2: 12
      3: 89
      4: 71
    That's enough, thanks.




    ------------------------------------------------------------------
    How many numbers for set 1 ? 4
    Type in the numbers (any size)
    The total for the numbers in this set is 228
```

In fact, we have already done that! ScreenMan is based on the window object. By declaring a window, we get an object which has data and procedures associated with it. When we look at how ScreenMan is implemented in Section 12.3, we shall develop this approach to oops in Pascal.

WHAT WE HAVE LEARNT

*This chapter dealt extensively with **text files**, how to declare them, open them, and use them, including the **eof** and **eoln** functions, and the management of **multiple input-output streams** in a program. By realizing that at times more that one logical stream is being directed at the screen, we introduced a special package called **ScreenMan** which gives modern screen handling facilities to standard Pascal. The effective use of multiple **windows** was discussed, and better user interaction explored. The ability to create **snapshots** of the screen via ScreenMan makes it a very powerful tool.*
Programming processes introduced were:

1. *Reading till end-of-file.*
2. *Manipulating several input and output streams via logical file names.*
3. *Relating the file concept to windows on the screen.*

QUIZ

1. What character is used to signal end-of-file from the keyboard on your Pascal system?
2. Is there a difference between the effect of the conditions in the following two loops?

   ```
   while not eof do …

   while not eof(input) do …
   ```

3. Give a simple loop to count the number of lines on a file declared as `fin`.
4. Investigate the means by which files are connected to devices on your Pascal system. Find out if there are any specially named devices that might be useful, for example a printer or the screen.
5. A clever programmer has written the following minimal code to copy text from one file to another. Will it work?

   ```
   reset (f);
   rewrite(g);
   while not eof(f) do begin
      read(f, ch);
      write(g, ch);
      if eoln(f) do begin
         readln(f);
         writeln(g);
      end;
   end;
   ```

6. Write calls to ScreenMan procedures to print out your name in the middle of a clear screen.
7. What are the five parameters to the `window` procedure and what are they used for?
8. How would you adapt Example 7.7 to print out a page of 16 blank labels?

9.   Give calls to ScreenMan to set up two windows called Top and Bottom occupying the top and bottom halves of the screen respectively.

10.   Why must special care be taken when reading numbers until end-of-file?

PROBLEMS

7.1   **Converting names** A very old file of people's names was created using all capital letters. Convert it to the usual capital and lower-case letters. Take account of initials, but do not go as far as handling surname prefixes properly, for example:

R A JONES	R A Jones
J. FOX-ROBINSON	J. Fox-Robinson
P DU PLESSIS	P Du Plessis

7.2   **Word length profile**   We already have a program to calculate the average length of words in a piece of text. Following on from this, process the same file, counting how many words are above the average length.

7.3   **Splitting a file** Suppose we have a file of numerical readings, some of which are negative and some of which are positive. We wish to create two new files, one with all the positive numbers, and one with the negative numbers, and then go back and print both out from the program, with the positive numbers file first.

7.4   **Comments** A piece of text is stored on a file. It is divided into paragraphs separated by blank lines. Write a program which reads in the text and prints it out again, ignoring all text between Pascal comment brackets { }. Print suitable warning messages if:

- a { is found inside a comment;
- a } is found without a matching { ;
- a paragraph ends without a matching }.

At the end of each paragraph print the percentage of text (excluding spaces) that occurred in comments.

```
Sample input                  Sample output

This is the same length       This is the same length
as the comment   {This        as the comment rest assured.
assured comment is the        *** No ending bracket
same length as the rest}
rest assured. {And so         Comment is 50% of the text
```

Use ScreenMan's windows to get the input and output side by side as shown here.

7.5   **Standard** A piece of text is stored on a file. It is divided into paragraphs separated by blank lines. Write a program which reads in the text and prints it out again, having made any changes necessary to have the text conform to the following standards:

- three spaces at the start of a paragraph;
- capital letter at the start of each sentence;

- two spaces between sentences or main clauses, that is, after a fullstop, question mark, exclamation mark, semicolon or colon;

- only one space between words otherwise.

```
Sample input                        Sample output
It is always hard to type     It is always hard to type
to a standard.Some people     to a standard.   Some people
use different ones: single    use different ones.      single
or            double   or no  or double or no spaces
spaces before a sentence.     before a sentence.    I think
i think double looks best.    double looks best.
```

Use ScreenMan's windows to get the input and output side by side as shown here.

7.6   **Contents page** Write a program to produce a contents page for a book using data supplied in a fixed format. The data should be read off a file and the output sent to a printer. Consider the following input:

```
(First steps (The computer, 5) (Problem Solving
(Definition, 10) (Outline, 15) (Algorithms,20)) (Programs
and Procedures, 25)) (Types and Looping (Types
(integers,30) (Character,36) (Boolean, 43)) (Looping
(Counting loops,49) (Conditional Loops, 52)))
```

The parentheses indicate the chapters, sections and subsections and the numbers following them are the page numbers. Page numbers are only given when there is no further subdivision. The output for the data above would be:

```
CONTENTS

1.    First Step
   1.1   The Computer                     5
   1.2   Problem Solving
      1.2.1    Definition                 10
      1.2.2    Outline                    15
      1.2.3    Algorithms                 20
   1.3   Programs and Procedures          25
2.    Types and Looping
   2.1   Types
      2.2.1    Integer                    30
      2.2.2    Character                  36
      2.2.3    Boolean                    43
   2.2   Looping
      2.2.1    Counting Loops             49
      2.2.2    Conditional Loops          52
```

Use ScreenMan to get the input and output on the same screen, one window above each other.

7.7   **More windows** In Example 3.1 and Problem 3.3 we considered how to print tables. Use ScreenMan with Example 3.1 to get the effect proposed by Problem 3.3.

7.8   **Counting assignments** We would like to count the number of assignment statements in a program. Make use of the buffer variable to write a program to do this.

7.9   **Two-up display** . Use windows to display a program from a file in two columns on the screen.

8 More about Procedures

8.1 Parameters again

Why do we use procedures? Our experience to date would probably suggest:

- to avoid duplication;

- as a conceptual tool for breaking up a problem into subproblems;

- as a documentation aid.

We have also seen that procedures can be made more powerful by allowing the effect to differ slightly each time the procedure is called, using the parameter mechanism. We can now consider parameters in a more formal way.

The parts of the procedure that are to be generalized are listed in the declaration, straight after the procedure name. These are the **formal parameters**. Correspondingly, when we call the procedure, we list the specific instances for those parts and these are known as **actual parameters**. The list of formal value parameters acts as a declaration of variables that are to be used in the procedure. As for any other variables, therefore, the appropriate types must be specified. Actual parameters can be variables, expressions, procedures or functions.

Procedure declaration

```
PROCEDURE name (formal parameters);
   declarations
   BEGIN
      statements
   END;  {name}
```


Procedure call

```
name (actual parameters);
```

Parameters fall into two categories, depending on the way in which the correspondence between the formals and actuals is set up, that is:

- **value parameters** for passing values in only, and

- **VAR parameters** for passing access to variables.

With value parameters, the value of the actual parameter is passed into the procedure, and may be changed under its formal name there, but any changes do not affect the actual parameter, even if it is a variable rather than an expression. For example, the following program:

```
PROGRAM Passing (input, output);
   VAR
      a : integer;
      b : char;

   PROCEDURE swallow (head : integer; tail : char);
      BEGIN
         writeln ('Swallow 1: ',head:4, tail:4);
         head := head*2;
         tail := succ(tail);
         writeln ('Swallow 2: ', head:4, tail:4);
      END; {swallow}

   BEGIN
      a := 25;
      b := 'X';
      writeln ('Main 1: ', a:4, b:4);
      swallow(a, b);
      writeln ('Main 2: ', a:4, b:4);
   END.
```

would produce the following output:

```
Main 1:              25    X
Swallow 1:           25    X
Swallow 2:           50    Y
Main 2:              25    X
```

The situation is different with VAR parameters. A procedure may have the task of calculating a result which needs to be passed back to the calling program. Pascal provides for this by means of parameters which are specially designated in the list of formals as VAR. These formal parameters act as channels to the actual parameters and any changes made to a formal parameter affect the actual parameter.

The form of a VAR parameter declaration is simply:

VAR parameter declaration

```
VAR   formal parameter identifiers : type identifier;
```

EXAMPLE 8.1   A swapping procedure

Suppose we have a number of occasions when we need to place two values in order. We could write a procedure that has two parameters, and alters them so that their values are in numeric order. The parameters would have to be declared as VAR.

```
PROCEDURE order (VAR n, m : integer);
   VAR temp : integer;
   BEGIN
      if n > m then begin
         temp := n;   n := m;   m := temp;
      end;
   END; {order}
```

If we have x as 9 and y as 5, then the call:

```
order (x, y);
```

will result in x becoming 5 and y becoming 9. If the parameters had been declared as value, then although the values of n and m would have been interchanged, this effect would not have been transmitted back to x and y.

EXAMPLE 8.2   Special integer read

Another useful procedure is one that can read in an integer followed by any character, not necessarily a space. In most Pascal implementations, numbers must be followed by a space, tab or end-of-line. So to read in an integer such as a measurement, for example 6 m or 5 s, we shall need to decode the characters ourselves. The procedure follows the description of integers in Section 6.2.

```
PROCEDURE readinteger (VAR n : integer);
 {Assumes at least one digit after a sign,
 but   the sign is not compulsory}
VAR
   negative        : boolean;
   ch              : char;
BEGIN
   n := 0;
   read(ch);
   if ch in ['+','-'] then begin
      negative := ch = '-';
      read(ch);
   end else negative := false;
   while ch in ['0'..'9'] do begin
      n := n * 10 + ord(ch) - ord('0');
      read(ch);
   end;
   if negative then n := -n;
END; {readinteger}
```

There will be an example of how this could be used in the next section.

Behind the scenes

In order to reinforce the notion of VAR parameters being channels to their actual counterparts, let us look at how they operate inside the computer. In essence, the formal VAR parameter is a variable which is supplied with the **reference** of the actual parameter at the time of the call. The effect of the actual parameters being changed by any changes to the formal parameters is a facility that should not be used lightly. It is also possible that it may not be exactly what is intended in a particular situation, as illustrated in the following example.

Suppose we wish to use the order procedure in another context, that is, we have my age and your age in two variables and we wish to put them in numerical order. If we call:

```
order (myage, yourage);
```

then the contents of the variables are described in Figure 8.1.

What has happened here? The actual parameters have been altered, which is not what we wanted in this case. We probably only wanted to *know* who was younger. What we need is a procedure with these two parameters as value parameters and another, VAR, parameter for the result. This gives:

```
PROCEDURE firstisyounger (n, m :  integer;  VAR b :
boolean);
   BEGIN
      b := n > m;
   END; {firstisyounger}
```

and we could call this with:

```
firstisyounger (myage, yourage, me);
if me then writeln('I am younger);
```

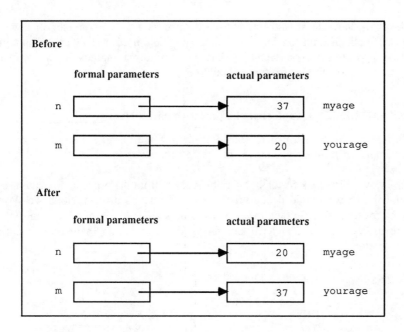

Figure 8.1   Contents of variables before and after a VAR parameter call.

Parameter passing rules

There are certain rules that apply to the correspondence of formal and actual parameters, known as parameter passing. When talking about value parameters, we refer to **pass-by-value** and when referring to VAR parameters, the term is **pass-by-reference**. The rules are:

1. The actual parameters supplied must agree with the formal parameters in number, order and type. Thus, the following are all incorrect calls.

    ```
    order (p);                 needs two parameters
    swallow ('+', 7);          wrong order
    swallow (4, 8);            tail must be a char
    ```

2. For value parameters, the actual parameters can be any constants, variables or expressions. For example, we could have:

    ```
    swallow (sqr(trunc(pi)) + 1, chr(ord(b) - ord('A')));
    ```

    For VAR parameters, the actual parameters must be variables. They may not be constants, because values of the actual parameters may be changed. It would therefore be incorrect to say:

    ```
    order (x, 8);           8 is not a variable
    ```

3. The names chosen for actual parameters are quite independent of those for the formals. However, one need not make them deliberately different. Comments are often useful to describe the meaning of formal parameters.

4.   A variable should only be used once as a VAR parameter in any one call. The reason for this is that a variable used, say twice, as an actual parameter would end up having two formal names, with confusing results. For example, we should not write order (a,a);

EXAMPLE 8.3 Counterfeit cheques with parameters _____

Problem We would like to consider whether the Checkacheque program in Example 4.3 cannot be better written using parameters.

Solution First look for global variable usage. Both the procedures make use of globals, so we should declare them with parameters instead. Next, we should look for repetition. In fact, the two procedures RecordZero and RecordnonZero are nearly identical, and we can rationalize by making them into one, with parameters.

Program Consider the two procedures:

```
PROCEDURE RecordZero;
   {Uses and updates globals : CountofZeros,
                               CountofNonzeros
                               Counterfeit}
   BEGIN
      CountofZeros := CountofZeros + 1;
      CountofNonzeros := 0;
      if CountofZeros = 3 then counterfeit := true;
   END; {RecordZero}

PROCEDURE RecordNonzero;
   {Uses and updates globals : CountofZeros,
                               CountofNonzeros
                               Counterfeit}
   BEGIN
      CountofNonzeros := CountofNonzeros + 1;
      CountofZeros := 0;
      if CountofNonzeros = 4 then counterfeit := true;
   END; {RecordNonzero}
```

We can write a single procedure which does the same operation as either, and would be called by one of the following:

```
if digit = 0
then Register (CountofZeros,CountofNonzeros,3,counterfeit);
else Register (CountofNonzeros,Countofzeros,4,counterfeit);
```

The procedure can be written generally in terms of runs as follows:

```
PROCEDURE Register (VAR CurrentRun, OtherRun : integer;
                        max : integer;
                        VAR counterfeit : boolean);
   BEGIN
      CurrentRun := CurrentRun + 1;
      OtherRun := 0;
      if CurrentRun = max then counterfeit := true;
   END; {Register}
```

Inserting this in the program and rerunning it is left as an exercise.

This example emphasizes that the choice of formal parameter names is important, but that one should not feel obliged to think of new names for the sake of it: counterfeit is a perfectly adequate name as a formal and an actual.

8.2 Functions

We have already seen the use of built-in functions such as sin, sqrt, abs and eof. In Pascal, we can also define our own functions, with the properties that they:

- return a single value as the function value, and

- are called as part of an expression.

Functions can have parameters, along the same lines as procedures. However, it is considered bad practice to have functions that alter their environment, and so generally, by convention, we restrict parameters to passing by value.

Form of a function

A function is declared in much the same way as a procedure, with the added bit of information being its type which may be integer, real, boolean or character. (Subranges of these and enumerated types are also permitted, as described in Chapter 9.) The form below shows how a function is declared. There is no form for a call: calls have to be part of an expression, appearing in another statement such as an assignment or writeln.

Function declaration

```
FUNCTION name (formal parameter declarations) : type;
   declarations
   BEGIN
      statements
   END;   {name}
```

The function must be assigned a value at least once somewhere inside its body before it terminates, and that value must be of the correct type. Although a function is called as part of an expression or assignment statement, the function name may not be used as if it were a variable inside its own body.

For example, suppose we wish to calculate the sum of all the numbers up to n. The temporary variable used to keep the running total is essential, and its value is assigned to the function name at the end.

```
FUNCTION Sigma (n : integer) : integer;
```

```
                    VAR i, total : integer;
                    BEGIN
                       total := 0;
                       for i := 1 to n do
                          total := total + i;
                       Sigma := total;
                    END; {Sigma}
```

EXAMPLE 8.4   Ticking clock _____

Problem   We wish to provide a digital clock which ticks over at the right speed.

Solution   Looking at a clock, the counters for the minutes and seconds go from 0
to 59 and round again, while the hour counter goes from 1 to 12. So we shall
provide a function called next which has three parameters – the counter and its
upper and lower bounds. The function will check the counter against the upper
bound and reset it if necessary.

Function

```
        FUNCTION next (c, lower, upper : integer) : integer;
           BEGIN
              if c = upper then next := lower else next := succ(c);
           END;  {next}
```

Testing   A suitable test would be to print out the time from a given start to a
given finish – carefully choosing these so that each of the hours, minutes and
seconds will tick over, without producing too much output. To keep it
manageable, we can list several times on each line, and in fact, use the modulo
counter to keep track of this too! The program would be:

```
        PROGRAM TestTicker (input, output);
           {Testing the next function using a clock and a counter}

           VAR
              H, startH, endH : 1..12;
              M, startM, endM,
              S, startS, endS : 0..59;
              counter,
              timesperline    : 1..10; {or so}

           FUNCTION next (c, lower, upper : integer) : integer;
              BEGIN
                 if c = upper then next := lower
                              else next := succ(c);
              END;   {next}

           BEGIN
              writeln('***** Testing the next function *****');
              write('Starting hours, minutes and seconds : ');
              readln(startH, startM, startS);
              write('Ending hours, minutes and seconds : ');
              readln(endH, endM, endS);
              write('How many times per line? ');
              readln(timesperline);
              H := startH;     M := startM;     S := startS;
              counter := 1;
```

```
      REPEAT
         write(H:2,':',M:2,':',S:2,'      ');
         counter := next(counter,1,timesperline);
         if counter = 1 then writeln;
         if S = 59 then begin
            if M = 59 then H := next (H,1,12);
            M := next (M, 0, 59);
         end;
         S := next(S, 0, 59);
      UNTIL  (H = endH) and (M = endM) and (S = endS);
      writeln(H:2,':',M:2,':',S:2,'      ');
   END.
```

A typical run would look like this:

```
***** Testing the next function *****
Starting hours, minutes and seconds : 12 59 50
Ending hours, minutes and seconds : 1  0   5
How many times per line? 5
12:59:50  12:59:51     12:59:52     12:59:53     12:59:54
12:59:55  12:59:56     12:59:57     12:59:58     12:59:59
   1:  0:  0        1:  0:  1          1:  0:  2
   1:  0:  3        1:  0:  4
   1:  0:  5
```

There is obviously a better way of outputting the clock time: it should be in a single place, and should 'tick over' in the same way that a digital watch does. To do this, we need to be able to position the cursor on the screen, using the gotoxy procedure discussed with ScreenMan in Section 7.3. This is left as an exercise for the reader.

EXAMPLE 8.5   Checksums

Problem   Zanyland University gives each student a student number which consists of four digits and ends with a checksum character which is computed by taking the sum of the preceding digits modulo 4. These checksums need to be verified.

Solution   Define a function which will take a number, analyse it, and return true or false, depending on whether the checksum digit is correct or not.

Examples   Some sample numbers might be:

1234 2	$1 + 2 + 3 + 4 = 10$;	$10 \bmod 4 = 2$;	correct
5682 1	$5 + 6 + 8 + 2 = 21$;	$21 \bmod 4 = 1$;	correct
7007 1	$7 + 0 + 0 + 7 = 14$;	$14 \bmod 4 = 2$;	incorrect

Algorithm   The number will have to be decomposed, digit by digit. This can be done simply by repeatedly taking modulo 10. At the same time, the digits can be added and then the sum checked against the check digit.

Program

```
FUNCTION checksum (number, digit: integer; ) : boolean;
   VAR
      i : 1 ..4;
      sum : 0..9999;

   BEGIN
      sum := 0;
      for i := 1 to 4 do begin
         sum := sum + number mod 10;
         number := number div 10;
      end;
      checksum := (sum mod 4) = digit;
   END;   {checksum}
```

Notice that in this function, one of the value parameters, number, is used as if it were a variable. This is quite permissible, and any changes made to number will not be reflected back in the calling program.

EXAMPLE 8.6   Length of a number

Problem   We would like to know how much space a number will occupy if printed.

Solution   Working from first principles, we can deduce how many digits an integer needs by looking at the characteristic of its logarithm.

Function

```
FUNCTION digits (n : integer) : integer;
   VAR d : integer;
   BEGIN
      if n < 0 then begin
         d :=1; n := abs(n);
      end else
      d := 0;   {plus sign not printed}
      d := d + trunc (ln(n) / ln(10) + 1);
      digits := d;
   END; {digits}
```

The function could be used in cases where formatting is required. For example, to find out if a number will fit on a line 60 characters wide on which count characters have already been written, we could use:

```
if   count + digits(number) > 60   ...
```

Notice that the function name cannot be used as a variable and therefore the local variable d had to be defined for the summing, and assigned to digits at the end.

8.3   Designing procedures and functions

In designing a Pascal program with procedures and functions, the easy part is breaking the work up into logical components. It is more difficult to do this well. Doing it well means creating components which are as self-contained as possible, and have a safe interface with the rest of the program.

It is generally held that parameters provide the best interface, because the names of the formals are defined by the procedure, and therefore do not depend on or conflict with anything that may be declared elsewhere. Thus we should strive to have procedures that only communicate via parameters, and do not make use of global variables.

This rule applies to constants as well. A procedure can rely on implicit constants, but this weakens its usefulness as a building block in other programs. Take for example the `checksum` function in Example 6.5. It mentions three constants: 1, 4 and 10. One may argue that 10 is genuinely intrinsic to the computation, since numbers are written in base 10, and that 1 is the start of a counting range. But the presence of 4 ties us to the specific case of a four digit number. It would be more general to have this as a parameter, giving:

```
FUNCTION checksum (number, digit, size: integer) : boolean;
   VAR
      i   : 1..maxint;
      sum  : 0..9999;

   BEGIN
      sum := 0;
      for i := 1 to size do begin
         sum := sum + number mod 10;
         number := number div 10;
      end;
      checksum := (sum mod size) = digit;
   END;   {checksum}
```

Not all procedures, of course, are intended to be reused in other programs. Some, particularly those that are declared nested inside another, serve a very specific purpose, and it is sometimes convenient for them to make use of non-local variables. These choices are illustrated in Example 8.7.

Choosing a procedure or a function

The choice of whether to use a function or procedure, when both are possible, can be made according to:

- how many values need to be returned, and

- how the routine is to be called.

If more than one value is to be returned, then necessity dictates that we use a procedure with VAR parameters. If we are only talking about a single value result, then a function is a nicer way of expressing things. However, if we need to know the result of the computation again later in the program, then we won't want to call the function again, and so would like to have the result stored somewhere. A procedure with the VAR parameter serves this purpose, but there is another way of doing it. The essential point is to record the result of the routine, and this can be done with the function. Recall the procedure:

```
PROCEDURE firstisyounger (n,m : integer;  VAR b : boolean);
  BEGIN
     b := n > m;
  END {firstisyounger }
```

We could replace this with a function:

```
FUNCTION isyounger (n, m : integer) : boolean;
  BEGIN
     isyounger := n > m;
  END;  {isyounger }
```

and call it with:

```
answer := isyounger (myage, yourage);
```

Both are correct, and the choice will depend largely on circumstances.

EXAMPLE 8.7   Calculating floor areas _____

Problem   Estate agents frequently provide information about houses that includes the dimensions of each room. It is very useful when comparing houses to be able to have a figure for the total floor area, based on these.

Solution   Enter the room dimensions into a data file, and have a program which reads them and calculates the area. We shall assume that the dimensions are given initially in feet and inches but that we wish to have them in metric as well.

Example   Assume we are dealing with input and output such as this:

```
14 Highfield Lane
-----------------------
Lounge  23'8"x11'2"   264.28sq ft 7.21m x 3.40m   24.55sq m
Bedroom1  12'3"x11'3" 137.81sq ft 3.73m x 3.43m   12.80sq m
```

Algorithm   We use step-wise refinement and start at the outer level, itemizing the tasks that need to be done, in the correct order, and making assumptions about procedures and parameters as seems fitting.

```
BEGIN
   Setupfiles;
   Copyheadings;
   CalculateRoomsandTotal;
END.
```

The idea is that there are no global variables at all (except the files), and that all the work is done inside the procedure CalculateRoomsandTotal. At the next level down, a likely sequence of events is given by this portion of the procedure:

```
BEGIN
    aBlankLine := false;
    WHILE not aBlankLine do begin

        Echoto(' ');
        readftins (ft1, ins1);
        Echoto('x');
        readftins(ft2, ins2);
        multiply (ft1, ins1, ft2, ins2, area);

        convert(ft1, ins1, m1);
        convert(ft2, ins2, m2);
        writeln(area, m1, m2, m1*m2);
                        {with units, of course}
        Addtototals;
        Checkforablankline;
    END;
END;
```

Each procedure can then be elaborated in turn, using as much old material as we can. For example, Readftins can make use of a version of the previously developed procedure, readinteger from Example 8.2.

```
PROCEDURE readftins (VAR ft, ins : integer);
    VAR  a : integer;
            next : char;

    PROCEDURE readinteger
                    (var n : integer; var follow : char);
        {Reads an integer and returns the following character}
        VAR ch : char;
        BEGIN
            n := 0;
            while ch in ['0'..'9'] do begin
                n := n * 10 + ord(ch) - ord('0');
                read(f, ch);
            end;
            follow := ch;
        END; {readinteger}

    BEGIN
        readinteger(a, next);
        if next = '''' then begin {feet}
            ft := a;
            readinteger (ins, next);
        end;
        ins := a;
    END;   {readftins}
```

This procedure illustrates nicely the use of a nested procedure called with different parameters. In fact, we could not have done without the parameters here.

Finally, consider the case of checking for a blank line being the end of the data. (We do not wish to use end-of-file because we are anticipating several sets of data coming in.) The results of the check will be stored in a boolean variable, which is defined outside the procedure, giving:

```
PROCEDURE Checkforablankline;
  BEGIN
    readln(data);  writeln(results);
    if eoln(data) then begin
      aBlankline := true;
      readln(data);  writeln(results);
    end;
  END; {Checkforablankline}
```

Alternatively, the outer procedure could send its boolean variable as a parameter which Checkforablankline could call the same name, and do exactly the same with it, that is:

```
PROCEDURE Checkforablankline
              (VAR aBlankline : boolean);
  BEGIN
    readln(data);  writeln(results);
    if eoln(data) then begin
      aBlankline := true;
      readln(data);  writeln(results);
    end;
  END; {Checkforablankline}
```

Which is better, is a moot point. Checkforablankline is a one-off procedure, defined entirely for ease of reading and it does not actually need a parameter. Addtototals is in a similar position. However, if the procedure were either at the outer level, or could conceivably be called more than once, then a parameter should be used.

Finer points about procedures

A program with procedures is said to consist of several **levels**. The outermost level is level 1, which is that of the program itself. Thus, all declarations made under the program header are at level 1. Level 1 is also known as the **global** level, and the variables and procedures declared there are called **globals**.

Within these outer procedures at level 1, further declarations can be made. These would then be at level 2. Procedures inside them would be at level 3, and so on, for as many levels of nesting as are required. Declarations within a procedure are called **local** declarations, and the identifiers that they introduce are known as local to that procedure. Parameters acquire the same level as the locals, not as the procedure. Thus, if we had the little skeleton program:

```
PROGRAM skeleton (input, output);
  VAR i, j : integer;

  PROCEDURE order (VAR n, m : integer);

    VAR temp : integer;
    ...
    END; {order}

BEGIN
  ...
END.
```

then i, j and order are at level 1, but n, m and temp are considered to be declared inside order and therefore are all at level 2.

Scope and visibility

With all these places where declarations can be made, it is necessary to sort out which identifiers are visible where, and what happens if the same name is used more than once. The **scope** of an identifier is the extent of the procedures over which the identifier is visible and can be used. This leads to Pascal's rule of scope.

Pascal's Rule of Scope

An identifier is visible in the block (i.e. program, procedure or function) in which it is first declared *and* in all enclosed blocks in which it is not redeclared.

The term 'enclosed blocks' refers to the nesting. If we view nested procedures as a set of nested boxes, then what the rule is saying is that the inner boxes can see outwards, but not vice versa. One way of remembering this is to imagine all the boxes being built with one-way glass: someone in a box can see out, but no one outside can see in.

As stated in the Rule of Scope, an identifier is not visible if it is redeclared in an inner block. The effect of this is that if two variables in the same scope have the same name, only the innermost one is visible. The proper name for this phenomenon is **occlusion**. The identifier which is hidden because of the inner declaration is said to be **occluded**.

The forward directive

The order in which declarations are made also affects visibility. Pascal requires that any use of an identifier must be preceded by its declaration. Thus, if two procedures are declared at the same level, their order of declaration will dictate who can call whom. The procedure currently being declared cannot actually see the following ones. This problem can be overcome by declaring the procedure as forward, then giving its details later on. For example, if procedure A calls B and vice versa, then we could declare them as follows:

```
PROCEDURE B;   forward;

PROCEDURE A;
  BEGIN
      ...
    B;
```

```
      END;

PROCEDURE B;
   BEGIN
      ...
      A;
   END;
```

8.4 Recursion

We now consider an aspect of procedures and functions which renders them very powerful indeed. Solutions to problems that involve iteration can often be expressed in the following general terms:

> **The operation**
>> Do something
>> If the data is not 'finished',
>>> then do the same operation on amended data.

An example of this kind of thinking would be counting people for party invitations. If a party list is written out as:

>>> John
>>> Mary & Peter
>>> David & Anne & Catherine & Thomas
>>> George
>>> William & Harry
>>> Aunt Edith
>>> Granny & Grandpa

and we wish to count both the people who are coming and the number of invitations needed, then we can express the algorithm as:

> **Count a person**
>> Read a name
>> Add one
>> If an ampersand follows, count a person

Essentially, we are reusing the operation by calling it from itself. This is known as **recursion**. In Pascal, the above operation could be part of another procedure as follows:

```
PROCEDURE partyplan;
   VAR
      people, invitations : 0..1000;

   PROCEDURE countaperson;
      BEGIN
         readname;
```

```
              people := people + 1;
              if ampersandfollows then
                 countaperson;
          END; {countaperson}

   BEGIN
      people := 0;
      invitations := 0;
      while not eof do begin
         countaperson;
         invitations := invitations + 1;
      end;
      writeln('For the ',people:1,' people, you will need ',
              invitations:1, ' invitations.');
   END.
```

where `ampersandfollows` and `readname` are suitably defined.

If the recursive call comes at the very end of the operation, then the recursion can be replaced directly by a loop. For example, we could have just as easily written:

```
   PROCEDURE countaperson;
      BEGIN
         repeat
            readname;
            people := people + 1;
         until not ampersandfollows;
      END; {countaperson}
```

Recursion usually only becomes preferable to looping when parameters are involved. Recursive algorithms share with loops the two essential properties that:

- there must be a stopping condition, and
- some variables must change their values each time.

Recursion with parameters

When a recursive call is made on a procedure with parameters, it follows the same execution pattern as an ordinary call. The parameters and local variables of the caller are remembered (or 'stacked') and the new procedure is entered with the new parameters. At the end of the call, the program returns to where it was, and the caller's parameters and variables become visible again. With a recursive procedure, the parameters and variables have the same name and meaning each time, though they may have different values, and thus they can record the state of a computation as time goes by. By deftly altering the order of the 'do something' and 'do the operation again' in the general algorithm above, we can obtain the effect of looking at the state in reverse. This is aptly illustrated by the next example.

EXAMPLE 8.8   Based number writing _____

Problem   Write a procedure to print out positive integers of any size to a given base.

Solution If we knew that the number had exactly, say, three digits, then we could calculate the hundreds first, the tens next and finally the units. But if we express the solution like this:

Print the left part of the number; write the rightmost digit

and consider that printing the left part is exactly the same operation again, then it is not necessary to know in advance how long the number is. When we eventually get down to a single digit then printing the left part does nothing, the rightmost digit is written, and we return to the previous piece of the number.

Example Suppose we print 102 to base 8. This proceeds in steps as follows:

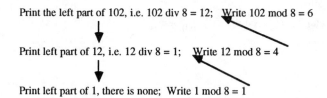

Print the left part of 102, i.e. 102 div 8 = 12; Write 102 mod 8 = 6

Print left part of 12, i.e. 12 div 8 = 1; Write 12 mod 8 = 4

Print left part of 1, there is none; Write 1 mod 8 = 1

and the digits printed out are 146, in that order.

Algorithm The stopping condition here coincides with the left part running out. We can confirm that the variables will change because the procedure is called with the value of parameter number being the number div base. In algorithmic terms, the solution becomes:

> **Print number to a base:**
> > If number < base, then write it out
> > Otherwise
> > > Print number div base to base
> > > Write out number mod base

The procedure, together with a test program, follows on easily.

Program
```
PROGRAM Basetester (input, output);
   VAR number, base : 0..maxint;

   PROCEDURE print (n, b : integer);
      BEGIN
         if n < b then write(n:1)
         else begin
            print (n div b, b);
            write(n mod b:1);
         end;
      END; {print}
   BEGIN
      writeln('****** Testing printing to a base ******');
```

```
      write ('Number and base (positive only): ');
      readln(number, base);
      write(number:1,' to ', base:1,' is ');
      print(number, base);
      writeln;
  END.
```

Multiple recursion

A procedure can also call itself from more than one point. This is usually done on either side of the actual work of the procedure. The general algorithm at the beginning of this section can be rephrased as:

The operation
> If the data is not finished, then do the operation on amended data
> Do something
> If the data is not finished, then do the operation on amended data

where the two amendments might be different. This sort of recursion is illustrated in the next example, and is taken up again in Chapters 14 and 15.

EXAMPLE 8.9   Towers of Hanoi

Problem   The Towers of Hanoi is a classic problem which has a very elegant computer solution. *n* discs of decreasing sizes on a rod need to be moved to another rod, using a third rod, with no disc ever being placed over a smaller one. Pictorially we have:

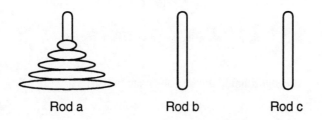

Rod a   Rod b   Rod c

Solution   The solution uses induction. Moving 5 discs from a to b is equivalent to moving 4 from a to c, followed by the fifth to b and then the four back from c to b. Pictorially this is:

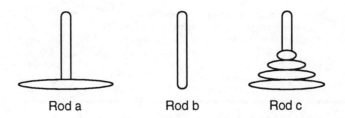

Rod a   Rod b   Rod c

Stage 1 Transfer $n-1$ discs from a to c

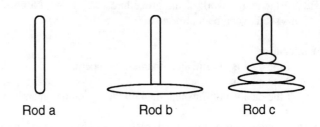

Rod a   Rod b   Rod c

Stage 2 Move the nth disc to b

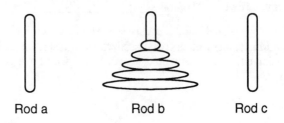

Rod a   Rod b   Rod c

Stage 3 Move the $n-1$ discs back from c to b

Algorithm   The algorithm to do this can be phrased as:

Transfer n discs from a to b using c
       If more than one disc, then transfer $n-1$ from a to c using b
       Move the remaining disc from a to b
       If more than one disc, then transfer the $n-1$ discs from c to b using a

Program   A simple program to test out the algorithm simply prints the movements required. In this version, we call the program for three discs.

```
PROGRAM TestHanoi (input, output);

    PROCEDURE Hanoi (discs : integer; p, q, r : char);
        BEGIN
            if discs > 1 then Hanoi (discs-1, p, r, q);
            writeln(p, '->', q);
            if discs > 1 then Hanoi (discs-1, r, q, p);
        END; {Hanoi}

    BEGIN
        Hanoi(3,'a','b','c');
    END.
```

Testing   The output from the program is:

```
a->b
a->c
b->c
a->b
c->a
c->b
a->b
```

and you can check this out by trying it on paper.

Enhancement   Although correct, a list of moves is hardly a satisfactory output for this problem, as it is very hard to see what is going on. We would like to actually display the rods on the screen and watch the discs moving around.

Solution 2   Clearly, we need to use ScreenMan. To display a single disc on the screen, we need to know:

- the rod it is on

- its position in the rod

- its size

as given in this picture:

	Position	Size
**	4	1
****	3	2
******	2	3
********	1	4

Thus, initially, we would display all the discs on rod a, with positions $n, n-1, \ldots$ and sizes $1, 2, \ldots$, calling the procedure

```
PROCEDURE DisplayDisc(rod : char;
        y : integer; size : integer; symbol : char);
    var x, j : integer;
    BEGIN
        x := ord(rod)-ord('a')+1;
        gotoxy(screen, x*20, 10-y);
        for j := 1 to size*2 do writech(screen,symbol);
    END;
```

with

```
for i := 1 to n do DisplayDisc('a',n - i + 1, i,' *');
```

The additional parameter `symbol` is used so that we can *wipe out* a disc when we move it off one of the rods.

In general, to wipe out a disc on rod *p* and redraw it in the correct position on rod *q*, we need to know how many discs are on each of the rods. Let us assume that the heights of the rods are kept in *pn*, *qn* and *rn*. Then, the sequence to redraw a disc is:

```
DisplayDisc(p,pn,discs,' ');
pn := pn-1;
qn := qn+1;
DisplayDisc(q,qn,discs,'*');
```

Now we have all the basics for animating the Towers of Hanoi. All we need to decide is how the heights of the rods are going to be passed around. Are they to global, local, value parameters or VAR parameters for the `Hanoi` procedure?

The different options will cause very different things to happen during the recursive process. First of all, we can eliminate the local option as local variables cannot retain their values between procedure calls. The same applies to the value parameter option, as any changes made to the heights would not be reflected once the procedure is exited. So we want the height values to be pervasive, and need to choose between global and VAR. If the heights are global, then their identifiers – say *an*, *bn*, *cn* – will refer always to those specific rods. However, within the `Hanoi` procedure, the rods are known by different names, as their usage changes. Thus, the correct option is VAR parameters.

Program Putting this all together with calls to Show and SnapShot in ScreenMan, we get:

```
PROGRAM TestHanoi (input, output);
  CONST
  {$I SM1.pas}

  VAR
    rod1, rod2, rod3,i : integer;
    screen : windows;
  {$I SM2.pas}

  PROCEDURE DisplayDisc(rod:char; y:integer;
                        size:integer; symbol:char);
    var x, j : integer;
  BEGIN
    x := ord(rod)-ord('a')+1;
    gotoxy(screen, x*20,10-y);
    for j := 1 to size*2 do writech(screen,symbol);
  END;

  PROCEDURE Hanoi (discs:integer; p, q, r:char;
                   var pn, qn, rn: integer);
  BEGIN
    if discs > 1
      then Hanoi (discs-1, p, r, q, pn, rn, qn);
    DisplayDisc(p,pn,discs,' ');
```

```
            pn := pn-1;
            qn := qn+1;
            DisplayDisc(q,qn,discs,'*');
            Show;
            SnapShot;
            if discs > 1
               then Hanoi (discs-1, r, q, p, rn, qn, pn);
         END; {Hanoi}
         BEGIN
            whole(screen);
            writestrln(screen,'***** Towers of Hanoi *****');
            writestr(screen,'Number of discs: ');
            readint(screen,rod1);
            gotoxy(screen,11, 20);
            writestr('a                 b                 c');
            rod2 := 0;
            rod3 := 0;
            for i := 1 to rod1 do DisplayDisc('a',rod1-i+1,i,'*');
            Show;
            SnapShot;
            Hanoi(rod1,'a','b','c',rod1,rod2, rod3);
         END.
```

Testing   There are eight snapshots taken for moving three discs. They are:

```
***** Towers of Hanoi *****
Number of discs: 3




            **
            ****
            ******
            a                 b                 c
```

```
***** Towers of Hanoi *****
Number of discs: 3




            ****
            ******          **
            a                 b                 c
```

```
***** Towers of Hanoi *****
Number of discs: 3




              ******           **              ****
                a              b                c
```

```
***** Towers of Hanoi *****
Number of discs: 3




                                               **
              ******                           ****
                a              b                c
```

```
***** Towers of Hanoi *****
Number of discs: 3




                                               **
                               ******          ****
                a              b                c
```

```
***** Towers of Hanoi *****
Number of discs: 3




              **               ******          ****
                a              b                c
```

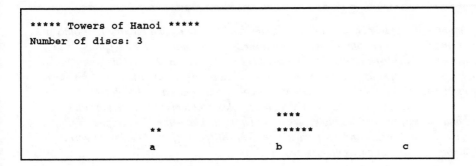

```
***** Towers of Hanoi *****
Number of discs: 3




                                     ****
               **                 ******
               a                     b                    c
```

```
***** Towers of Hanoi *****
Number of discs: 3




                                     **
                                   ****
                                 ******
               a                     b                    c
```

This sort of output is much easier to check!

Backtracking with recursion

Recursion effectively enables us to build up a history of values and then go back and use them again. It is very effective if there is a choice of paths to follow at a given time. One can travel recursively down one, find it no good, come back up to the crossroads with everything restored to what it was before, and proceed down some other path. This technique is used widely in game-playing programs, for chess, noughts and crosses, or any situation where there are choices to be made. A full discussion of this fascinating area is beyond the scope of this book, but is sure to be taken up again in future courses in advanced programming, recursive techniques or data structures.

Recursive data types

A data type which is still to be discussed (in Chapter 14) is the **pointer**. The structures that can be built with pointers are inherently recursive. Hence, many of the algorithms to create and manipulate such structures are excellent examples of recursion at work.

WHAT WE HAVE LEARNT

*The three main topics of this chapter are **var** parameters, **functions** and **recursion**. Both var parameters and functions enable results to be returned from a routine, and the choice as to which to use depends on a) how many values need to be returned and b) how the routine is to be called. Var parameters are used when there is more than one result. Functions are more typically used when there is only one result and its computation has no side-effects.*

Recursive procedures enable complex problems with evolving state to be expressed and implemented very simply. We looked at simple last-line recursion, as well as multiple recursion with value and var parameters. The different effect of declaring variables as local, global, var or value was highlighted.

QUIZ AND PROBLEMS

These are included with Chapter 9's.

Arrays

9.1   The type statement

There are five predefined types in Standard Pascal – integer, real, char, boolean and text. The first four are known as **scalar** types. and the last is a **structured** type, in that it forms a collection of characters in a certain structure. Pascal also provides for another structured type of character – the string – which was the first type we encountered. However, in Standard Pascal there is no predefined type name *string*.

In the next few chapters we shall be looking at the seven ways Pascal provides for creating new types from existing values and types. Figure 9.1 gives the full list of Standard Pascal's predefined types and existing type mechanisms.

The user-defined types are created by means of a type statement, which gives a name to a chosen new structure. In any declaration section, the keyword TYPE appears only once, but several types may be listed under it, as is done in the CONST and VAR sections.The order of the three sections is fixed as: CONST, TYPE, VAR. Although in some implementations (such as Turbo Pascal) these sections may be freely intermingled and repeated, this is not so for Standard Pascal.

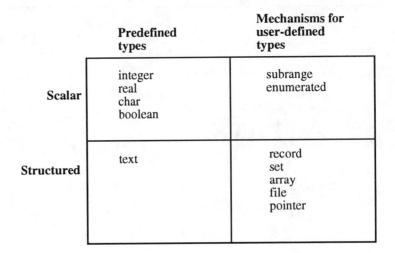

	Predefined types	Mechanisms for user-defined types
Scalar	integer real char boolean	subrange enumerated
Structured	text	record set array file pointer

Figure 9.1 Pascal's types and type mechanisms.

Form of the type statement

A type statement associates a name with a type formation as follows:

```
Type declaration

TYPE
    identifier = type;
    identifier = type;
        . . .
    identifier = type;
```

9.2 Subrange types revisited

The first type enables constraints to be placed on the range of values available in three of the other scalar types – integer, char and enumerated. This is done by specifying precise lower and upper bound values. In earlier chapters, bounds were given for individual variables; now they will have official status and can be used over and over again by name. As before, any such bounds will used by the Pascal system to check that the use of variables conforms with their declaration. The form for defining a subrange type is:

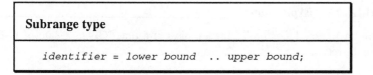

Subrange type

```
identifier = lower bound  .. upper bound;
```

where the bounds must both be of the same type, known as the **base type**. Permissible base types are integer, char or enumerated. The bounds must be constant values or named constants: they may not be expressions. Note that the symbol .. must not have a space between the dots. Examples of subrange types are:

```
TYPE
        weights      = 0..200;    {kgs}
        temperatures = -50..60;   {degrees Celsius}
        money        = 0..maxint;
        initials     = 'A'..'Z';
        digits       = '0'..'9';
        counters     = 1..10;
        marks        = 0..100;
```

Variables of these types can then be declared, as in:

```
VAR
        myweight,
        yourweight   :  weights;
        income, tax  :  money;
        initial      :  initials;
        i, j, counter :  counters;
```

The importance of subrange types

Variables of subrange types can only take values in the specified range. If assignment of a value outside this range is attempted, the program should stop with a 'value out of range' error. For example, the following are erroneous:

```
initial := 'p';   and   counter := 0;
```

It is possible to assign an expression of the base type to a subrange variable, and the Pascal system will then check at runtime that the values are compatible. For example, in:

```
counter := counter + 1;
```

the Pascal system should always check that the range of `counter` is not exceeded.

'Value out of range' errors often indicate that the original algorithm is defective in some way. In other words, the declarations stated that the variables have certain properties, but the statements were not keeping the values within these. Without the proper use of subranges, many of these errors go undetected or are very hard to find.

A subrange type inherits the operators and functions from its base type. However, care must be taken with the functions `succ` and `pred` so that the range is not exceeded.

EXAMPLE 9.1 Expiry dates _____

Problem A library lends books for ten days at a time. Given a date of issue, calculate the return date.

Solution The basic calculation is to add the 10 days to the day of issue, and to check whether this takes us into the next month. By making various simplifying assumptions, the solution breaks up into several parts. In the first place, we assume that all months have the same number of days, say 31, and we set this up as a named constant in the CONST section. Then, we assume that the months will be known by number, not by name, as we intend doing simple arithmetic on the months. Given these assumptions, the calculation becomes:

> Add 10 to the issue day, taking modulo days in the month
> If the issue day plus 10 is more than the days in the month,
> add 1 to the issue month

Program Because this seems such a simple solution, we go straight into the program, using suitable subranges for the day and month types, and a named constant for the borrowing period.

```
PROGRAM LibraryReturns1 (input, output);
   CONST
      daysinmonth = 31;   {for now}
      period      = 10;   {days}

   TYPE
      days        = 1..daysinmonth;
         months   = 1..12;

   VAR
         issueday,
         returnday   : days;
         issuemonth,
         returnmonth : months;

   BEGIN
      writeln('****** Book dates ******');
      write('Type in the day and month: ');
      readln(issueday, issuemonth);
      returnday := (issueday + period) mod daysinmonth;
         if issueday + period > daysinmonth then
            returnmonth := issuemonth + 1
         else
            returnmonth := issuemonth;
         writeln('Due back on ', returnday:1,
                 '/', returnmonth:1);
   END.
```

Testing Running the program with a selection of values seems to work, until we try to take out a book on the 21st. The Pascal system stops the program and complains that a value is out of range on the line:

```
returnday := (issueday + period) mod daysinmonth;
```

Studying this, we see that the computer *has* detected a mistake: (21 + 10) mod 31 is 0, which is not a valid day. The correct answer is 31.   Suppose we quickly change the statement to:

```
returnday := (issueday + period) mod daysinmonth - 1;
```

and rerun the program. The 21st is still incorrect and now the 22nd gives the wrong answer as well: 0 instead of 1.

From all this, we realize that this statement is really not correct, and that using mod is not going to work because it will sometimes return a zero, which we don't want. The answer is to treat the two cases of being within a month and going over a month boundary separately. The revised program becomes:

Program 2
```
PROGRAM LibraryReturns2 (input, output);
    CONST
        daysinmonth  = 31;   {for now}
        period       = 10;   {days}
    TYPE
        days         = 1..daysinmonth;
        months       = 1..12;
    VAR
        issueday,
        returnday    : days;
        issuemonth,
        returnmonth  : months;

    BEGIN
        writeln ('****** Book dates ******');
        write ('Type in the day and month: ');
        readln (issueday, issuemonth);
        if issueday + period > daysinmonth then begin
            returnday := issueday + period - daysinmonth;
            returnmonth := issuemonth + 1;
          end else begin
            returnday := issueday + period;
            returnmonth := issuemonth;
          end;
        writeln('Due back on ', returnday:1,
            '/', returnmonth:1);
    END.
```

Testing 2   Testing proceeds as before, and all seems well until we try Christmas Day – 25 and 12. The system stops again and says a value is out of range on the line:

```
returnmonth := issuemonth + 1;
```

This makes sense, because there is no such month as 13! The use of a subrange has caused another silly error to be detected. To fix this one, another circular addition is needed, as in:

```
if issuemonth = 12
   then returnmonth := 1
   else returnmonth := issuemonth + 1;
```

Solution 2   Turning now to the days in the month, we recall that a case-statement was used in Chapter 5 to set up the maximum. This can be incorporated in the beginning of the program.

Program 3

```
PROGRAM LibraryReturns3 (input, output);
{Calculates the date 10 days hence}

CONST
    period  = 10;    {days}

TYPE
    days    = 1..31;
    months  = 1..12;
    years   = 1900 .. 2500;

VAR
        issueday,
        returnday    : days;
        issuemonth,
        returnmonth  : months;
        daysinmonth  : days;
        year         : years;

FUNCTION daysof(month : months): days;
BEGIN
    CASE month of
        9, 4, 6, 11 : daysof := 30;
        1, 3, 5, 7, 8, 10, 12 : daysof := 31;
        2  :  begin
                 write('In what year? ');
                 readln(year);
                 if (year mod 4 = 0)
                        and not ((year mod 100 = 0)
                        and not (year mod 400 = 0))
                 then daysof := 29
                 else daysof := 28;
              end;
    END; {CASE}
END;   {daysof}

BEGIN
    writeln ('****** Book dates ******');
    write ('Type in the day and month: ');
    readln (issueday, issuemonth);
    if issueday + period > daysof(issuemonth) then begin
        returnday := issueday +
                        period - daysof(issuemonth);
        if issuemonth = 12
            then returnmonth := 1
            else returnmonth := issuemonth + 1
        end else begin
        returnday := issueday + period;
        returnmonth := issuemonth;
        end;
    writeln('Due back on ', returnday:1,
                '/', returnmonth:1);
END.
```

Testing   For the record, a sample run would produce:

```
****** Book dates ******
Type in the day and month: 22  2
In what year? 1986
Due back on 4/3
```

Reading into a subrange

There is a general method for reading integer subranges which makes use of the
following procedure:

```
PROCEDURE readrange
        (VAR x : integer;  min, max : integer);
   BEGIN
     REPEAT
       read(x);
       if (x < min) or (x > max)
       then writeln('NO! Range is ',min:1,'..',
          max:1,' : ');
     UNTIL (x >= min) and (x <= max);
   END;  {readrange}
```

The caller supplies an integer variable with the two relevant ranges and
readrange will repeatedly read numbers until it receives one within the given
range. The caller follows this up with an assignment into the actual variable that
is to be read. So, for example, with the declarations:

```
TYPE
   weights       =  0..200;
   temperatures  = -50..60;   {degrees Celsius}
VAR
   myweight       : weights;
   temperature    : temperatures;
   num            : integer;

readrange (num, 0, 200);    myweight := num;
readrange (num, -50, 60);   temperature := num;
```

Similar procedures could be written for the other base types.

Hints on using subranges

1. The **bounds** required for a subrange are not always as clear cut as the
    above examples for days or months might suggest. Numbers of children,
    amount of tax, even the year should have upper limits, but these have to be
    decided on the basis of what is sensible. A comment to the effect that the
    bounds are 'for now' or 'approximately' will be useful as documentation.

2. Notice that subranges cannot apply to **real numbers**. Instead, we
    continue to use comments to define the range of reals to be used for each
    variable.

3. Subranges are always checked when a variable is **assigned to** or when an
    expression is passed as a **value parameter** to a procedure or function.
    Most Pascal systems do not check the value when a subrange variable is

read into.

4. The **shorthand** for subrange types with the range specified directly on a variable declaration as in:

```
VAR   age : 0..140;
```

is not good practice. Often the same range is needed again, for example as a parameter type, and without a type name to unify the properties, mismatches can occur.

5. To distinguish between **type names** and variable names, a nice convention (used in this book and elsewhere) is to make types plural. Thus, we have the variable day of type days, and so on.

6. Making use of **named constants** as subrange bounds is very helpful if the ranges have to be changed.

9.3 Simple arrays

We are beginning to realize that there is a need to be able to store and manipulate multiple values in a program. If there are relatively few values, simple variables can possibly be used, but consider the following example.

Suppose we have several hundred scores between 0 and 20 which have to be analysed for frequency of occurrence of each score. We could set up 21 counters, one for each score. As the scores are read in, the counter corresponding to the score could be incremented. It would be very unwieldy if we had to invent 21 different names for the counters, and then use a big case-statement every time one of them needed updating. What we need is the concept of the *i*th **variable** so that we can read a value, say *i*, and then update *counter$_i$*. Pascal provides for this facility with the **array**.

Form of an array type

An array is a bounded collection of elements of the same type, each of which can be selected by indexing. The relevant form is:

Array type

```
TYPE identifier = ARRAY [bound type] OF element type;
```

---

where the bound type is a subrange of integer, char, boolean or enumerated type and the element type is any type not containing a file type. Examples of declarations are:

```
TYPE
     scores       =  0..20;
```

```
classrange   =   0..100;
frequencies  =   ARRAY [scores] of classrange;
capitals         =   'A'..'Z';
occurrences  =   ARRAY [capitals] of boolean;
daysofweek   =   1..7;
daycounts    =   ARRAY [daysofweek] of integer;
```

To use an array, we must first declare a variable of that type, then each element can be accessed by mentioning the name of the array variable and an index expression enclosed in square brackets. The index is sometimes known as the **subscript**. For example, we have:

```
VAR
    counter    : frequencies;
    occurred   : occurrences;
    daycount   : daycounts;

FOR score := 0 to 20 do counter[score] := 0;
occurred['Z'] := false;
daycount[5] := daycount [5] + 1;
```

EXAMPLE 9.2   Frequency count _____

Problem   The frequencies of several hundred scores between 0 and 20 have to be calculated as well as the frequency of occurrence of the code for the club they belong to, which is a character.

Example   Suppose we have a file with the data:

```
19   J        Smith A
10   B        Jones P G
19   A        Brown T
```

then the result required would be that all the score frequencies would be zero, except:

$$scorecount_{19} = 2 \qquad\qquad scorecount_{10} = 1$$

and all the club frequencies would be zero except those for J, B and A which would be one.

Solution   The solution has already been outlined at the beginning of the section. We set up two arrays and as each score is read, the appropriate element of the array is incremented. Similarly for the clubs. The algorithm is so simple that we go straight on to the program.

Program

```
PROGRAM CountingFrequencies (input, output, inp);
    CONST
        maxscore      = 20;
        playerlimit   = 250;


    TYPE
        scores        = 0..maxscore;
```

```
           players       = 0..playerlimit;
           clubs         = 'A'..'Z';
           scorearrays   = ARRAY [scores] of players;
           clubarrays    = ARRAY [clubs] of players;

      VAR
           scorecount    : scorearrays;
           clubcount     : clubarrays;
           score         : scores;
           club : char;
           filename      : string[12];
           inp           : text;

      BEGIN
           writeln('****** Frequency counting ******');
           write('What file for the data? ');
           readln(filename);
           assign(inp, filename);
           reset (inp);

           {Initialize the arrays}
           FOR score := 0 to maxscore do
              scorecount[score] := 0;
           FOR club := 'A' to 'Z' do
              clubcount[club] := 0;

           {Count the scores and clubs}
           WHILE not eof(inp) do begin
              read(inp, score);
              scorecount [score] := scorecount [score] + 1;
              repeat read(inp, club) until club <> ' ';
              clubcount[club] := clubcount[club]+ 1;
           END;

           {Print the frequencies}
           writeln('Table of Score Frequencies');
           for score := 0 to maxscore do
              writeln(score, scorecount[score]:6);
           writeln;
           writeln('Table of Club Frequencies');
           for club := 'A' to 'Z' do
              writeln(club, clubcount[club]:6);
      END.
```

This program has been written without procedures or functions. Clearly, it could have been formally broken up and parameter interfaces created. However, in this case, we deemed it simpler to present the program as one unit, so that the idea of arrays can be understood on its own. In later examples, we shall see how arrays can be passed as parameters and procedures written which operate on arrays.

Properties of array types

Arrays can be formed of any type. This includes arrays themselves, leading to multi-dimensional arrays, discussed in detail later. The size of an array is limited only by the computer's memory, which is usually adequate for most applications. Most computers, though, will probably baulk at an array with subscripts given as [integer].

As with records, there are no operators that apply to whole arrays. However, assignment is possible. For example, given:

```
TYPE
   range      = 1..100;
   vectors    = array[range] of real;

VAR a, b   : vectors;
```

we can say:

```
   b := a;
```

Operations on the elements of an array depend on their type. Whole arrays cannot be read or written from text files; they must be treated element by element.

A note on security

Pascal is quite firm about only allowing access to array elements that actually exist. Every time an array is accessed, the index supplied is checked against the bounds given in the type definition. If the index is out of bounds, an error message such as 'Invalid subscript' is given and the program halts.

These checks are done at compile time whenever possible. Thus, the following may all result in compilation errors:

```
scorecount[25]
initialcount['a']
initialcount['*']
```

Arrays as an abstraction

In this book, we delayed introducing arrays in order to emphasize the control operations in processing data. Very often, one will find a solution to a problem that makes use of an array, where in fact it is not strictly necessary. Is this wrong? No, it is not wrong; it merely represents a different abstraction of a solution.

Consider the following problem: we need to read in 20 values and find the smallest and the largest. There are two approaches to the solution:

1.   Read in the 20 values, keeping track of the smallest and largest 'on the fly'.

2.   Read the 20 values into an array, then scan the array through twice to find the smallest and then the largest values.

Instinctively, the first approach seems more efficient, and on the face of it, it is no more complicated than the second. But the balance changes if we take into account procedures and functions that we already have in stock.

Suppose we already have functions to calculate the minimum and maximum values from a given array. Then, the comparative algorithms would be:

Min and max on the fly

Initialize min and max

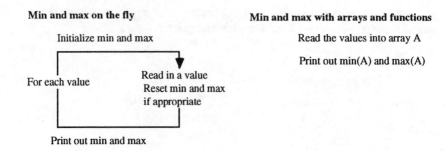

For each value

Read in a value
Reset min and max
if appropriate

Print out min and max

Min and max with arrays and functions

Read the values into array A

Print out min(A) and max(A)

The concept we are highlighting here is called *separation of concerns*. In the first algorithm, all the operations are mixed up in one process. In the second, we identify three concerns which can be handled separately in both time and space. These are the reading, finding the minimum and finding the maximum. The development of each process can proceed independently in time, and are also identified separately in space as three different procedures. In the long run, the second approach can be more efficient and easier to manage.

These ideas are illustrated in the Example 9.3, which strictly speaking, does not *need* an array, but which uses one to good effect to make an easily understandable program. On the other hand, Example 9.4 does need an array, as did Example 9.2.

EXAMPLE 9.3   Diving competitions

Problem   The judging of diving competitions relies on judges from several countries or states. In order to avoid bias (a judge rewarding competitors from home), the result for a dive is calculated as the average of all the scores, less the highest and lowest score. We would like to computerize these calulations.

Algorithm   As outlined just above, there are two possible approaches to this problem. The three values required, that is, the sum, the lowest and the highest scores, can all be calulated on the fly while the scores are read in. Alternatively, we can read the values in and then assess them. Assuming we choose the second approach, then there are once again two options. These are to compute the three values simultaneously in a single loop, or to have three different loops, perhaps in three different functions, to calculate them. Since the calculations are really so simple, we shall adopt the first approach this time, and do them all together.

Program
```
PROGRAM Diving (input, output);
  CONST
    noofdives  = 3;
    noofjudges = 8;

  TYPE
    results    = real;
    rawscores  = 0..10;
    judges     = 1..noofjudges;
    scorearray = array [judges] of rawscores;
```

```
    dives       = 1..noofdives;

  VAR
    dive                : dives;
    scores              : scorearray;
    min, max            : rawscores;
    sum, result, total  : real;
    minjudge, maxjudge  : judges;

PROCEDURE GetJudges(var s : scorearray);
    VAR
      i : judges;
    BEGIN
      for i := 1 to noofjudges do begin
        write(i:8,': ');
          read(s[i]);
        if i div 4 = 0 then writeln;
        end;
    END; {GetJudges}

PROCEDURE Assess (s : scorearray; var sum : results;
               var min : rawscores; var minj : judges;
               var max : rawscores; var maxj : judges);
    VAR
      i : judges;
    BEGIN
      min := 10;
      max := 0;
      sum := 0;
      for i := 1 to noofjudges do begin
        sum := sum + s[i];
          if s[i] < min then
                begin min := s[i]; minj := i; end;
          if s[i] > max then
                begin max := s[i]; maxj := i; end;
        end;
    END;

BEGIN
    writeln('**** Diving Score Calculator ****');
    writeln;
    total := 0;
    FOR dive := 1 to noofdives do begin
      writeln('Dive no: ',dive:1);
      GetJudges(scores);
      Assess(scores,sum,min,minjudge,max,maxjudge);
      result := (sum - min - max) / (noofjudges-2);
      total := total + result;
      writeln('Scores ',min:1, ' from judge ',
          minjudge:1,' and ',max:1,
            ' from judge ',maxjudge:1,' excluded.');
      writeln('Result is: ',result:5:1);
      end;
    writeln('Diving average is : ',total/noofdives:5:1);
END.
```

Testing   The following is a typical test for three dives:

```
**** Diving Score Calculator ****
Dive no: 1
1: 7          2: 8          3: 7          4: 4
5: 8          6: 6          7: 9          8: 7
Scores 4 from judge 4 and 9 from judge 7 excluded.
Result is:    7.2
Dive no: 2
1: 8          2: 8          3 : 8         4: 8
5: 4          6: 8          7: 10         8: 8
Scores 4 from judge 5 and 10 from judge 7 excluded.
Result is:    8.0
Dive no: 3
 1: 7         2: 7          3: 7          4: 7
5: 7          6: 7          7: 7          8: 7
Scores 7 from judge 1 and 7 from judge 1 excluded.
Result is:    7.0
Diving average is :    7.4
```

EXAMPLE 9.4   The lifetime of light bulbs _____

Problem   A factory manufactures light bulbs, and from the production line, bulbs are chosen at random to see how long they last. For quality control purposes, there must be regular reports on the mean lifetime and standard deviation in hours.

Solution   If we have a set of measurements x_i we can analyse them to find the mean $\bar{x}$ which gives the average measurement, and the standard deviation s, which shows the amount by which measurements are likely to differ from the mean. In other words, the standard deviation indicates the spread of the measurements.

The mean of a set of measurements x_i $(i = 1, n)$ is defined to be:

$$\bar{x} = \frac{\sum_{i=1}^{n} x_i}{n}$$

and the formula for the standard deviation is:

$$s = \sqrt{\frac{\sum_{i=1}^{n}(x_i - \bar{x})^2}{n - 1}}$$

We can allow for expected errors and intrinsic randomness by saying that the result of a set of measurements will be within a certain standard deviation. In many cases we can say that the true result is in the range $\bar{x} \pm 2s$, that is, the mean plus or minus twice the standard deviation.

Algorithm   Calculating the mean – or average – can be done fairly simply on the fly, as shown in Examples 7.1 and 7.3. However, because the formula for the standard deviation uses the mean, we have to calculate it after the mean has been decided. Thus, we store the values in an array, and process them from there in a second stage.

We declare a vector a_i, with $i = 1$ to *nmax*. In a run of the program we first ask the size of the data set n, then read n real numbers into a_i ($i = 1$ to n). Because the formula for s includes division by $n - 1$, we check whether $n = 1$, to prevent a runtime error.

We also choose to set up the two formulae as functions, making them self-contained, and therefore able to be reused in other programs. In the functions, the vector has its usual name of a; but in the main program we use a name more specific to the problem, that is, hourreadings.

Program

```
PROGRAM LightBulbAnalysis (input,output);
  CONST
     nmax = 100; {Maximum vector size handled}
  TYPE
     range  = 1..nmax;
     vector = ARRAY[range] of real;
  VAR
     hourreadings : vector;
     num          : range;
     ave          : real;

  PROCEDURE initialize;
     VAR
        i : range;
     BEGIN
        writeln('********Light Bulb Analysis********');
        writeln;
        writeln('Statistical analysis of the lifetime ',
             'of light bulbs');
        writeln('with  no. of readings <= 100 at present.');
        writeln;
        write('How many readings? n =');
        readln(num);
        writeln('Enter the ', num:1,
           ' readings followed by return:');
     END; {initialize}

  PROCEDURE Getdata (var a : vector; n : range);
     VAR i : range;
     BEGIN
        FOR i := 1 to n do
           read(a[i]);
        readln;
     END; {Getdata}

  FUNCTION mean (a : vector; n : range) : real;
     VAR i : range;
        sum : real;
     BEGIN
        sum := 0.0;
        FOR i := 1 to n do
           sum := sum + a[i];
        mean := sum / n;
     END; {Mean}

  FUNCTION sigma (a:vector; n: range; m : real) : real;
```

```
        VAR sum : real;
            i : range;
        BEGIN
           sum := 0.0;
           FOR i := 1 to n do
              sum := sum + sqr(m - a[i]);
           sigma := sqrt(sum / (n - 1));
        END;  {sigma}

    BEGIN
       initialize;
       Getdata(hourreadings, num);
       IF num = 1 then
          writeln('Mean = ',hourreadings[1]:10:6,
             '  Standard deviation not defined for n = 1')
       else begin
          ave := mean(hourreadings, num);
          writeln('Mean =  ', round(ave):1, ' hours ');
          writeln('Standard deviation = ',
             round(sigma(hourreadings, num, ave)):1,
             ' hours ');
       END;  {IF}
    END.
```

Testing

```
    ********Light Bulb Analysis*********

    Statistical analysis of the lifetime of light bulbs
    with  no. of readings <= 100 at present.

    How many readings? n = 5
    Enter the 5 readings followed by return:
    1105    909    1043    989    961
    Mean = 1001 hours
    Standard deviation = 75 hours
```

9.4 Strings

Pascal recognizes that character elements are frequently replicated to form strings for storing names, addresses, sentences and in fact any kind of text data. Strings have a special place in Pascal's array mechanism. Unfortunately, the extra privileges accorded to strings do not go far enough for many applications, and most Pascal systems have extended them. These extensions are usually sensible enough, but using them renders a program non-standard and hence difficult to move to other Pascal systems. For that reason, we mention only the most important ones at the end of this section, and advise strongly that the use of extensions is kept to a minimum, and clearly marked in a program.

The form of strings

In order to ensure that strings are stored efficiently, there is a special form of array declaration for them:

```
String type

    TYPE identifier = PACKED ARRAY [bound type] of char;
```

The addition of the word PACKED informs the Pascal system that it can squeeze up the items, several to a memory word. Words usually contain 32 bits, large enough for four characters, so that a saving in space is made. The computer can also deal more efficiently with characters stored in this way, rather than one per word. In recognition of such features, Pascal has a few additional properties for strings.

String values and operators

String constants, which were introduced right at the start of the book, consist of characters enclosed in quotes. A string constant of n characters is considered to be of the type:

```
PACKED ARRAY [1..n] of char;
```

which enables them to be used in expressions with array variables of the same type.

Strings may be compared using all six relational operators. For example, we can declare:

```
CONST
    n          = 6;
    default    = 'Holmes';
TYPE
    namerange = 1..n;
    names      = PACKED ARRAY [namerange] of char;
VAR
    yourname, myname : names;
```

and then have:

```
myname := 'Watson';
yourname := default;
if myname = yourname then ...
if myname < yourname then ...
```

However, strings are of fixed length, so it is not possible to say:

```
myname := 'Wu';
yourname := 'Moriarty';
```

as these constants do not have exactly six characters, as required by this particular type.

Reading and writing strings

Writing out constant strings is a familiar operation. Since there is an equivalent type, and variables of it can be defined, it is also possible to write out string variables. This does not apply to plain arrays of characters, which is why it is so important to include the keyword PACKED in the declaration.

Pascal does not give any additional assistance for reading a string. Thus, a string has to be read character by character. This is fine if the data is exactly the same length as the string. Take for example the declarations:

```
CONST
   namemax   = 10;
TYPE
   namerange = 1..namemax;
   names   = packed array [namerange] of char;
VAR
   name : names;
```

Then, the data J Robinson which is exactly 10 characters long can be read with the loop:

```
FOR i := 1 to namemax do read(name[i]);
```

However, if the name is shorter or longer than will fit, additional checks and reactions are needed. The usual conventions are that:

- shorter strings are padded with blanks,

- longer strings are truncated.

Given this, it becomes reasonable to define a special readname procedure:

```
PROCEDURE readname (VAR name : names);
   CONST
      space = ' ';
   VAR
      i : namerange;
   BEGIN
      for i := 1 to namemax do
         if  eoln  then name[i] := space else read(name[i]);
      readln;
   END; {readname}
```

EXAMPLE 9.5   Multilingual interfaces _____

Problem   A program is being written for general use within several countries, and it is a requirement that the output should be in whatever language is spoken in that country. However, we do not want to change the program every time. How can the words printed out be made independent of the Pascal code?

Solution   The solution is to make the words data and store them in files, one for each language. At the start of the program, the language required is set, and the words from that file are read into one or more arrays. Instead of writing out actual strings, the program is altered to write out the contents of the array instead.

Algorithm   As an example, take the days of the week. Within the program, we can refer to these by numbers, with 1 being Monday, and so on. This leads to a subrange:

```
TYPE
    daysofweek = 1..7;   {1 is Monday}
```

The actual words to be printed will be stored in a file. For example, the French versions are:

> lundi
>
> mardi
>
> mercredi
>
> jeudi
>
> vendredi
>
> samedi
>
> dimanche

and could be stored in a file called `French.days`.

Although in French the longest name is eight letters long, in English it is nine, and in some other languages it may be longer. To be safe, we allow 10 characters for a name. So the declarations for name, as given above, will be appropriate, as will the `readname` procedure. The array of day names is then simply an array of this type.

Program The declarations required are:

```
CONST
    namemax     = 10;
TYPE
    namerange   = 1.. namemax;
    names       = packed array [namerange] of char;
    daysofweek = 1..7; {1 is Monday}
    daynames    =  array [daysofweek] of names;
```

Then, the reading in of the French names and writing them can be done by first reading in the filename, and then the strings, as in:

```
PROCEDURE SettheLanguage(var dayname : daynames);
    VAR
        filename : names;
        dayfile : text;
        day : daysofweek;
    BEGIN
        write('Which file for the day names? ');
        readln(filename);
        reset (dayfile, filename);
        for day := Monday to Sunday do
            readname(dayfile,dayname[day]);
    END;
```

Now consider writing day names. We could say:

```
write(dayname[4]);
```

which will write out :

```
jeudi- - - - -
```

where – represents a space. The full 10 characters for each string are written, which may not be what is required in all circumstances. For that reason, a procedure similar to `readname` can be written, which will only write out the letters of a name, omitting any trailing blanks.

```
PROCEDURE writename (name : names);
   CONST
      space = ' ';
   VAR
      i : namerange;
   BEGIN
      FOR  i := 1 to namemax do
         if name[i] <> space then write(name[i]);
   END; {writename}
```

Switching to another language would be done by calling again and giving a new file name for the new words.

9.5 Multi-dimensional arrays

Arrays are very useful for storing tables of information, such as data in rows and columns, or matrices. Since Pascal permits array elements to be of any type, including arrays themselves, arrays of multiple dimensions can be built up. For a typical matrix such as:

the declarations might be:

```
CONST
   rowmax       = 4;
   columnmax    = 5;

TYPE
   rowrange    = 1..rowmax;
   columnrange = 1..columnmax;
   rows        = array [columnrange] of real;
   matrices    = array [rowrange] of rows;

VAR
   matrix : matrices;
   r,i,j  : rowrange;
   c      : columnrange;
```

Then, a single row of the matrix is represented by:

```
matrix[r]
```

Each element of the row can also be selected, as in:

```
matrix [r] [c]
```
or:
```
matrix [r, c]
```

The two forms are equivalent, although the second one is more natural when a matrix is defined as a single type, without defining the row type first. This can be achieved by declarations such as:

```
TYPE
    rectangles  = array [rowrange, columnrange] of real;
```

The difference between the two forms is that an array declared with subscripts listed in one declaration, like `rectangles`, cannot then be broken up into rows that can be manipulated independently. With the two-stage declaration, as for `matrices`, a row variable could be defined such as:

```
VAR
    row : rows;
```

and rows from the matrix assigned directly to it. Thus, to swap two rows of the matrix, we could say:

```
row := matrix[i];
matrix[i] := matrix[j];
matrix[j] := row;
```

EXAMPLE 9.6 Gold exploration _____

Problem   ZanyLand Exploration Inc. has obtained data of infrared readings of a portion of desert where gold is believed to be present. The data should show up the boundaries of a gold reef, based on readings which are greater than the average of those around them. Can you help find the gold?

Solution   The map of the readings can be considered, a point at a time, and a corresponding map printed out showing those with higher than average infrared levels. For example, given the following data on a sample 8×8 grid:

```
21  21  22  30  40  21  34  45
21  22  23  30  45  21  37  40
22  23  24  35  46  47  38  39
22  23  24  35  46  47  38  38
23  24  25  36  46  49  37  36
23  24  25  37  39  48  36  35
23  24  25  25  26  25  26  25
23  25  26  27  28  29  30  31
```

we could deduce the corresponding map:

```
Map of possible boundaries of the gold reef
=============================================

     1 2 3 4 5 6 7 8
  1
  2            *   *
  3     *    * * *
  4           * *
  5     *    * * *
  6           *   *
  7
  8
```

Algorithm   The high-level algorithm is:

Gold exploration
> Read in the data
> Assess each point, creating the corresponding map of blanks and asterisks
> Print the map

Each of these steps can now be refined, into double loops scanning the whole matrix. Assessing a point consists of:

```
point := data[i,j];
average := (data[i-1,j]+data[i+1,j]
              +data[i,j-1]+data[i,j+1])/4;
if point > average then map[i,j] := cover;
```

However, we must consider how to deal with data points on the edge of the grid. We shall assume that there is sufficient redundancy in the grid to allow us to ignore the boundary points. Thus we run the assessing loops from 2 to rowmax and 2 to colmax respectively.

Program   The program makes good use of matrices, defining two on the same ranges, but with different elements – real for the data and char for the map.

```
PROGRAM Exploration (input, output);
   CONST
      rowmax = 8;
      colmax = 8;
   TYPE
      rowrange = 1..rowmax;
      colrange = 1..colmax;
      matrix   = array[rowrange, colrange] of real;
      maps     = array[rowrange, colrange] of char;
       VAR
      data : matrix;
      map  : maps;

   PROCEDURE Readin(var data:matrix);
      VAR
         f : text;
         i : rowrange;
         j : colrange;
      BEGIN
       writeln('Reading from EXPLORE.DAT ...');
       reset(f,'explore.dat');
```

```
      for i := 1 to rowmax do begin
        for j := 1 to colmax do
          read(f,data[i,j]);
        readln(f);
      end;
      writeln('Data read in successfully');
    END; {Readin}

  PROCEDURE Assess(data : matrix; var map : maps);
      CONST
        cover = '*';
        blank = ' ';
      VAR
        i : rowrange;
        j : colrange;
        point, average : real;

      BEGIN
        for i := 1 to rowmax do
          for j := 1 to colmax do
            map[i,j] := blank;
          for i := 2 to rowmax-1 do begin
            for j := 2 to colmax-1 do begin
                point := data[i,j];
                average := (data[i-1,j]+data[i+1,j]
                              +data[i,j-1]+data[i,j+1])/4;
                if point > average then map[i,j]:= cover;
            end;
          end;
      END; {Assess}

  PROCEDURE Print (map : maps);
      VAR
        i : rowrange;
        j : colrange;
        f : text;
      BEGIN
        writeln('Map being written to EXPLORE.OUT ...');
        rewrite(f,'explore.out');
        writeln(f,'Map of possible boundaries of ',
                  'the gold reef');
        writeln(f,'==========================================');
        writeln(f);
        write(f,'    ');
        for j := 1 to colmax do write(f,j:2); writeln(f);
        for i := 1 to rowmax do begin
          write(f,i:2,' ');
          for j := 1 to colmax do
            write(f,map[i,j]:2);
          writeln(f);
        end;
        writeln('Good luck');
      END; {Print}

  BEGIN
    writeln('**** ZanyLand Exploration Inc *****');
    writeln('We will find gold!');
      Readin(data);
      Assess(data,map);
      Print(map);
  END.
```

Testing   The expected output to the file has already been given. The narrative on the screen will be:

```
**** ZanyLand Exploration Inc *****
We will find gold!
Reading from EXPLORE.DAT ...
Data read in successfully'
Map being written to EXPLORE.OUT ...
```

Example 9.7   Rainfall statistics

Problem   The Zanyland Weather Department has kept statistics on monthly rainfall figures for the past 20 years. Now they would like to calculate:

• the average rainfall for each month, and

• the standard deviation for each month.

Solution   The table of rainfall figures that is provided by a clerk will look something like this:

Year	Jan	Feb	Mar	Apr	May	Jun	Jul	Aug	Sep	Oct	Nov	Dec
1982	20	22	17	14	5	0	0	0	7	12	30	20
1983	22	24	19	12	0	0	3	0	8	15	20	25
1984	17	17	17	15	0	0	0	0	6	17	8	20
1985	10	10	10	5	0	0	0	0	0	12	10	15
1986	10	10	10	5	0	0	0	0	0	12	10	15
1987	20	22	17	14	5	0	0	0	7	12	30	20
1988	22	24	19	12	0	0	3	0	8	15	20	25
1989	17	17	17	15	0	0	0	0	6	17	8	20
1990	25	30	25	15	7	0	0	0	20	15	20	30
1991	25	30	25	15	7	0	0	0	20	15	20	30

The data can be read in nicely by drawing such a table on the screen and letting the user type in each value in turn, or by reading the values off a file. As the values are read in, they are stored in a matrix which is indexed by both the months and the years. Since the rainfall for a month seems to be the crucial figure, the matrix should be structured so that a whole column can be moved around at once. To do this, we make months the first subscript, and the range of years the second, that is:

```
CONST
   maxyear = 30;

TYPE
   months       = 1..12;
   yearrange    = 1..maxyear;
   rainfalls    = real;
   monthlyrains = array[yearrange] of rainfalls;
   raintables   = array[months] of monthlyrains;
VAR
   raintable : raintables;
```

Once the figures are safely in the matrix, procedures can be designed to perform the required calculations. Each will make use of the matrix and be passed either a column of one month's rainfall figures or an index to such a column.

Algorithm   We have discussed the formulae for the mean and standard deviation in Example 9.4. The function to calculate the monthly average could be declared as:

```
FUNCTION monthlyaverage (rain:monthlyrains; n : yearrange)
        : rainfalls;
```

Alternatively, the declaration could be:

```
FUNCTION monthlyaverage (m : months; n : years)
        : rainfalls;
```

where the parameter indicates an index into the rain table. If the index alone is sent as a parameter, then the function has to access the rainfall table as a global variable, which affects its self-containedness, and it has to perform double indexing to get to each element. If the whole column is sent, there is an initial overhead in copying the values into the function, but accessing the elements is by single indexing, and the self-containedness of the function is preserved. On balance, the first is a better choice.

If the value calculated by monthlyaverage is assigned to a variable a it can be passed to the next function which uses it to calculate the standard deviation. The declaration for this function is therefore:

```
FUNCTION monthlystddev (rain : monthlyrains;  n : years;
                        mean : rainfalls) : rainfalls;
```

Program   This version of the program assumes input from a file called rain.dat with output to rain.out.

```
PROGRAM Weather (input, output);
  CONST
    maxyear = 30;
  TYPE
    months       = 1..12;
    years        = 1950..2100;
    yearrange    = 1..maxyear;
    rainfalls    = real;
    monthlyrains = array[yearrange] of rainfalls;
    raintables   = array[months] of monthlyrains;

  VAR
    raintable           : raintables;
    startyear, endyear  : years;

  FUNCTION monthlyaverage(rain:monthlyrains; n : yearrange)
            : rainfalls;
    VAR
      total : rainfalls;
      y     : yearrange;
    BEGIN
      total := 0.0;
      for y := 1 to n do total := total + rain[y];
```

```
        monthlyaverage := total / n;
    END; {monthlyaverage}

FUNCTION monthlystddev(rain:monthlyrains;
        mean : rainfalls; n : yearrange) : rainfalls;
    VAR
      total : rainfalls;
      y     : yearrange;
    BEGIN
      total := 0.0;
      for y := 1 to n do
        total := total + sqr(mean-rain[y]);
      monthlystddev := sqrt(total / (n-1));
    END; {monthlystddev}

PROCEDURE ReadinData(var startyear, endyear : years);
    VAR
      year : 0..maxyear;
      y    : integer{years};
      data : text;
      m    : months;

    BEGIN
      writeln('Reading from RAIN.DAT ...');
      reset(data,'rain.dat');
      year := 0;
      WHILE not eof(data) do begin
        read(data,y);write(year);
        if year = 0 then startyear := y;
        year := year + 1;
        for m := 1 to 12 do begin
          read(data,raintable[m][year]);
          write(raintable[m][year]:4:1);
        end;
        writeln;
      END;
      endyear := y;
      writeln('Data read for years ',
        startyear, ' to ', endyear);
    END; {ReadinData}

PROCEDURE PrintResults(startyear, endyear : years);
    VAR
      m       : months;
      a       : rainfalls;
      results : text;
      nyears  : years;
    BEGIN
      writeln('Writing to RAIN.OUT ...');
      rewrite(results,'rain.out');
      writeln(results,'Rainfall statistics for ',
        startyear:1, ' to ',endyear:1);
      writeln(results,'=================================');
      writeln(results);
      writeln(results,'Month    Average     Std Deviation');
      nyears := endyear-startyear+1;
      for m := 1 to 12 do begin
        a := monthlyaverage(raintable[m],nyears);
        writeln(results,m:4, a:12:2,
          monthlystddev(raintable[m],a,nyears):12:2);
      end;
```

```
   close(results);
END; {PrintResults}

BEGIN
   writeln('******* Rainfall statistics ******');
   ReadinData(startyear,endyear);
   PrintResults(startyear,endyear);
END.
```

Testing   For the data shown above, the output to the file would be:

```
Rainfall statistics for 1982 to 1991
=====================================

Month        Average      Std Deviation
  1          18.80         5.39
  2          20.60         7.11
  3          17.60         5.06
  4          12.20         3.97
  5           2.40         3.17
  6           0.00         0.00
  7           0.60         1.26
  8           0.00         0.00
  9           8.20         6.88
 10          14.20         2.04
 11          17.60         8.37
 12          22.00         5.37
```

WHAT WE HAVE LEARNT

*We discussed the important data type – the **array**. The array maps subscripts to elements, and we saw that it was important to declare both as their own types in a **type statement**. The convention of setting up a **range type** for subscripts was emphasised. With subranges, Pascal gives a good deal of protection against silly mistakes and off by one errors. The two enhancements or simple arrays – **strings** and **multi-dimensional arrays** were also discussed. Only the standard approach to strings was covered. Methods discussed in this chapter are:*

- *Arrays as an abstraction for computation.*
- *Calculations on the fly versus stored values.*
- *Accessing coded values through arrays.*
- *Separation of concerns as a means of controlling complexity.*
- *Processing matrices in two-dimensions, or as rows of vectors.*

QUIZ

1. Is the following a valid subrange? `kilograms = 0.4 ..20.0`
2. Can subscripts for arrays be negative integers?

3. Can part of a matrix be passed as a parameter? If so, what part?

4. Can an array be the result to a function?

5. If s has the value 'Winter' and is of the type `names` as defined in Example 9.5, what will be the difference between calling

```
            writeln(s,'!')
   and
            writename(s); writeln('!');
```

6. Write the declaration for a procedure P which needs two integer value parameters, a real VAR parameter and real value parameter.

7. Is it permissible for corresponding actual and formal parameters to have the same name?

8. Is it permissible for a formal parameter to have the same name as a local variable in its procedure?

9. Study the following program.

```
         PROGRAM Picture (output);
            VAR row, length : integer;
            PROCEDURE modify (v : integer;  VAR x : integer);
               BEGIN
                  x := v * v - v;
               END; {modify}

            PROCEDURE line (long : integer);
               VAR index : integer;
               BEGIN
                  for index := 1 to long do write(row:2);
                  writeln;
               END; {line}

         BEGIN
            FOR row := 1 to 4 do begin
               modify (row, length);
               write (row:2, length:4);
               line (length);
            END;
         END.
```

What will `Picture` print out when it is run?

10. If we declare an array of strings, can we get at the individual characters of each string?

PROBLEMS

9.1 **Mains voltage** The mains voltage supplied by a substation is measured at hourly intervals over a 72-hour period, and a report made. Write a program to read in the 72 readings and determine:

- the mean voltage measured;

- the hours at which the recorded voltage varies from the mean by more than 10%;
- any adjacent hours when the change from one reading to the next was greater than 15% of the mean value.

Include in your program an option to display a histogram of the voltage over the 72 hours, using the procedure developed in Example 6.14.

9.2 **Useful procedures** Write and test procedures which take an array of integers as one of their parameters and do the following:

- find the maximum of all the elements;
- find the maximum of all the elements, plus all the positions where it occurs;
- determine the range of values spanned by the array;
- determine whether all the quantities in the array are equal;
- determine the number of times a value greater than a given level occurs.

9.3 **Sum of squares** Write a function which is given two integers as parameters, and returns as its value the sum of the squares of the numbers between and inclusive of the two parameters. Show how to call the function to print the value of $\sum i^2$ where i runs from 1 to 10. How would the program change if the data was to be read in and stored initially in an array?

9.4 **Validating codes** Example 6.4 checks whether a word is a valid course code. Convert the checking part into a boolean function and verify that the program still works correctly.

9.5 **Recursive functions** Define and test simple recursive functions for the following:

- factorial;
- the Fibonnacci sequence;
- the length of a string;
- the highest common factor of two numbers.

9.6 **Codes** A simple coding system depends on an arrangement of 25 letters in a square depending on a keyword. The remaining letter is transmitted as itself. For example, if the keyword is PLANT and the letter to be sent unaltered is V, then the square would be

```
P L A N T
B C D E F
G H I J K
M O Q R S
U W X Y Z
```

The code works by considering pairs of letters and replacing each one by the one in the same row but in the column of the other. So M A becomes Q N. (The row of M is 4 and the column of A is 3 => Q, the row of A and column of M => N.) Thus

```
GO TO OUR CAVE NOW    =>    OGLSMWOEVNEWO
```

Write a program which reads in the five letter keyword and letter to remain unaltered and passes these to a procedure which reads a single line message and prints the coded form. Write another procedure to decode such a message.

9.7 **Standard passes** The Senate at Zanyland University has decreed that at least 75% of students in each class must pass. This means that the pass mark for each class will differ. Write a program which will read in a file of marks and determine the highest pass such that the Senate's rule applies.

9.8 **Palindromes** A palindrome is a word or sentence that reads the same forwards as backwards, disregarding punctuation. Famous palindromic sentences are:

> Madam, I'm Adam!
> Able was I, ere I saw Elba.

Checking for a palindrome involves successively comparing pairs of characters, one from each end of the input. This can be expressed nicely as a recursive check:

> It is a palindrome if the leftmost and rightmost chars are the same
> and the inner portion of the sentence is a palindrome.

Write a recursive function which tests whether a given string (stripped of all punctuation and spaces) is a palindrome or not. Test the function in a short program.

10 More User-Defined Types

10.1 Enumerated types
10.2 Records
10.3 Files
10.4 Sets
10.5 Case study: designing a database

10.1 Enumerated types

The objects that programs have to deal with go beyond the predefined types, which provide only for numbers, characters and boolean values. Good examples come from the data in a passport, with the following three items not falling into any predefined category:

sex	male or female
marital status	single, married, widowed, divorced, separated
colour of eyes	blue, grey, brown, hazel, green

In older languages, such values had to be forced into one of the predefined types, leading to **codes**, which were usually numeric. For example, male would be 1 and female 2. The disadvantage of this scheme is that it can easily lead to errors by using the wrong code, and there is no obvious check that a code is valid at all.

Pascal recognizes that its predefined types do not cover everything and provides for new types to be constructed with the individual values listed as identifiers. This is known as **enumerating** the values, and hence these types are called **enumerated types**.

Form of an enumerated type

An enumerated type is declared in a type statement, with the type formation being a list of identifiers. Formally, this gives:

> **Enumerated type**
>
> *identifier* = (*list of identifiers*);

Examples are:

```
TYPE
    sex         = (male, female);
    status      = (single, married, widowed, divorced,
                      separated);
    eyecolours  = (blue, grey, brown, hazel, green);
    machines    = (micro, mini, mainframe);
    states      = (found, notthere, looking);
    suits       = (clubs, diamonds, hearts, spades);
```

Enumerated values

Each enumerated type can have as many values as one likes, but each must be a distinct identifier, and the identifiers must not clash with other identifiers within the same scope. Specifically, a given identifier cannot be a value in two different types, as in:

```
TYPE
    lights      = (red, amber, green);
    eyecolours  = (blue, grey, brown, hazel, green);
```

However, subranges of newly-declared enumerated types are possible, and can often be used to good effect, as in:

```
TYPE
    daysoftheweek = (Monday, Tuesday, Wednesday, Thursday,
                       Friday, Saturday, Sunday);
    weekdays      = Monday..Friday;
    weekend       = Saturday..Sunday;
    midweekbreak  = Tuesday..Saturday;
```

Unfortunately, these types are linear, and do not 'wrap around'. Subranges therefore must refer to values in order. For example, we cannot follow the above declarations with:

```
    longweekend  =  Friday..Monday;
```

The notation for an enumerated value is simply an identifier like `boolean`. As for any other identifier, the case of letter is unimportant. Thus, the following all refer to the same value:

```
Monday
monday
MONDAY
```

Enumerated functions and operators

There are three functions that apply to all enumerated types:

`ord(id)`	gives the ordinal value of `id` in the list of the type
`succ(id)`	gives the next value in the list, if it exists
`pred(id)`	gives the previous value in the list, if it exists.

The values in an enumerated type are said to be ordered, and there exist equivalent ordinal values starting from 0. Thus, in the `eyecolours` type, `ord(blue)` is 0 and `ord(brown)` is 2. The ordering can be used to loop through the values, either using a for-statement, as in:

```
VAR day : daysoftheweek;
for day := Tuesday to Saturday do
```

or with `succ` or `pred`, as in:

```
day := Tuesday;
while day <= Saturday do begin
      {whatever}
      day := succ(day);
end;
```

One problem with using `succ` and `pred` is that they are not defined for the last and first values in a list respectively. Thus, `succ(Saturday)` is alright, but `succ(Sunday)` should cause a value out of range error.

The operators that are available for enumerated types are the same as those for characters, that is, the conditional operators = <> <= >= < and >. The interpretation of the inequalities is once again based on the order of the values as specified in the declaration of the type.

EXAMPLE 10.1   Calculating bills _____

The Relaxeeze Holiday Camp in Zanyland has a basic charge of D120 per person per week, but has three billing strategies, depending on the season and the day on which the guests arrive:

> Arrive on Saturday, Sunday or Monday: standard charge
> Arrive after Monday: half price
> In summer: add 50%

Given the day of arrival, the season and the number of people, we can write a function which will use these to work out the cost of the holiday.

```
TYPE
      daysofweek = (Saturday, Sunday, Monday,Tuesday,
                    Wednesday, Thursday, Friday);
```

```
seasons     = (spring, summer, autumn, winter);
peoplerange = 0..100;   {can't take more}
dollies     = 0..maxint;   {sky's the limit}

FUNCTION holidaycost  (
                arrival : daysofweek;
                season  : seasons;
                people  : peoplerange) : dollies;

    CONST
       basicrate = 120;   {dollies}
    VAR
       sofar : dollies;
    BEGIN
       sofar := basicrate;
       if arrival > Monday then sofar := sofar div 2;
       if season = summer then sofar := round(sofar * 1.5);
       holidaycost := sofar * people;
    END;  {holidaycost}
```

Notice that the declaration for the days of the week was altered to start on Saturday so that the > could be used to good effect with the arrival day.

Input and output of enumerated types

Input and output is not available for enumerated types in Pascal. Thus, the use of enumerated types is often confined to manipulations inside a program. However, it is sometimes essential to get values from the outside world into a program and to store them in an enumerated type. In order to do this, the ordinal values referred to above might have to be employed. Alternatively, the words used as the values can be read in and decoded.

In the same way, outputting an enumerated value involves a translation from the identifier values to items that can be printed, that is, numbers or strings or characters. Both of these processes can be neatly packaged in procedures, so that for any given new enumerated type, x, readx and writex routines can be written. For debugging purposes, the ord of a value can always be printed.

EXAMPLE 10.2   Coding days _____

Problem   The days of the week form a very useful type in many applications. We would like to be able to use it sensibly in a program, including reading and writing values.

Solution   Coding the days as numbers is not very secure: not everyone would agree that Monday is day 1, and confusion could result. It is far better to use an enumerated type within the program, and provide procedures to supplement the operations which are available.

Algorithm   Printing is easy, as it simply employs a case statement to map the non-printable enumerated values on to printable strings.

```
PROCEDURE writeday (d : daysofweek);
   BEGIN
      case d of
         Monday          : write ('Monday');
         Tuesday         : write ('Tuesday');
         Wednesday       : write ('Wednesday');
         Thursday        : write ('Thursday');
         Friday          : write ('Friday');
         Saturday        : write ('Saturday');
         Sunday          : write ('Sunday');
      end;
   END; {writeday}
```

Reading is more difficult. We have to take an unknown quantity in the input –
suspected of being a day name – and check it against one of the seven
possibilities. There are two ways of tackling this:

1.   Check each letter as it comes in, and make a decision based on the first
      few letters.

2.   Read in the whole word and check it against a table of possibilities.

Let us consider the first approach. The procedure must read characters until it
can be sure as to what day is intended; then it can skip characters until a space is
reached. Monday, Wednesday and Friday can be established on the first letter, but
the others need two letters. The procedure is:

```
PROCEDURE readday (var d : daysofweek);
   VAR
      ch     : char;
      valid : boolean;
   BEGIN
      REPEAT
         valid := true;
         read(ch);
         if ch in ['M','T','W','F','S'] then
         case ch of
            'M' : d := Monday;
            'W' : d := Wednesday;
            'F' : d := Friday;
            'T' : begin
                     read(ch);
                     if ch = 'h' then d := Thursday else
                     if ch = 'u' then d := Tuesday else
                     valid := false;
                  end;
            'S' : begin
                     read(ch);
                     if ch = 'a' then d := Saturday else
                     if ch = 'u' then d := Sunday else
                     valid := false;
                  end;
         end
         else valid := false;
         if not valid
         then writeln('*** Wrong spelling. Try again');
      UNTIL valid;
      repeat read(ch) until ch = space;
   END; {readday}
```

One feels slightly uneasy about this procedure because it is only checking one or sometimes two letters, and making an assumption that these are the beginnings of words for days. Thus, given any of the following:

> Saturn
> Saturday
> Sat.
> Satsuma

`readday` would decide that the word was Saturday.

Discussion Within the confines of reading a date, the dangers of the procedure being given something quite silly are minimal. However, Example 11.3 explores how the ideas in Example 9.5 can be used to good effect to obtain a much better read procedure.

EXAMPLE 10.3 Prime numbers

Problem Given a positive integer, decide whether it is prime or not.

Solution The basic method for deciding whether a number is prime is to divide it by successive smaller numbers and if any divide evenly, then the number is not prime. There are several well-known refinements to this outline, that is:

- 1, 2 and 3 are prime;
- try dividing by 2 first;
- then start dividing from 3, and skip all even numbers as divisors;
- stop dividing when the divisor exceeds the square root of the number.

To explain the last refinement, note that if the number has a divisor, and that divisor is greater than the square root, then a divisor smaller than the square root must already have been found. So, once all the smaller numbers have been tried, the process can stop.

An enumerated type will be used inside a program, to make manipulating the three states natural and clear.

Examples

Number : 37	Approx. square root : 6
Divisors : 2 3 5	Result : Prime
Number : 217	Approx. square root : 14
Divisors : 2 3 5 7	Result : Not prime
Number : 211	Approx. square root : 14
Divisors : 2 3 5 7 9 11 13	Result : Prime

Algorithm The algorithm can be phrased in a pseudo-code chart as shown overleaf. There are two points at which the loop can stop, and neither is at the start or end of the loop; so a while statement or repeat statement is not immediately applicable. What we do is regard the loop as having **states**, which can be expressed in the symbolic type:

```
TYPE states = (stilldividing, factorfound, nofactors);
```

The state of the loop starts off as `stilldividing`. Then, when one of the stopping conditions becomes true, the state changes. After the loop, the state can be tested to establish the result.

Prime number tester

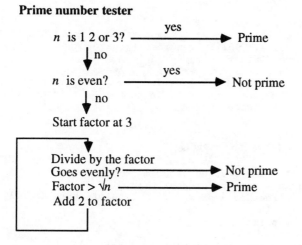

Program   The actual prime tester is written as a function, so that it may be called from other programs. The program itself is very basic, and just calls the function for one number at a time.

```
PROGRAM Primetesting (input, output);
   VAR
      number : integer;

   FUNCTION prime (n : integer) : boolean;
      TYPE
         natural = 0..maxint;
         states = (stilldividing, factorfound, nofactors);
      VAR
         factor   : integer;
         root     : natural;
         state    : states;
      BEGIN
         if (n <= 3) then prime := true else
         if not odd(n) then prime := false else
         BEGIN
            root := trunc(sqrt(n));
            write('Square root is approx: ', root:1,
                  '         Trial factors are: ');
            factor := 3;
            state := stilldividing;
            REPEAT
               write('  ', factor:1);
```

```
                    if n mod factor = 0
                    then state := factorfound
                    else
                        if factor > root
                        then state := nofactors
                        else
                            factor := factor + 2;
                UNTIL state <> stilldividing;
                writeln;
                prime := not (state = factorfound);
            END;
        END; {prime}

    BEGIN
        writeln('****** Prime testing program ******');
        write('Type in a number (greater than 0): ');
        readln(number);
        case prime(number) of
            true        : writeln(number:1, ' is prime');
            false       : writeln(number:1, ' is not prime');
        end; {case}
    END.
```

Testing   Sample test runs might be:

```
****** Prime testing program ******
Type in a number (greater than 0):  211
Square root is approx: 14      Trial factors are: 3   5   7   9
11   13   15
211 is prime

****** Prime testing program ******
Type in a number (greater than 0):  213
Square root is approx: 14      Trial factors are: 3
213 is not prime

****** Prime testing program ******
Type in a number (greater than 0):  12343
Square root is approx: 111      Trial factors are:   3   5   7
9   11   13   15   17   19   21   23   25   27   29   31   33   35   37
39   41   43   45   47   49   51   53   55   57   59   61   63   65   67
69   71   73   75   77   79   81   83   85   87   89   91   93   95   97
99   101   103   105   107   109   111   113
12343 is prime
```

It may seem wasteful in this last example to be dividing by multiples of 3, when we know that 3 doesn't go. The same applies to multiples of 5 and 7 and so on. However, recognizing multiples in order to exclude them as divisors will take a division operation in itself, which will not save anything. There are other methods of testing for primes, and a good one is discussed in the problems.

10.2 Records

Many programming applications are centred around the processing of data, which may assume a fairly complicated form. An example would be the full information required for a passport, which would include names, date of birth, sex, marital status, various facial characteristics and so on. All these items combine to form a single unit and there will be times when they need to be treated as such. Pascal provides for such a grouping mechanism in its record construct.

Form of a record type

A record type is declared as a list of fields of other types, enclosed in keywords. The types of the fields can be anything, either all different or all the same or a mixture.

Record type

```
identifier = RECORD
                field : type;
                field : type;
                     . . .
                field : type;
             END;
```

An example of a natural application of a record type would be a date: this comprises three fields, but may well be treated as a unit by itself on occasion. Such a definition, with its subsidiary definitions, would be:

```
CONST
      past   = 1750;
      future = 2500;

TYPE
      days   = 1..31;
      months = 1..12;
      years  = past..future;
                  {The limit of the program's lifetime!}

      dates  = RECORD
                day   : days;
                month : months;
                year  : years;
              END;
```

Since a field can be of any type, it could be a record itself. For example:

```
TYPE
      sexes    = (male, female);
      newborns = RECORD
```

```
                                sex        : sexes;
                                birth      : dates;
                  END;
```

Record operators

It went without saying for the scalar types that assignment was defined, but it is worth emphasizing that this is also true for records. If we declare:

```
VAR mybirthday, today, happyday : dates;
```

and define appropriate values for the first two, then we can say:

```
if mybirthday = today
    then writeln('Happy Birthday to me!');
happyday := mybirthday;
```

The important operator as far as records are concerned is that for **field selection**, which is indicated by a dot. Any field of a record can be selected by giving the record variable name (not the type name) followed by a dot and the field name. If there are records within records, then several dots can be used to access the lower fields as in:

```
VAR
    baby : newborns;

baby.sex := female;
baby.birth.day := 21;
baby.birth.month := 3;
baby.birth.year := 1986;
```

Record values

The range of values for any one record is the product of every value of every field. In other words, any kind of composite value can be accommodated in a record type. However, there is no facility in Standard Pascal to write down a record constant in a program. To set values for a record, each field must be treated separately, as in the previous examples.

The with-statement

Writing out long selected field names can be tedious. Pascal provides a shorthand which factorizes out the common parts of a field name – the with-statement. The usual form of the with-statement is:

With-statement

```
WITH  record  variable name DO BEGIN
    statements;
END; {with}
```

The scope of the with-statement extends from the BEGIN to the END and within this scope any reference to the fields of the record mentioned can be given without their prefix. For example, the group of statements above could be rewritten as:

```
baby.sex := female;
WITH baby.birth DO BEGIN
      day := 21;
      month := 3;
      year := 1986;
END; {WITH}
```

This version is not any shorter, but it is perhaps easier to read and to write, because there is less repetition.

The syntax of the with-statement includes a version for having a list of record names, an example of which would be:

```
WITH baby, baby.birth DO BEGIN
      sex := female;
      day := 21;
      month := 3;
      year := 1986;
END; {WITH}
```

It is permissible to mention a record more than once, as was done here, but it is not correct to mention two records of the same type. In this case, the Pascal system would not know to which record each field belonged.

It is also possible to have a with-statement applying to only one statement, in which case the begin-end is omitted. The good use of this option is with read and write statements, as in:

```
with baby.birth do write(day, month, year);
```

Reading and writing records

Record values cannot be read or written in their entirety by the predefined read and write statements. It is necessary to treat each scalar field separately. As for enumerated types, it is a good idea to construct procedures for each of these operations. So, for example, one would define `readdate` and `writedate` procedures to handle variables of the type `dates`. However, entire records can be input from and output to files as discussed in the next section.

10.3   Files

The text files that we have used up to now consist of items of type character and include special end-of-line markers. Pascal actually permits new file types to be declared. These files can consist of items of any type, and in particular of records. This means that programs that process many items of data and then have to store the processed form, can do so efficiently. Files can be accessed sequentially, from the first item to the last: there is no provision for random access to files, although some (non-standard) implementations do provide such a feature.

Form of a file declaration

A file type is declared as follows:

```
┌─────────────────────────────────────────────────────────────┐
│ File type declaration                                         │
├─────────────────────────────────────────────────────────────┤
│     TYPE identifier = FILE OF type identifier ;               │
└─────────────────────────────────────────────────────────────┘
```

Variables of this type can then be defined. For example, in Section 10.4, a record for type newborns was defined. A corresponding file would be declared as in:

```
TYPE
    babyfiles = FILE of newborns;

VAR
    babyfile : babyfiles;
```

File values and operators

A file can contain theoretically an infinite number of items. In practice, there will be some limitation imposed by the available disk size.

Files must be opened, connected and closed (if necessary) as described before in Section 7.2. The procedures and function that can be used are:

```
reset (F)        opens the file for reading
rewrite(F)       opens the file for writing
eof(F)           returns true if the file is positioned past its end
```

The same extension to reset is used to make an association between the file name and a file on the disk. Note that both typed files and text files do not actually have to exist on some external device: Pascal does allow the concept of a **local file**. Thus, it is possible to declare and use a file within a program, without connecting it to any device. At the end of the program, then, no record of the file would remain.

With each file is associated a file pointer. The file pointer can be used to consult the buffer variable, which is known by the name of the file followed by an up-arrow, for example, Roomfile↑. At any time, the file pointer indicates the current position in the file, and the buffer variable contains the value of the item at that position, if one exists.

Reading and writing the file is done by using the buffer variable in conjunction with the following two procedures:

```
get (F)          moves the pointer to the next item in the file
                 and copies the value there into the buffer
put (F)          appends the item in the buffer to the end of the file
```

When a file is opened for reading, the first item is copied into the buffer, provided that the file is not empty. If x is a variable of the same type as the file's items, then the sequence for reading is:

```
X := F↑;
get(F);
```

This copies the contents of the buffer into x and then moves the file pointer on. The sequence for writing is:

```
F↑ := X;
put(x);
```

This assigns the value in x to the buffer variable and then transfers this to the end of the file. When a file is opened for writing, the value of the function eof is always true, and it is an error to inspect the contents of the buffer variable.

In many earlier versions of Pascal, get and put were the only procedures for accessing items in files. The most recent standard permits the read and write statements to be used as well, which means that the buffer variable can be ignored. Thus to read a value from a file we have:

```
read(F, X);
```

and to write a value we use simply:

```
write(F, X);
```

As with text files, several items can be listed as parameters, so that the following are also valid:

```
read(F, X, Y);
write(F, P, Q, R);
```

EXAMPLE 10.4   Archiving _____

Problem   We have an array of records containing important data, and would like to save this onto disk, to be reused later.

Solution   Essentially, the data is to be 'dumped' as-is onto disk, and is not to be read via a text editor when it is there. It is therefore not necessary to pass each field through the text write procedures. Instead we use a typed file.

Algorithm   We shall call the two operations 'save' and 'restore'. They have slightly different algorithms. When saving, we know how many records we have, and therefore use a for-loop, simply writing out each element of the array. When restoring, we may be in a different program, and have no idea of how many records were saved. We therefore use a 'while not end-of-file' loop.

Procedures   We can phrase the procedures in a general way, using italics for those parts that must be filled in for the actual record type involved. Notice that the file itself is declared within each procedure, as it is only used during the save or restore process.

```
PROCEDURE Save (a:arrayofrecords; n : range);
   VAR
   i : range;
   filename : string;
   f : file of records;
   BEGIN
      write('Save to what file? ');
      readln(filename);
      rewrite(f,filename);
      for i := 1 to n do
         write(f,a[i]);
      close(f);
      writeln(n, ' records saved');
   END; {Save}

PROCEDURE Restore (var a:arrayofrecords; var n : range);
   VAR
    filename : string;
    i : range;
    f : file of records;
   BEGIN
      write('Restore from what file? ');
      readln(filename);
      reset(f,filename);
      i := 1;
      while not eof(f) do begin
         read(f,a[i]);
         i := i + 1;
      end;
      n := i-1;
      close(f);
      write(n,' records restored');
   END; {Restore}
```

The name of the file is supplied by the user, so that different saved files could be restored.

10.4 Sets

Pascal is one of a few languages that provides for grouping and manipulating items without respect to order. The type mechanism is the **set**, which has most of the properties and operations of the mathematical concept of a set.

By far and away the most common use of sets is the test for set membership. This has already been introduced in Chapter 5, along with the `in` operator. To recapitulate, examples of such uses of **set literals** are:

```
if month in [sep, apr, jun, nov] then days := 30;
borderlines := mark in [49, 59, 69, 74];
isadigit := ch in ['0'..'9'];
```

If the sets are to be used more often, or manipulated in any way, then a **set type** should be defined, along with **set variables** of that type. The declaration can be split into four stages.

Form of a set type

1.   **Define the base type**. A set has to be defined on a base type, which may be a small subrange of integer, char, boolean or enumerated or any subrange of these. Examples of base types are:

```
TYPE
    months        = (jan, feb, mar, apr, may, jun, jul,
                      aug, sep, oct, nov, dec);
    markrange     = 0..100;
    smallrange    = 'a'..'z';
    capitalrange  = 'A'..'Z';
```

2.   **Define the set type**. The form of a set type definition is:

Set type

```
identifier = SET OF base type;
```

Examples of set types are:

```
TYPE
    monthsets  = set of months;
    marksets   = set of markrange;
    smallsets  = set of smallrange;
    capsets    = set of capitalrange;
    charsets   = set of char;
```

Notice the use of the suffixes '-range' and '-set' to distinguish between bases and the sets themselves.

3.   **Declare the set variables**. Set types, like any other types, do not exist as items that can be manipulated. We first have to declare variables of that type. Examples are:

```
VAR
    allmonths, months30 : monthsets;
    class, border       : marksets;
    smalls              : smallsets;
    letters, digits     : charsets;
```

4.   **Initialize the sets**. Like any other variable, a set variable does not have an initial value. That is, it does not start off as the empty set, any more than an integer variable starts off as zero. It is necessary, therefore, to initialize the set to some value, by listing the elements, or ranges of them, in square brackets, for example:

```
allmonths  := [jan..dec];
months30   := [sep, apr, jun, nov];
class      := [50, 60, 70, 75];
digits     := ['0'..'9'];
letters    := [  ];  {to start with}
smalls     := ['a' ..'z'];
```

Note the special case of [ ] which denotes the empty set, and is a set literal compatible with any set type.

Set values and operators

Theoretically, the range of a set is restricted only by the range of its base type. However, because of the way sets are implemented, there is usually a limit placed on the maximum ordinal value in a base type. Turbo Pascal's limit is 256, so that the following would be valid base types:

```
TYPE
   secondcentury = 100..199;
   charsets      = set of char;
```

but the following would not be valid:

```
TYPE
   numbers       = integer;
   fifthcentury  = 400..499;
```

Even though `fifthcentury` has only 100 possible values, it exceeds the limit on the maximum ordinal value.

As we have already noted, literal sets are enclosed in square brackets, and may contain individual elements and ranges of elements, where the elements can be constants or expressions of the base type.

There are several operators applicable to sets. The relational ones are:

in	set membership
= <>	set equality and inequality
<= >=	set inclusion

For manipulation of sets, the three operators are:

+	set union
*	set intersection
−	set difference

We shall now see how these are used in typical cases.

There are no predefined functions defined for whole sets. Sets can be passed as parameters to user-defined functions.

Neither input nor output to text files is possible for whole sets – a restriction that we have already seen for whole records and whole arrays. Procedures for accomplishing this are described below.

Manipulating sets

1. **Creating sets from sets**. A large set may have disjoint subsets, which can be formed by set difference, rather than by listing the elements in each case. For example, we can declare and initialize:

```
VAR
months31 : monthsets;

months31 := allmonths - months30 - [feb];
```

(This is exactly what the old rhyme says: '... all the rest have thirty-one, excepting February alone ...'.) Notice that the set operations work on sets, not elements, and it would have been incorrect to say – feb instead of – [feb].

2. **Creating sets from data**. The elements of a set cannot always be fixed as constants in a program. For example, not all schools and universities have the same class borders for marks as given earlier. To create a set dynamically, we initialize it to the empty set and use set union:

```
class := [ ];    border := [ ];
for i := 1 to 4 do begin
   read (mark);
   class := class + [mark];
   border := border + [mark - 1];
end;
```

3. **Printing a set**. A set is not a simple type, and it cannot be printed in its entirety using a simple Pascal write statement. To print all the elements present in a set, we have to loop over the whole base type and use tests on set membership. For example:

```
for mark := 0 to 100 do if mark in classes then
   write (mark);
```

There is no simpler way. In fact, to perform any operation on all elements of a set, we need such a combination of a for-statement and an if-statement.

4. **Cardinality of a set**. Sometimes it is necessary to know how many elements there are in a set (its cardinality). To count the elements, once again we have to loop through all possibilities and use tests on set membership. In general, such a function could be defined as:

```
FUNCTION cardinality (s : someset) : integer;
   VAR
      i      : somebase;
      count   : integer;   {0..maxsetsize}
   BEGIN
      count := 0;
      for i := lower to upper do if i in s then
         count := count + 1;
      cardinality := count;
   END; {cardinality}
```

The parts in italics will need to be specified for the particular set type and different versions of the function will have to be included for each set type for which it is required.

EXAMPLE 10.5   Generalized menus _____

Problem   In Example 5.3, we investigated ways of making menus for controlling programs that will run for some time. We would like to create a menu system where the options and the commands can vary as data, rather than be built into the program.

Solution   There are actually two problems here:

- varying the messages associated with each choice, and
- varying and checking the commands.

To solve the first, we can declare an array of messages and read the appropriate strings off a text file. The file would be created and maintained via an ordinary text editor.

For the second, we assume that each message on the file is preceded by its command letter, and that in addition we provide the facility for the message numbers to be valid commands as well. Suppose the file looks like this:

```
N   read in New data
D   Display
S   Save
R   Restore
Q   Quit
```

Then the valid set of commands will be:

```
['N', '1', 'D', '2', 'S', '3', 'R', '4', 'Q', '5']
```

Careful design of the messages will ensure that the commands are not ambiguous. This set is then used to check the user's responses. Notice the convention of a capital letter used in a message to indicate the command.

Algorithm   We shall assume that the menu is to be displayed in some command window, and we shall use ScreenMan to control the window. The window may look something like this:

```
***** Main menu *****
1   N   read in New data
2   D   Display
3   S   Save
4   R   Restore
5   Q   Quit
messages here
```

The command window has certain *x* and *y* boundaries which can be preset. However, when an operation (such as Save) wishes to give some status message, then it uses the line in the window directly after the last option. The position of this line must be set up. The operations required by our menu system are:

- SetUpMenu   read in the menu options from a file, set up the command set and message line position;
- DisplayMenu   display the menu in the command window;
- GetRequest   get a command, check it is valid, and refresh the menu.

The purpose of refreshing the menu is to remove any status messages that might have been printed in response to previous commands. However, we are careful to leave these messages on the screen while the user is entering the next command because the information might be relevant.

Program   The command window coordinates will position it in the upper left quadrant of the screen. The maximum number of menu options is set to 10, which is quite a lot.

```
CONST
   maxmenu = 10;
      {Command window}
         cx1      = 1;      cx2 = 39;
         cy1      = 3;      cy2 = 12;
         mx       = 1;      {my is a variable}
TYPE
   commandsets  = set of char;
   options      = string[30];
   optionrange  = 1..maxmenu;
   optionarrays = array [optionrange] of options;

VAR
{These variables used by all the menu procedures}
   commands    : commandset;
   optionslist : optionarrays;
   noptions    : optionrange;
   my          : 1..25;  {for messages - set to noptions+1;}
   comwin      : windows;

PROCEDURE SetUpMenu;
   VAR
      menu     : text;
      filename : string;
      ch       : char;
      n        : 0..optionsmax;

   BEGIN
      write('What menu file? ');
      readln(filename);
      reset (menu, filename);
      noptions := 0;
      commands := [   ];

      while not eof(menu) do begin
         noptions := noptions + 1;
         readln(ch1, optionslist[noptions]);
         commands := commands + optionslist[ch1];
```

```
            end;
            close(menu);
            my := noptions+2;
            window(comwin,cx1, cy1, cx2, cy2)
     END; {SetUpMenu}

     PROCEDURE DisplayMenu;
        BEGIN
            gotoxy(comwin, cx1, cy1+1);
            for i := 1 to noptions do
               writestrln (comwin,optionslist[i]);
        END; {DisplayMenu}

     PROCEDURE GetRequest (var c : commands);
        BEGIN
           repeat
              readch(comwin,c);
              newline(comwin,1);
              DisplayMenu;
              if c in ['a'..'z']
                 then c := chr(ord(ch)-ord('a')+ord('A'));
              if not (c in  commands) then
                 writestrln(comwin, 'Not a valid command');
           until c in commands;
        END;   {GetRequest}
```

10.5   Case study – designing a database

It is often the case that one's manual data records get out of hand, and the idea of using a computer seems very attractive. Let us consider such a real problem.

Problem

The leader of the 1st ZanyLand Cub Scouts finds that she is constantly being required to produce lists of cubs with certain characteristics, and in different orders. It is very tedious to write these out by hand, so she would like to computerize all her records and have a small tailor-made program to produce the lists she wants. It is clear that we shall need the following data structures:

- a **record** for the details of one cub;
- an **array** to keep the details of all cubs while the program is running;
- a **file** to store the details in between runs.

Background

When starting out to write a specific database, one must ask about the fields that will be required in each record, and the operations that are going to be applied. For this we need a bit of background.

In ZanyLand, cubs are young boys and girls between the ages of 7 and 11. There are usually 24 in a *pack*, but there may be more, and they will be divided into groups called *sixes* which have roughly six members each. The leader will want to record the usual data about people – name, address, age – as well as the school the cub goes to, and the six. The training for cubs consists of going through a series of trails, which are known as Cheetah, Leopard, Lion and Leaping Wolf. Before the first trail, a cub is known as a 'new chum'.

At different times, the leader will want to produce lists of cubs arranged by name, by age, by trail, by six or even by school. This will require *sorting* the records, and must be left till the next chapter. Meanwhile, we can set up the basic infrastructure for the database, and use the material covered in this chapter to good advantage.

The basic and advanced database

A basic database requires the following:

- the definition of the data record;
- operations to:
        read one record
        display one record
        read all records
        display all records
        add a new record to all records
        save all records on disk
        restore records from disk;
- a menu manager to provide access to the above operations.

An advanced database will have in addition

- perhaps additional data fields;
- operations to:
        find a record with given characteristics
        extract all records with given characteristics
        sort all records or all extracted records on a given key
        produce printed lists of records
        merge forms with the information in the records;
- more sophisticated menu systems and help facilities.

In this case study we shall develop the basic database, and most of the advanced features will be picked up in later chapters.

Defining the data record

The basic data record can be built up using some of the types defined in earlier sections:

```
TYPE
   cubs = record
      firstname,
      surname  : names;
      birth    : dates;
```

```
          age       : ages;
          six       : sixes;
          trail     : trails;
          school    : schools;
     end;
```

We have omitted the address, for brevity's sake. The first four fields have fairly obvious types, but the last three need some thought. Should they be strings or enumerated types? The decision should be made on the basis of what we want to do with them. For example, we may wish to sort on trails, and a string sort would put Leaping Wolf before Lion, which is wrong. So trails should be an enumerated type. On the other hand, the list of schools that could be represented is not known at the time the program is written, so strings are more appropriate. Sixes could go either way, and for variety, we shall make them type char. There may be a time when a new six is created, and it is more difficult to update an enumerated type. On the other hand, we shall have to avoid conflicting first letters, for example, Blue and Brown.

The additional types needed, therefore are:

```
CONST
   namemax = 20;
TYPE
   namerange = 1..namemax;
   names = packed array[namerange] of char;
   dates = RECORD
               day : 1..31;
               months : 1..12;
               years : 1960 .. 2050;
            end;
   ages     = 7..11;
   sixes    = char;
   trails   = (newchum, cheetah, leopard, lion, leapingwolf);
   schools  = names;
```

Defining the data structures

There are two structures that need to be defined, both holding a full pack of cubs. The first is the array, which is used when the program is running, and the other is the file, for backup storage. The declarations required here are:

```
CONST
   packmax = 48;
TYPE
   packrange = 1..packmax;
   packs     = array[packrange] of cubs;
   packfiles = file of cubs;
VAR
   pack     : packs;
   packfile : packfiles;
```

Notice that we have to leave enough space in the array for the largest possible pack, even though we may only use half of it most of the time.

Setting up the controlling menu and windows

The next step is to establish the overall control within the database, from whence
we can start defining the individual operations. Menus have been considered in
Example 5.3 and again in example 10.3. The program below uses a specialized
version of the general menu system of Example 10.3. The screen is divided into
three windows as follows:

```
***** Cubs V1 Main Menu *****            ***** Output Window *****

1 N   read in New data
2 D   Display data
3 S   Save to disk
4 R   Restore from disk
5 A   Add or update a record
9 T   Take a snapshot
0 Q   Quit




***** Input Window *****
```

The purpose of separating the input and output is to enable a display to remain on
the screen while changes are being made. Notice that we have included taking a
snapshot as a user-driven option: thus, the status of the input and output can be
recorded at any stage, to be printed out from a snapshot file later. The above
display was created from such a snapshot.

The main program, with the main loop activating all the operations is:

```
PROGRAM CubsDatabase1 (input, output);

   BEGIN
      whole(screen);
      writestrln(screen,'***** Cubs V1 Main Menu *****');
      gotoxy(screen,ix1, iy1-2);
      writestrln(screen,'***** Input Window *****');
      gotoxy(screen,ox1, oy1-2);
      writestrln(screen,'***** Output Window *****');

      window(inwin,ix1,iy1,ix2,iy2,'Input');
```

```
window(outwin,ox1,oy1,ox2,oy2,'');
window(comwin,cx1,cy1,cx2,cy2,'Command');

DisplayMenu;
allcommands :=
   ['1'..'5','9','N','D','S','R','A','T','Q'];
available := ['1','N','4','R','9','T','0','Q'];
Repeat
   GetRequest(command);
   case command of
   '1','N' : ReadPack(pack, n);
   '2','D' : WritePack(pack,n);
   '3','S' : Save(pack, n);
   '4','R' : Restore(pack, n);
   '5','A' : Update(pack, n);
   '9','T' : Snapshot;
   '0','Q' : ;
   end;
   until command = 'Q';
END.
```

In addition to the set of all commands, we have defined another one which indicates the commands that are logically available. When the program starts, there is no data loaded, so we want to require the user to choose the read or restore options before trying any of the others. Once data has been read in, the available set can be increased.

The following snapshot shows the screen after a file has been restored from disk and displayed.

```
***** Cubs V1 Main Menu *****        ***** Output Window *****

1 N   read in New data              Pack details
2 D   Display data                  1. John    9
3 S   Save to disk                  2. Peter   9
4 R   Restore from disk             3. Alice   10
5 A   Add or update a record        4. Sue     10
9 T   Take a snapshot               5. Simon   10
0 Q   Quit



***** Input Window *****
```

The operations

The operations proposed for this version involve reading and displaying one record or all records, saving and restoring to disk (covered in example 10.4) and updating or adding a new record. The last one deserves more explanation.

In order to update a record, we need to ask for the record number. In its simplest form, which we shall employ, updating merely means re-entering the data for that record. Adding a record is then similar, except that we add one to the number of records, thus creating a new space. The procedure is:

```
PROCEDURE Update(var pack : packs; var n : packrange);
    var i : integer;
    ch : char;
    BEGIN
        gotoxy(comwin,mx,my);
        writestr(comwin,'Add or Update? ');
        readch(comwin,ch);
        case ch of
            'A','a' : begin
                n:=n+1; i:=n;
                writestr(comwin,'Type in record ');
                writeintln(comwin,n);
                end;
            'U','u' : repeat
                writestr(comwin,'Which record number? ');
                readint(comwin,i);
                until i in [1..n];
            end;
        readcub(pack[i]);
    END; {Update}
```

Notice how sets are used once again to force the user to type in the number of an existing record, if the update option is chosen. The following snapshot shows the screen after a new record has been read in (Mary), an existing one updated (Peter) and the pack redisplayed.

Notice that the information typed in on the input window remains there. This can be helpful for looking back at how a file was built up. The input window will scroll on its own, as will the output window. However, each display operation clears the window before putting out the data.

The program

In the program that follows, we have restricted the actual cub record to just two fields – the name and age. The other fields can be easily added, with the changes affecting only ReadCub, WriteCub and Update.

The program makes use of screen manager via the {$I} comments. Including ScreenMan, the program is about 500 lines long: quite a substantial piece of work!

In addition, we have made use of a variable string reading facility with a copy command in order to be able to type in names neatly. Most Pascal compilers have such or similar.

```
***** Cubs V1 Main Menu *****        ***** Output Window *****

1 N  read in New data                Pack details
2 D  Display data                    1. John    9
3 S  Save to disk                    2. Peter   10
4 R  Restore from disk               3. Alice   10
5 A  Add or update a record          4. Sue     10
9 T  Take a snapshot                 5. Simon   10
0 Q  Quit                            6. Mary     8



***** Input Window *****

Name: Mary
Age:  8
Name: Peter
Age:  10
```

```pascal
PROGRAM CubsDatabase1 (input, output);

CONST
        packmax = 30;
    {Window coords}
        {Command window}
          cx1 = 1;   cx2 = 39; cy1 = 3; cy2 = 12;
          mx = 1;    my = 7; {for messages}
        {Input window}
          ix1 = 1;   ix2 = 39; iy1 = 15; iy2 = 24;
        {Output window}
          ox1 = 41; ox2 = 80; oy1 = 3; oy2 = 24;

{$I SM1.pas}

    TYPE
      names    = string[20];
      ages     = integer; {tp restriction 7..11;}
      cubs     = record
                    name : names;
                    age      : ages;
                  end;
      commands    = char;
      commandset  = set of commands;
      packrange   = 1..packmax;
      packs       = array [packrange] of Cubs;

      VAR
```

```
   command     : commands;
   available,
   allcommands : commandset;
   pack        : packs;
   n           : packrange;
   screen,
   comwin,
   inwin,
   outwin      : windows;

   {$I SM2.pas}

PROCEDURE ReadCub (var c : cubs);
   var s : longstring;
   BEGIN
     writestr(inwin,'Name: ');
     readstr(inwin,s); c.name := copy(s,1,length(s));
     if c.name <> '' then begin
        writestr(inwin,'Age:      ');
        readint(inwin,c.age);
     end;
   END; {ReadCub}

PROCEDURE WriteCub (c : cubs);
   BEGIN
     writestr(outwin,c.name);
     writestr(outwin,'        ');
     writeintln(outwin,c.age);
   END; {WriteCub}

   PROCEDURE ReadPack(var pack : packs; var n:packrange);
    var i : 0..packmax;
    BEGIN
     writestrln(inwin,'Type return to finish');
     i := 0;
     repeat
        i := i+1;
        readcub(pack[i]);
     until pack[i].name = '';
     n := i-1;
     writeint(comwin,n);
     writestrln(comwin,' records read');
     available := allcommands;
   END; {ReadPack}

PROCEDURE WritePack (p : packs; n : packrange);
   var i : packrange;
   BEGIN
     clear(outwin);
     writestrln(outwin,'Pack details');
     for i := 1 to n do begin
        writeint(outwin,i);
        writestr(outwin,'.  ');
        writecub(p[i]);
     end;
   END; {writepack}

PROCEDURE Save (pack : packs; n : packrange);
   VAR
     i : packrange;
     filename : longstring;
```

```
              f : file of cubs;
          BEGIN
              writestr(comwin,'Save to what file? ');
              readstr(comwin,filename);
              rewrite(f,filename);
              for i := 1 to n do
                 write(f,pack[i]);
              close(f);
              writeint(comwin,n);
              writestrln(comwin,' records saved');
          END; {Save}

      PROCEDURE Restore (var pack : packs; var n : packrange);
          VAR
              filename : longstring;
              i : packrange;
              f : file of cubs;
          BEGIN
              writestr(comwin,'Restore from what file? ');
              readstr(comwin,filename);
              reset(f,filename);
              i := 1;
              while not eof(f) do begin
                 read(f,pack[i]);
                  n := i + 1;
              end;
              n := i-1;
              close(f);
              writeint(comwin,n);
              writestrln(comwin,' records restored');
              available := allcommands;
          END; {Restore}

      PROCEDURE Update(var pack : packs; var n : packrange);
          var i : integer;
          ch : char;
          BEGIN
              gotoxy(comwin,mx,my);
              writestr(comwin,'Add or Update? ');
              readch(comwin,ch);
              case ch of
                 'A','a' : begin
                     n:=n+1; i:=n;
                     writestr(comwin,'Type in record ');
                     writeintln(comwin,n);
                     end;
                 'U','u' : repeat
                     writestr(comwin,'Which record number? ');
                     readint(comwin,i);
                     until i in [1..n];
                 end;
              readcub(pack[i]);
          END; {Update}

      PROCEDURE DisplayMenu;
          BEGIN
              clear(comwin);
              writestrln(comwin,'1 N  read in New data');
              writestrln(comwin,'2 D  Display data');
              writestrln(comwin,'3 S  Save to disk');
              writestrln(comwin,'4 R  Restore from disk');
```

```
        writestrln(comwin,'5 A  Add or update a record');
        writestrln(comwin,'9 T  Take a snapshot');
        writestrln(comwin,'0 Q  Quit');
    END; {Display menu}

PROCEDURE GetRequest(var command : commands);
    BEGIN
        repeat
          readch(comwin,command);
          DisplayMenu;
          if command in ['a'..'z'] then
             command := chr(ord(command)-ord('a')+ord('A'));
          gotoxy(comwin,mx, my);
          if command in (allcommands - available) then
             writestrln(comwin,'Not available now');
        until command in available;
        gotoxy(comwin,mx, my);
    END; {GetRequest}

BEGIN
    whole(screen);
    writestrln(screen,'***** Cubs V1 Main Menu *****');
    gotoxy(screen,ix1, iy1-2);
    writestrln(screen,'***** Input Window *****');
    gotoxy(screen,ox1, oy1-2);
    writestrln(screen,'***** Output Window *****');
    window(inwin,ix1,iy1,ix2,iy2,'Input');
    window(outwin,ox1,oy1,ox2,oy2,'');
    window(comwin,cx1,cy1,cx2,cy2,'Command');

    DisplayMenu;

    allcommands :=
         ['1'..'5','9','N','D','S','R','A','T','Q'];
    available := ['1','N','4','R','9','T','0','Q'];
    Repeat
      GetRequest(command);
      case command of
      '1','N' : ReadPack(pack, n);
      '2','D' : WritePack(pack,n);
      '3','S' : Save(pack, n);
      '4','R' : Restore(pack, n);
      '5','A' : Update(pack, n);
      '9','T' : Snapshot;
      '0','Q' : ;
      end;
    until command = 'Q';
END.
```

Testing   Sample output was given earlier.

WHAT WE HAVE LEARNT

Four separate ways of creating new types were discussed. **Enumerated types** *provide a coded version of integers that can reduce errors in programs and make them more readable.* **Records, sets and files** *provide for composite data types. Records can have elements of several types, whereas sets and files are based on a single type. Care is taken to explore the choice of the most appropriate data structure for each situation.*
Methods discussed in this chapter are:

1. *Converting between enumerated types and strings.*
2. *Using enumerated types as state variable.*
3. *Files for archiving.*
4. *Generalizing menus using text files, arrays and sets.*
5. *Designing the infrastructure for a small database.*

QUIZ

---

1. Is the following a valid enumerated type?

   ```
   Roman = ('M', 'D', 'C', 'L', 'X', 'V', 'I');
   ```

2. If the variable day is of an enumerated type days, can one say:

   ```
   read(days)? write(days)?
   ```

3. Can one record be assigned to another of the same type?

4. Give a sequence of statements to copy the contents of file f to file g, where both files are of the same type.

5. If we have two records a and b of the same type, can we say the following:

   ```
   with a,b do ...
   ```

6. Can a set of strings be declared?

7. Find all the errors in the following excerpt.

   ```
   TYPE
       coins = (1, 2, 5, 10, 20, 50);
       coinset = SET OF coins;
   VAR
       n : coins;

   BEGIN
       read (n);
       if n in coinset then ....
   ```

8. An illness can be identified by possible symptoms, which are catered for by the enumerated type:

   ```
   TYPE
       symptoms = (temperature, headache, stomach ache, cough,
                   runny nose, sore eyes, spots);
   ```

Declare a type called `illness` which is a set of symptoms.

9.   Given that `flu` and `cold` are both illnesses, write an expression that represents those symptoms that are common to both.

10.   What is the expression to convert a lower-case letter to upper case?

PROBLEMS

10.1   **Scalar product**   One of the more common operations on vectors is finding the scalar product defined as the sum of the product of each of the elements of the two vectors, that is:

$$\sum_{i=1}^{n} a_i b_i$$

Write a procedure to calculate the scalar product which can accommodate vectors of different lengths. Write a suitable test program to test it out.

10.2   **Judges' countries**   In Example 9.4, instead of printing out the judges' numbers when a score is diskarded, we would like to print out the country they come from. Use the techniques developed in Example 9.6 to read and store the countries for each judge, and print them out as appropriate. Consider carefully whether to have an array of countries alongside the scores, or to incorporate the country name and score in a record.

10.3   **Improving cubs**   Add additional fields to the cubs' records database. These should record the six, school and trail of each cub. Consider how the display will have to change to display full records, and whether this is desirable. Improve the Update operation to require only one field to be entered, not the whole record.

10.4   **Training schedules**   Employees at Zanyland Inc. attend training courses and a record of each course attended is kept on a file. Set up a system to record this information, and to list the employees who have attended each course. Assume that employees are known by three digit numbers, and that the courses are known by a single letter. **Hint:** The solution should use sets.

10.5   **Better training schedules**   Starting with the program in exercise 10.4 on employee training schedules, adapt it to print out the names, rather than the numbers, of employees. Then use sets to work out how many employees are doing the same combination of any two courses.

10.6   **AD and BC dates**   A historian is studying the period of the Roman Empire, which extends either side of 1 AD. He wishes to computerize some of his data and to be able to compare and make simple calculations about the dates. Typical dates and calculations might be:

54 BC – 64 BC = 10 years

4 BC – 33 AD = 37 years

Decide on a method of inputting, storing and outputting such dates, and write procedures to read a date, write a date and subtract two dates.

10.7 **Student marks** Define a record type which contains fields for a student number, a year mark, an examination mark, a total mark and an indicator as to whether the total mark is above a subminimum or not. Write a procedure that:

- has parameters for a student and a subminimum;
- reads the student number, year mark and exam mark;
- calculates the total mark as the average of the two marks read in;
- sets the subminimum indicator according to a given subminimum.

Test your procedure with a suitable test program and data.

10.8 **Population increase** Since 1970, the Zanyland population statistics have been stored on a file, with each line containing the year followed by the total people counted for that year. Write a program that will read this file and find the two consecutive years in which there was the greatest percentage increase in population. Use a record to store the year–population pair. Write the program without using any arrays.

10.9 **Club records** Choose an activity with which you are familiar and design a record data structure to store information about the people, equipment or events associated with the activity. What operations would be needed for this information?

10.10 **Inventory** Design a record to hold a typical inventory of wares in a hardware shop. Write a program which will allow inventory data to be read off a text file, and which will print out the complete record of any item whose stock has fallen below its reorder level.

10.11 **Sieve of Eratosthenes** The usual method for finding prime numbers, discussed in the answer to the previous question, seems very inefficient in that division by 9, 15, 21, and so on is still attempted after division by 3 had failed. One of the ancient Greek philosophers, Eratosthenes, discovered a better method. The idea is to put all the numbers in a 'sieve'. The first number is taken out, then all multiples of it removed. Then the next number is taken out, and all its multiples removed. By this process, all of the 'taken out' numbers will be prime. Write a Pascal program to implement the Sieve of Eratosthenes, using sets.

10.12 **Supermarket competition** A supermarket is running a competition in which a customer wins a prize for collecting cards with four lucky numbers. The cards are numbered from 1 to 60 and are handed out at the tills. Each Friday the four lucky numbers are announced and any customer holding cards with those numbers may claim a prize. Write a Pascal program which will check a given list of four numbers (from a customer) against a list of four read off a file and indicate whether a prize has been won or not. Use sets and set operations.

11 Sorting and Searching

11.1 Simple sorting

Sorting is a very common operation in computing, and many systems provide high level commands which enable data to be sorted in any specified way. These commands rely on one of a number of sorting algorithms and every programmer should know at least one such sorting algorithm off by heart. We start by introducing a simple one – selection sort – which performs in time proportional to the square of the number of items being sorted. Other algorithms (for example, Quicksort) perform faster, but are perhaps more difficult to understand and remember. Quicksort is examined in Section 11.4.

Selection sort

Sorting items means moving them around in a methodical way until they are all in order. A method used by some card players is to sort cards by holding them in the right hand, finding the lowest one and taking it out into the left hand, then finding the next lowest and taking it out, until all the cards have been selected, and the left hand holds the cards in order. The following sequence illustrates how this method works.

Left hand	Right hand
	7 3 9 0 2 5
0	7 3 9 – 2 5
0 2	7 3 9 – – 5
0 2 3	7 – 9 – – 5
0 2 3 5	7 – 9 – – –
0 2 3 5 7	– – 9 – – –
0 2 3 5 7 9	– – – – – –

We could implement this by having two arrays and picking the numbers out of one, adding them to the other. However, there is a way of keeping both lists in the same array, the one growing as the other shrinks. Each time an element is picked out, the gap it leaves is moved to one end, thus creating a contiguous gap, which is used to hold the new list. The move is done by a simple swap with the leftmost element of the right hand. So, the example would proceed as follows:

Left hand	Right hand
	7 3 9 0 2 5
0	3 9 7 2 5
0 2	9 7 3 5
0 2 3	7 9 5
0 2 3 5	9 7
0 2 3 5 7	9
0 2 3 5 7 9	

Each time, a reduced list is considered, until only one element is left. The algorithm can be phrased more precisely as:

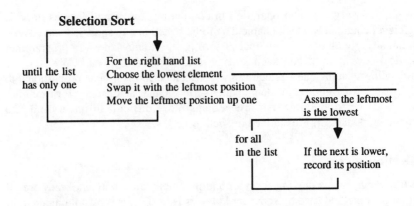

Selection Sort

until the list has only one

For the right hand list
Choose the lowest element
Swap it with the leftmost position
Move the leftmost position up one

Assume the leftmost is the lowest

for all in the list

If the next is lower, record its position

Because sorting is clearly going to be useful in many contexts, it makes sense to put it in a procedure from the beginning. The types that it will need are:

```
TYPE
    items    = integer;   {for testing}
    range    = 1..max;
    tables   = array [range] of items;
```

The parameters would be the array to be sorted, and the number of items that are active in it. (The array may be 100 long, and only have, say, 56 items stored in it.)

```
PROCEDURE sort (VAR a : tables;  n : range);
    VAR
        temp : items;
        i,
        chosen,
        leftmost   : range;

    BEGIN
        FOR leftmost := 1 to n - 1 do begin
            chosen := leftmost;
            for i := leftmost + 1 to n do
                if a[i] < a[chosen] then chosen := i;
            temp := a[chosen];
            a[chosen] := a[leftmost];
            a[leftmost] := temp;
        END;
    END; {sort}
```

EXAMPLE 11.1   Ocean temperatures sorted _____

Problem   An ocean-going research ship records the sea temperature at each hour of the day. The scientists on board like to see a sorted list of the temperatures in order to get a feel for the spread.

Solution   Read in the temperatures, sort them and print out the temperatures for each day. The sorting procedure above can be used as is.

Program   The program starts by defining the types needed by the sort – items, range and tables. The output is in three columns for ease of reading.

```
PROGRAM SortingTemperatures (input, output);
    CONST
        max  = 24;
    TYPE
        items   = real;   {degrees celsius}
        range   = 1..max;
        tables  = array [range] of items;

    VAR
        i : range;
        temps : tables;

    PROCEDURE readdata (VAR a : tables);
        VAR i : range;
        BEGIN
            writeln('Type in the 24 temperatures');
            for i := 1 to 24 do read(a[i]);
            readln;
```

```
        END; {readdata}

        PROCEDURE sort (VAR a : tables;  n : range);
        {As defined above}
        END; {sort}

    BEGIN
        writeln('****** Ocean temperatures in ',
                'order ******');
            readdata(temps);
        sort (temps, max);
        writeln('The temperatures in order are: ');
        for i := 1 to 8 do
        writeln(temps[i]:6:2,'        ',
                temps[i+8]:6:2,'        ',
                temps[i+16]:6:2,'        ');
        writeln;
    END.
```

Testing

```
****** Ocean temperatures in order ******
Type in the 24 temperatures
11.1   11.08  11.03   11.56   11.98   12.01    12.0    12.13
12.13    12.5   12.4    12.09   12.5   12.8    13.01    13.1
14.5    14.6   14.51   13.5    13.32   13.04   12.9    12.8
The temperatures in order are
11.03   12.13  13.01
11.08   12.13  13.04
11.10   12.40  13.10
11.56   12.50  13.32
11.98   12.50  13.50
12.01   12.80  14.50
12.01   12.80  14.51
12.09   12.90  14.60
```

Sorting is a frequent requirement in computing, and it is useful to have a sorting algorithm handy. As will be seen in following sections, the algorithm can be applied to arrays of any size, and containing any elements, and can be used to sort in ascending order just by changing the comparison from < to >.

Notice, however, that if we wish to sort from highest to lowest, then the value that moves to the left each time will be the largest, not the smallest.

EXAMPLE 11.2   Sorting names and marks _____

Problem   Suppose that the names and marks of a class of students have to be printed in alphabetical order.

Solution   Use a computer. Read all the name–mark pairs into an array, sort them according to the name using selection sort, and then print out the contents of the array.

Algorithm   The first step is to define the data and the data structure. The data will look like this:

```
67    Jones K L
51    MacDeedle P
```

with the mark first and then the name. This enables the end-of-line to be used as a string terminator. We define a record with two fields – one for the name and one for the mark. In the sorting process, the name is used in the comparison part, but when the swapping is done, the whole record is copied. Thus, the mark will move around with the name while sorting is proceeding.

Program   The program is really just a rework of the sort given in the previous example, but we give it in full here to emphasize the versatility of the method. Because the types of the array being sorted are different, the sort procedure has had to be changed accordingly.

```
PROGRAM Sortingmarks (input, output, data);
   CONST
      classmax    = 200;
      namemax     = 24;
   TYPE
      namerange   = 1..namemax;
      names       = packed array [namerange] of char;
      marks       = 0..100;
      students    = record
                          name : names;
                          mark : marks;
                    end;
      classrange  = 1..classmax;
                          {assumes at least one student}
      classes     = array [classrange] of students;

   VAR
      class       : classes;
      noofstudents,
      i           : classrange;
      data        : text;

   PROCEDURE readname (VAR name : names);
      VAR i : namerange;
      BEGIN
         for i := 1 to namemax do
            if eoln(data) then
               name[i] := ' ' else read(data,name[i]);
         readln(data);
      END;  { readname }

   PROCEDURE sortname(var a : classes;  n : classrange);
      VAR
         i,
         chosen,
         leftmost  : classrange;
         temp      : students;  {used in swapping}
      BEGIN
         FOR leftmost := 1 to n - 1 do begin
            chosen := leftmost;
            for i := leftmost + 1 to n do
               if a[i].name < a[chosen].name
               then chosen := i;
            temp := a[chosen];
```

```
            a[chosen] := a[leftmost];
            a[leftmost] := temp;
        END;
    END; {sortname}

BEGIN
    writeln('****** Sorting names and marks ******');
    write('For the data file use student.data');
    reset(data, 'student.data');
    noofstudents := 0;
    while not eof(data) do begin
        noofstudents := noofstudents + 1;
        with class[noofstudents] do begin
            read(data, mark);
            readname(name);
        end;
        readln(data);
    end;

    sortname(class, noofstudents);

    writeln('The class in alphabetical order is: ');
    for i := 1 to noofstudents do
        with class[i] do
            writeln(name:namemax,'    ', mark:3);
END.
```

Multi-way sorting

The selection sorting procedure sorts in a defined order. In Example 11.1 we sorted in ascending order, and in example 11.2 in descending order. The change was effected by changing the comparison operator inside the sort itself. It would be nice if we could choose the order at runtime. Furthermore, when sorting records, it would also be useful to be able to choose the field that must be used for the ordering. For example, in the previous example, we sorted on alphabetical order, that is, on the name field, but we should be able to sort on the mark field just as easily.

There are two ways of achieving such multi-way sorting in Pascal. The one uses procedural parameters, which are not very common, and are covered in Chapter 13. The other method, which we shall discuss here, uses a combination of enumerated types and case statements to provide a surprising degree of flexibility.

First, we decide on all the possible orderings that we would wish to use on the given data. Let us suppose that for Example 11.2, these are the following:

```
TYPE orderings = (onname, onmarksup, onmarksdown);
```

Then the definition of the procedure must include a parameter of this type, as in:

```
PROCEDURE sort (var a:somearray; n:range; direction:orderings);
```

and inside the procedure, the comparison is replaced by a case-statement which selects the appropriate order and assigns the result to a local boolean variable, relation, as in:

```
case direction of
   onname : relation := a[i].name < a[chosen].name;
   onmarksdown : relation := a[i].mark > a[chosen].mark;
   onmarksup : relation := a[i].mark < a[chosen].mark;
end;
if relation then ...
```

Incorporating this method into a program is explored in the case study at the end of the chapter.

11.2 Linear searching

Just as sorting is a common operation, so is searching. If we have a sequence of values stored in an array or in a file, then we can search the sequence for a particular value by starting at the beginning of the sequence and comparing each element in turn. This is called linear searching, because we scan the sequence in a linear way.

The linear searching algorithm is an example of a double-exit loop: either the value is found in the sequence, or the end of the sequence is reached before the value is found. We use a technique known as **state indicators** to keep track of the state of the search while it is progressing. This state starts out as *searching*, then can change to either *found* or *not found*, depending on the outcome. We are therefore looking towards an enumerated type defined as:

```
TYPE
   state = (searching, found, notthere);
```

and the algorithm in pseudo-chart form is :

Linear Search

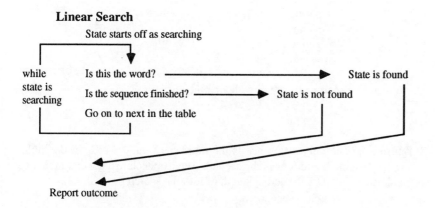

State starts off as searching

while state is searching

Is this the word? — State is found

Is the sequence finished? — State is not found

Go on to next in the table

Report outcome

Linear search can be nicely packaged up in a procedure. The one issue to settle is how the procedure should report that the value required did not match any in the sequence. The best way is to have a boolean as a parameter, and to rely on the caller checking it before assuming that the index returned is meaningful.

EXAMPLE 11.3   Searching string tables _____

Problem   In the program that wrote out foreign spellings for days of the week
(Example 9.5), there is also a requirement that it read them. The user should be
able to type in a word, and the program check whether it is a valid day or not.

Solution   The words for days are stored in a file, and read into an array of
strings. A potential day can then be read and passed to a **search** procedure,
which will return the index to the array for that string, or some error code if the
string is not a valid name.

   If we reflect on this, we realize that searching is an operation that could be
applicable in many circumstances. Reading a month name, or a department
name, or even a person's name, and checking that it appears on a list could be
done in the same way. The only difficulty is that different enumerated types
could not be used for the subscripts. If we sacrifice the use of enumerated types
at this level, and use integer subranges instead, we can come up with a very nice
generalized procedure for reading and identifying strings.

   Given a table containing days of the week in French:

lundi	vendredi
mardi	samedi
mercredi	dimanche
jeudi	

then passing the word:

   vendredi

as a parameter to the proposed search procedure should return a 5. With the data:

   spring
   summer
   autumn
   winter

a call to the same search procedure with a parameter:

   summer

will return a 2. The only difference is the number of valid words in the table:
seven in the first case, and four in the second. We can declare a general table of a
reasonable size, and pass the actual length of it to the search procedure.

Algorithm   The searching algorithm was described above. We go straight on to
the program.

Program   In the program that follows, three string tables are set up and
searched. Moreover, reading in a table is also an operation that can be
generalized, and this is done as well in ReadStringTable.

```
PROGRAM Searchingtables (input, output);

   CONST
      tablemax = 30;
      wordmax = 20;

   TYPE
      string        = packed array[1..wordmax] of char
      tablerange    = 1..tablemax;
      tableindex    = 0..tablemax;
      stringtables  = array[tablerange] of string;
      dayrange      = 1..7;
      seasonrange   = 1..4;
      deptrange     = 1.. 20;

   VAR
      daytable,
      seasontable,
      depttable    : stringtables;
      word         : words;
      there, stop  : boolean;
      ndays,
      nseasons,
      ndepts
      n                : tableindex;

   PROCEDURE ReadStringTable (
                              VAR n : stringindex;
                              VAR T : stringtables;
                              filename : string);
      VAR f : text;

      BEGIN
         reset (f, filename);
         n := 0;
         while not eof(f) do begin
            n := n + 1;
            readln(f,T[n]);
         end;
         writeln('Table with ', n,
                 ' elements read from ', filename);
      END; {ReadStringTable}

   PROCEDURE Search (
            T : stringtables;
            n : stringindex;
            x : string;
            VAR index : stringrange;
            VAR result : boolean);
      TYPE
         states = (searching, found, notthere);
      VAR
         i : stringrange;
         state    : states;
      BEGIN
         if i = 0 then state := notthere else begin
         state := searching;
         i := 1;
         REPEAT
            if x = T[i] then state := found else
            if i = n then state := notthere else
```

```
            i := succ(i);
        UNTIL state <> searching;
        end;
        CASE state of
           found :  begin
                    index := i;
                    result := true;
                    end;
           notthere :  result := false;
        END;
     END; {search}

BEGIN
   writeln('****** Searching string arrays ******');

   ReadStringTable(daytable, ndays, 'day names');
   ReadStringTable(seasontable, nseasons,
                   'season names');
   ReadStringTable(f, depttable, ndepts,
                   'department names');

   stop := false;
   repeat
      writeln('Type in a day, a season, ',
              'a department or QUIT');
      readln(word);
      if word = 'QUIT'
      then stop := true
      else begin
         Search (daytable, ndays, word, n, there);
         if there
         then writeln('This is day No. ', n)
         else begin
            Search (seasontable, nseasons, word, n, there);
            if there
            then writeln('This is season No. ', n:1)
            else begin
               search (depttable, ndepts, word, n , there);
               if there
               then writeln ('This is department No. ', n:1)
               else writeln ('This word is not ',
                       'in any of the tables.');
            end;
         end;
      end;
   until stop;
END.
```

Discussion A point to note is that in Standard Pascal, there is a facility to pass to a procedure arrays that are actually of different lengths. These are called **conformant array parameters** and are considered in Chapter 13.

Simpler searches

If one is absolutely sure that the value being sought is definitely in the sequence – perhaps it was inserted there by the same program – then there is a simpler search algorithm that can be used. In Pascal it is:

```
i := 1;
while a[i] <> x do i := i+1;
```

Many textbooks will propose augmented versions of this loop which involve checking whether i has reached n and so on, but it is our belief that once past the very simple case, the state variable approach is the safest and cleanest.

11.3 Binary searching

The search procedure implements a **linear search**. If the data to be searched is ordered, that is, sorted, then there are more efficient searching methods. The archetypal one is called **binary search**. It involves splitting the sequence in half, and only searching that part where the value must lie. One can be certain about which half the value is in, because the sequence is assumed to be sorted.

For example, suppose we have the sorted sequence:

    23   45   61   65   67   70   82   89   90   99

and are searching for the value 90. Informally, we could divide the sequence in two between 67 and 70 and see that 90 must be in the right-hand side.

    23   45   61   65   67   70   82   89   90   99

We divide this subsequence in two between 89 and 90 and move to the right again.

                    70 82 89   90 99

The sequence we are interested in is now too long, but we still divide and move to the left, where we find 90.

                    90   99

This took 4 divides and compares, compared to 9 with a linear search.

Clearly, binary search is faster *on average* but not every time. If the value being sought was 23 (the first in the sequence), binary search would still start in the centre and move gradually to the left to find it.

The best way to formulate such a binary search is by using recursion. The algorithm is:

> **Binary search a sequence for *x***
>> If the sequence has one element,
>>> compare *x* to it and return found or not found.
>> Otherwise consider the element in the middle of the sequence.
>>> If *x* < middle element, then search left subsequence for *x*
>>> else search the right subsequence for *x*.

In many cases, the sequence or subsequence to be split will not have an even number of elements and so we make the convention that the extra element goes to the left sublist. Looking at the algorithm, one can see that an improvement would be to add an additional case in the second part, to consider whether the value being sought is in fact the middle element at the time.

Conditions for binary search

Binary searching relies on the values being ordered, but it also relies on being able to index the sequence. Thus, binary searching is not possible on ordinary sequential Pascal files. For files, linear searching must be used.

EXAMPLE 11.4   Animated binary search

Problem   In order to illustrate binary search, we shall develop the Pascal to implement the algorithm above, and shall show the stages of the search as it develops.

Solution   We start off with a line of numbers and every time we split the sequence, we shall print out only those numbers. This begs the question of how we 'split a sequence'. The answer is that we don't! What we do is we keep only one sequence, globally to the searching procedure, and pass in to the search the left and right limits each time.

Algorithm   There is a slightly difficult part in splitting a sequence: once the list no longer starts at 1, the expression for the midpoint is different. If the sequence starts at 1, we are used to finding the midpoint at $(n-1)$ *div* 2. However, if a subsequence runs from j to k in a larger sequence, then the midpoint of the subsequence is at position $(j + k)$ *div* 2. You should verify that you understand why this is so.

Program   The program to animate the binary search follows. We have chosen to set up test data by means of simple loop: data could also be read in, but remember to keep it sorted, or the program will not function correctly. (Alternatively, slot in the sort procedure and sort the data first, just to make sure.)

```
PROGRAM Anisearch (input, output);
  CONST
    indexmax = 20;
  TYPE
    values = integer;
    index = 1..indexmax;
    sequence = array[index] of values;

  VAR
    a : sequence;
    x : values;
    result : boolean;
    where : index;

  PROCEDURE SetupSequence(var a : sequence);
    VAR i : index;
```

```
      BEGIN
        writeln('***** Animated binary search *****');
        for i := 1 to indexmax do begin
          write(i:3);
          a[i]:=indexmax+i*3;
        end;
        writeln;
        for i := 1 to indexmax do write(a[i]:3); writeln;
      END; {SetupSequence}

  PROCEDURE BinSearch (left, right : index;
                       x:values;
                       var found : boolean;
                       var i : index);
      VAR midindex : index;

      PROCEDURE Display;
        VAR j : index;
        BEGIN
          for j:= 1 to left-1 do write(' ':3);
          for j := left to right do write(a[j]:3);
          writeln; readln;
      END;

      BEGIN
        Display;
        if left=right then begin
          found := x = a[left];
          i := left;
        end
        else begin
          midindex := (right+left) div 2;
          if x = a[midindex] then begin
            found := true;
            i := midindex;
          end
          else
          if x < a[midindex] then
            Binsearch (left, midindex, x, found, i)
          else
            Binsearch (midindex+1, right, x, found, i);
        end;
      END; {BinSearch}

BEGIN
  SetupSequence(a);
  write('What value do you wish to find? ');
  readln(x);
  BinSearch (1, indexmax, x, result, where);
  if result then writeln(x,' found at ',where)
  else writeln(x, ' not found.');
  readln;
END.
```

Testing   Two tests are shown: one where the number was found, and the other where it wasn't.

```
***** Animated binary search *****
 1   2   3   4   5   6   7   8   9  10  11  12  13  14  15  16  17  18  19  20
23  26  29  32  35  38  41  44  47  50  53  56  59  62  65  68  70  74  77  80
23  26  29  32  35  38  41  44  47  50  53  56  59  62  65  68  70  74  77  80
                                        53  56  59  62  65  68  70  74  77  80
                                                            68  70  74  77  80
                                                            68  70  74
70 found at 17

***** Animated binary search *****
 1   2   3   4   5   6   7   8   9  10  11  12  13  14  15  16  17  18  19  20
23  26  29  32  35  38  41  44  47  50  53  56  59  62  65  68  71  74  77  80
23  26  29  32  35  38  41  44  47  50  53  56  59  62  65  68  71  74  77  80
23  26  29  32  35  38  41  44  47  50
                        38  41  44  47  50
                        38  41  44
                        38  41
                        38
36 not found.
```

11.4 Quicksort

There are many different algorithms for sorting, but one that is a classic because of its overall good performance is known as Quicksort.

Sorting is based on the twin operations of comparing and exchanging; quicksort is based on the principle that any exchange must take place over the greatest distance possible. Thus, instead of exchanging adjacent elements, we select elements which are at virtually opposite ends of the sequence. To do this, we adopt the split-in-half idea used in binary search. Basically, we split the sequence at a certain point and move all the bigger items to the right and the smaller items to the left , using 'long exchanges'. This done, we concentrate on each subsequence in turn, doing the same until only one item remains in each. Quicksort does not split each subsequence exactly in half, as binary search did, but divides on the position around which the last exchange was made.

Put in algorithmic terms, Quicksort is:

Quicksort
> Provided the sequence has more than one item
>> Choose an item as a pivot (e.g. the midpoint)
>> Move all items less than it to the left
>> Move all items more than it to the right
>> Quicksort the left subsequence
>> Quicksort the right subsequence

where the algorithm for the Move is given below.

Quicksort is quite complicated, and strangely enough, animating it, or performing an example in detail does not make it clearer. It is one of those algorithms that one has to understand in theory, and then accept as correct. It is, however, possible to program it quite concretely in Pascal.

Move

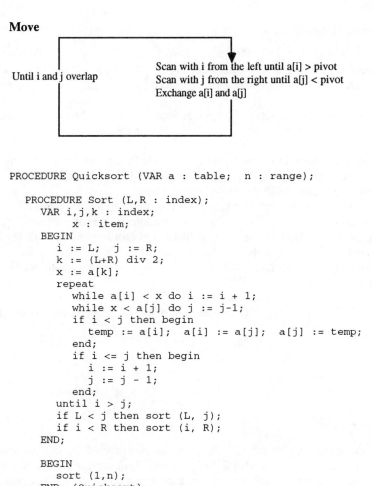

Until i and j overlap

Scan with i from the left until a[i] > pivot
Scan with j from the right until a[j] < pivot
Exchange a[i] and a[j]

```
PROCEDURE Quicksort (VAR a : table;  n : range);

  PROCEDURE Sort (L,R : index);
    VAR i,j,k : index;
        x : item;
    BEGIN
      i := L;   j := R;
      k := (L+R) div 2;
      x := a[k];
      repeat
        while a[i] < x do i := i + 1;
        while x < a[j] do j := j-1;
        if i < j then begin
           temp := a[i];  a[i] := a[j];  a[j] := temp;
        end;
        if i <= j then begin
           i := i + 1;
           j := j - 1;
        end;
      until i > j;
      if L < j then sort (L, j);
      if i < R then sort (i, R);
    END;

  BEGIN
    sort (1,n);
  END; {Quicksort}
```

11.5 A look at performance

The need to look for different algorithms to solve the same problem stems from a desire for speed: newer algorithms may be faster, and therefore in everyone's eyes, better. What differences in speed are found? With searching and sorting algorithms, they can be quite considerable. Moreover, the speed of the algorithms is proportional to the number of items involved, and therefore can become quite significant once there are thousands or millions of items.

There are two ways of comparing performance: theoretical and experimental. Let us look first at the theoretical performance. We calculate the speed of an algorithm based on the number of 'basic operations' it has to perform. These basic operations are rationalized to include only comparisons and exchanges, and assessing the performance boils down to counting the occurrence of these inside loops.

Comparison of sorts

Consider selection sort. The outer loop goes for $n-1$, and includes $n-1$ exchanges. The inner loop runs from i to $n - 1$ and so reduces by one at each iteration. The number of comparisons is therefore:

$$(n-1) + (n-2) + (n-3) + \ldots + 1 = n(n-1)/2$$
$$= (n^2 - n)/2$$

To simplify matters, we ignore the coefficients in the number of exchanges and simply say that there are of the order n^2. If we add in the number of exchanges, the whole process is still dominated by the n^2 term.

Quicksort, on the other hand, uses a partitioning algorithm, which in rough terms involves log_2 iterations. On each iteration, n comparisons are done, and roughly $n/6$ exchanges. Quicksort is therefore considered to operate at a speed proportional to $n \ log_2 n$. In real terms, how does this compare to the order of performance of selection sort? The table below evaluates both formulae for various values of n.

n	Selection sort order n^2	Quicksort order $n \ log_2 n$
10	100	30
50	2 500	300
100	10 000	700
1 000	1 000 000	10 000
10 000	100 000 000	130 000
100 000	10 000 000 000	1 600 000
1 000 000	1 000 000 000 000	20 000 000

The difference is phenomenal. Suppose the unit of time for one iteration is 1 microsecond (10^{-6}). Then for a million items, Quicksort will take 20 seconds, whereas selection sort will take around eleven and a half days! It is interesting, though, that at this rate of $1\mu s$, the difference between the two sorts would not really be noticeable until n exceeds 1000. At this point, selection sort will take a full second, whereas Quicksort will only take 1/100 of a second. In an interactive environment, the difference may not even be noticed.

So why don't we use Quicksort all the time? The answer is begged by the other performance indicator we have: space. Pascal procedures occupy space in memory for their instructions, as well as for their data. Both the algorithms have roughly the same number of statements, so there is not much to choose on the instruction side. However, there is a big difference in data space used. Selection sort declares four local variables and uses them throughout. Quicksort declares 6 local variables and parameters for each recursive call. Since recursive calls are stacked up, it may be in the worst case that for a million items, there are 120 items stacked up by Quicksort.

Yet even this is not a lot, and therefore we can probably conclude that the slight wariness with which ordinary programmers regard Quicksort is probably due to an unfamiliarity with recursion.

Comparison of searches

The two searches we looked at can easily be seen to have performances related to n (linear) and log_2n (binary). Here, the difference in speed is even more dramatic than sorting.

n	Linear Search order n	Binary search order log_2n
10	10	3
50	50	6
100	100	7
1 000	1 000	10
10 000	10 000	13
100 000	100 000	16
1 000 000	1 000 000	20

Put in real terms, this means that to search a telephone directory of 1 million entries by means of binary search, we should be able find any entry in no more than 20 goes. Very much better than an entry-by-entry linear slog!

Where is this leading?

The study of algorithms, and their analysis of performance, is a cornerstone of computer science, and a major part of a second computer science course. In addition to the two sorting algorithms mentioned here, you will learn other sorts such as bubble sort (very slow), merge sort and tree sort (very fast), and pigeonhole sort (extremely fast, but fussy). You will learn how to choose an algorithm for a given solution, and look at the limits of algorithms: how fast can they really get? It is a fascinating study, and we have merely touched on it here.

11.6   Case study – database continued

In the case study at the end of Chapter 10 we proposed an advanced database which would perhaps contain additional fields, and would have, among others, the operations:

- find a record with given characteristics;
- extract all records with given characteristics;
- sort all records or all extracted records on a given key.

Clearly, we can link in the sorting and searching algorithms developed here to provide these facilities, extending the menu at the same time. However, there are two considerations: the first is which algorithms to use, and the second is a question of the 'given characteristics' and 'given key'.

Which algorithm?

The question of which algorithm to use in a given circumstance is a very important one in computer science. We are faced here with only two algorithms in each instance, and we can probably make an optimal choice based on common sense. In later computer science courses, you will encounter more difficult cases, and study further the criteria on which decisions should be based.

For sorting, both algorithms will perform equally well. Although Quicksort is on average faster, for the small numbers of records that we have (less than 50), there is little to choose between them. Since selection sort is perhaps easier to remember, let's include it this time.

For searching, there is a more solid criterion: binary search needs sorted data, and it must be sorted on the same key that we shall be searching on. This cannot always be guaranteed in a database where the user is free to choose operations in any order. Moreover, linear searching will not be noticeably slower for only 50 items.

On characteristics and keys

The issue of characteristics and keys needs more careful consideration. Once the data for the Cubs is fully collected, there could be eight or more ways of sorting the data, and an equal number of fields for which to search. In both the sort and the search algorithms there is a statement where the comparison is made. Specifically, for the sort, this is:

```
if a[i] < a[chosen] then …
```

and for the linear search, it is:

```
if x = T[i] then …
```

In both cases, we need to augment this to allow for a multi-way comparison, as described in Section 11.1. But since the multi-way comparison is to be done more than once, we could endeavour to put it in a function, which can be called in either case. In other words, we are looking at saying:

```
if compare(a[i], lessthan, a[chosen], thekey) then …
```

or

```
if compare(x, equal, T[i], thekey) then …
```

where `thekey` is an enumerated value related to the field under consideration, and the second parameter is another enumerated value which indicates the type of comparison required. The function can then use case-statements to make the appropriate selection and return the answer.

On converting old data

If we are to build on the program of the previous chapter, we have one problem: the files of data that may have been archived will be in the old format. That is, they only have the name and age fields, and now we want many more. This is a very real problem in data processing, and it is as well to build into any new system a facility to read in files of the old sort. We can declare the old record and the file type inside a procedure, so that it does not have to conflict with the new record at all.

The program

The new program follows. It is over 500 lines long, but not all of that needs to be given here. First of all, ScreenMan is still included as before, so is not obviously listed in the program. Secondly, there are five procedures which did not change at all between this version and the previous one, and so we have put them in a separate include file as well, called cubsutils.pas (utils standing for Utilities). Still, what is shown here is nearly 300 lines, and is a substantial program.

```
PROGRAM CubsDatabase2 (input, output);

CONST
        packmax = 30;
    {Window coords}
        {Command window}
            cx1 = 1; cx2 = 39; cy1 = 3; cy2 = 12;
            mx = 1;   my = 10; {for messages}
        {Input window}
            ix1 = 1; ix2 = 39; iy1 = 15; iy2 = 24;
        {Output window}
            ox1 = 41; ox2 = 80; oy1 = 3; oy2 = 24;

{$I SM1.pas}

    TYPE
        names = string[20];
        ages = 7..11;
        sixes = char;
        trails = (unknown, newchum, cheetah, leopard,
                  lion, leapingwolf);
        schools = string[20];
        cubs = record
          name : names;
          age  : ages;
          six : sixes;
          trail : trails;
          school : schools;
        end;
        commands    = char;
        commandset  = set of commands;
        packrange   = 1..packmax;
        packs       = array [packrange] of Cubs;
        onkeys      = (onname, onage, onsix, ontrail, onschool);
        operators   = (equal, lessthan);

    VAR
        command     : commands;
        available,
        allcommands : commandset;
        pack        : packs;
        n           : packrange;
```

```
        screen,
        comwin,
        inwin,
        outwin       : windows;

    {$I SM2.pas}

PROCEDURE ReadTrail (var w : windows; var t : trails);
  VAR ch : char;
  BEGIN
     readch(w,ch);
     case ch of
      'n': t := newchum;
      'c' : t := cheetah;
      'l' : begin
                readch(w,ch);
                if ch = 'i' then t:= lion else
                begin
                  readch(w,ch);
                  if ch = 'o' then t:= leopard else
                  if ch = 'a' then t := leapingwolf
                  else t := unknown;
                end;
              end;
     end;
 END; {ReadTrail}

PROCEDURE WriteTrail(var w : windows; t : trails);
  BEGIN
    case t of
      unknown: ;
      newchum : writestr(w,'new chum');
      cheetah : writestr(w,'cheetah');
      leopard : writestr(w,'leopard');
      lion : writestr(w, 'lion');
      leapingwolf : writestr(w,'leaping wolf');
    end;
  END; {Writetrail}

PROCEDURE ReadCub (var c : cubs);
  var s : longstring;
  BEGIN
    writestr(inwin,'Name: ');
    readstr(inwin,s); c.name := copy(s,1,length(s));
    if c.name <> '' then begin
      writestr(inwin,'Age:  ');   readint(inwin,c.age);
      writestr(inwin,'Six: '); readch(inwin, c.six);
      writestr(inwin,'Trail: ');
      readtrail(inwin,c.trail);
      writestr(inwin,'School: ');
      readstr(inwin,s); c.school := copy(s,1,length(s));
    end;
  END;   {ReadCub}

PROCEDURE WriteCub (c : cubs);
  BEGIN
    writestrln(outwin,c.name);
    writestr(outwin,'    ');
    writeint(outwin,c.age);
    writestr(outwin,'    ');
    writech(outwin,c.six);
```

```
      writestr(outwin,'    ');
      writetrail(outwin,c.trail);
      newline(outwin,1);
      writestr(outwin,'    ');
      writestrln(outwin,c.school);
   END;  {WriteCub}

 PROCEDURE DisplayMenu;
  BEGIN
     clear(comwin);
     writestrln(comwin,'1 N   read in New data');
     writestrln(comwin,'2 D   Display data');
     writestrln(comwin,'3 A   Archive to disk');
     writestrln(comwin,'4 R   Restore from disk');
     writestrln(comwin,'5 U   Update');
     writestrln(comwin,'6 S   Sort');
     writestrln(comwin,'7 C   Convert from old file');
     writestrln(comwin,'9 T   Take a snapshot');
     writestrln(comwin,'0 Q   Quit');
   END; {Display menu}

  {$I cubutils.pas
     PROCEDURE ReadPack(var pack : packs; var n : packrange);
     PROCEDURE WritePack (p : packs; n : packrange);
     PROCEDURE Save (pack : packs; n : packrange);
     PROCEDURE Restore (var pack : packs; var n : packrange);
     PROCEDURE GetRequest(var command : commands);
  }

 PROCEDURE RestorefromOld (var pack : packs; var n : packrange);
  TYPE
     oldcubs = record
         name : names;
         age  : ages;
     end;
  VAR
     filename : longstring;
     i : packrange;
     oldpack : array[packrange] of oldcubs;
     f : file of oldcubs;
  BEGIN
     writestr(comwin,'Restore from what file? ');
     readstr(comwin,filename);
     reset(f,filename);
     i := 1;
     while not eof(f) do begin
        read(f,oldpack[i]);
        with pack[i] do begin
          name := oldpack[i].name;
          age := oldpack[i].age;
          six := ' ';
          trail := unknown;
          school := '';
        end;
        i := i + 1;
     end;
     n := i-1;
     close(f);
     writeint(comwin,n);
     writestrln(comwin,' records restored and copied');
     available := allcommands;
```

```
                END; {Restore}

        FUNCTION compare (a: cubs;
                          op : operators;
                          b : cubs;
                          key : onkeys) : boolean;
          VAR r : boolean;
          BEGIN
            case key of
              onname : if op = equal
                          then r := a.name=b.name
                          else r := a.name<b.name;
              onage :  if op = equal
                          then r := a.age=b.age
                          else r := a.age<b.age;
              onsix :  if op = equal
                          then r := a.six=b.six
                          else r := a.six<b.six;
              ontrail : if op = equal
                          then r := a.trail=b.trail
                          else r := a.trail<b.trail;
              onschool: if op = equal
                          then r := a.school=b.school
                          else r := a.school<b.school;
            end;
            compare := r;
          END; {compare}

        PROCEDURE Search (pack : packs;
                          n : packrange;
                          x : cubs;
                          key : onkeys;
                          var result : boolean;
                          var index : packrange);

          VAR state : (searching, found, notthere);
              i : packrange;
          BEGIN
           state := searching;
           i := 1;
           REPEAT
             if compare(x, equal, pack[i], key)
               then state := found
               else if i = n
                  then state := notthere
                  else i := succ(i);
           UNTIL state <> searching;
           case state of
             found : begin
                       index := i;
                       result := true;
                     end;
             notthere : result := false;
           end;
          END; {Search}


        PROCEDURE Update(var pack : packs; var n : packrange);
         VAR
           age : string;
           s : longstring;
```

```
      field  : char;
      result : boolean;
      where : packrange;
      c : cubs;
  BEGIN
    repeat
      writestr(inwin,'What cub''s name: ?');
      readstr(inwin,s); c.name := copy(s,1,length(s));
      search(pack,n,c,onname,result,where);
    until result=true;
    repeat
     writestr(inwin,'Field: Name Age 6 Trail School? ');
     readch(inwin,field);
    until field in ['N','A','6','T','S'];
    case field of
     'N': begin
            writestr(inwin,'Name: ');
            readstr(inwin,s);
            pack[where].name := copy(s,1,length(s));
          end;
     'A' : begin
             writestr(inwin,'Age:  ');
             readint(inwin,pack[where].age);
           end;
     '6': begin
             writestr(inwin,'Six: ');
             readch(inwin, pack[where].six);
           end;
     'T' : begin
             writestr(inwin,'Trail: ');
             readtrail(inwin,pack[where].trail);
           end;
     'S' : begin
             writestr(inwin,'School: ');
             readstr(inwin,s);
             pack[where].school := copy(s,1,length(s));
           end;
    end;
  END; {Update}


PROCEDURE SortPack(var a : packs; n : packrange);
  VAR temp : Cubs;
     i, j, left : packrange;
     field : char;
     key : onkeys;
  BEGIN
   repeat
     writestr(inwin,'What field? Name Age 6 Trail School');
     readch(inwin,field);
   until field in ['N','A','6','T','S'];
   case field of
   'N' : key := onname;
   'A' : key := onage;
   '6': key := onsix;
   'T' : key := ontrail;
   'S' : key := onschool;
   end;
   for left := 1 to n-1 do begin
     j := left;
     for i := left+1 to n do
       if compare (a[i], lessthan, a[j], key) then j := i;
```

```
            temp := a[j];
            a[j] := a[left];
            a[left] := temp;
             end;
        END; {Sort}


    BEGIN
      whole(screen);
      writestrln(screen,'***** Cubs V1 Main Menu *****');
      gotoxy(screen,ix1, iy1-2);
      writestrln(screen,'***** Input Window *****');
      gotoxy(screen,ox1, oy1-2);
      writestrln(screen,'***** Output Window *****');

      window(inwin,ix1,iy1,ix2,iy2,'Input');
      window(outwin,ox1,oy1,ox2,oy2,'');
      window(comwin,cx1,cy1,cx2,cy2,'Command');

      DisplayMenu;

      allcommands :=
         ['1'..'7','9','N','D','A','R','U','S','C','T','Q'];
      available := ['1','N','4','R','9','T','C','7','0','Q'];
      n := 1;
      Repeat
        GetRequest(command);
        case command of
          '1','N' : ReadPack(pack, n);
          '2','D' : WritePack(pack,n);
          '3','A' : Save(pack, n);
          '4','R' : Restore(pack, n);
          '5','U' : Update(pack, n);
          '6','S' : SortPack(pack,n);
          '7','C' : RestorefromOld(pack,n);
          '9','T' : Snapshot;
          '0','Q' : ;
        end;
      until command = 'Q';
    END.
```

Testing the database

Testing the new database will require time and patience. Fortunately, we have
built in two useful test aids: the snapshots of ScreenMan, which enable us to get
'hard copy' of the screen at any point, and the archiving feature which means that
we can build on past data and not always enter it anew. Here, we show just one
screen.

We start by reading in the previous data from cubs.save, converting it to
the new format, sorting by name, and updating some of Mary's fields. The result
is then displayed.

```
***** Cubs V1 Main Menu *****          ***** Output Window *****

1 N   read in New data                 1. Alice
2 D   Display data                         10
3 A   Archive to disk
4 R   Restore from disk                 2. John
5 U   Update                               9
6 S   Sort
7 C   Convert from old file            3. Mary
9 T   Take a snapshot                     8   B
0 Q   Quit
                                            Greenside
***** Input Window *****              4. Peter
                                         10
What field? Name Age 6 Trail Schooln
What field? Name Age 6 Trail SchoolN    5. Simon
What cub's name: ?Mary                     10
What field? Name Age 6 Trail School6
Six: B                                 6. Sue
What cub's name: ?Mary                    10
What field? Name Age 6 Trail School]
What field? Name Age 6 Trail SchoolS
School: Greenside
```

WHAT WE HAVE LEARNT

We looked at two **sorting** methods and two **searching** methods. Selection sort and Quicksort were explained and it was emphasized that the sorting algorithm was **independent of the type** of data being sorted. Moreover, techniques exist to select any particular field on which to sort. Alternative approaches to linear searching were discussed with a completely safe method using state indicators being favoured. We showed how to **animate** binary search and how not to bother for Quicksort, and ended up with a look at the **relative performance** of all four algorithms. In the case study, we gave examples of how an algorithm might be chosen to fit specific criteria.

QUIZ

1.   Show how 35 would be found by binary search in the following list of numbers:
     8 17 25 35 41 52 60 75
2.   If 86 was added as the last number, how many comparisons would it take to find 35?

3. With a list of 1000 records, what is the average number of comparisons needed to find a value by linear search?

4. By binary search?

5. For 50 000 items with one iteration per μs, compare the time taken by Quicksort and selection sort.

6. What is the fundamental difference between linear search and binary search, apart from speed?

7. Given 1000 unsorted items, which will be quicker on average for finding a given item:

   a) linear search

   b) Quicksort followed by binary search?

8. What is the formula for the midpoint of a subsequence $[j, k]$?

9. What are the possible dangers of using the simple statements:

   ```
   i := 1;
   while a[i] <> x do i := i + 1;
   ```

   for linear searching?

10. Is there a limit to the number of items that can be sorted with selection sort?

PROBLEMS

11.1 **Ocean temperatures** Consider Example 11.1 which sorts ocean temperatures. The scientists are interested in the spread, but would like to have the relevant hour indicated next to each temperature. Adapt the program to keep the hour with the temperature in a record, perform the sort as before, and print out both values in the table.

11.2 **Long stops** A set of data values (integers) has been read into an array which has space for an extra element. Derive a procedure to search the data for a given item using a simple while search and a 'stopping' item at the end of the data. What value should such a stopping value take on?

11.3 **Marker** First year students at Zanyland take four courses and in each they write an examination and do an assignment. Design and implement a program which will maintain a database of names and marks as they come in and provide lists of students sorted on any mark. The final list, produced when all the marks are in, should give all the eight marks input, plus a composite mark for each course, and a final mark for the year. Assume that examinations and assignments count 50% each for a course, and that each course counts 25% of the final mark.

11.4 **Translation** Translating from one© language to another is possible if the language and grammar are severely restricted. Consider the case of restaurant menus, and devise a program which will translate menus from English to another language.

11.5 **Concordance** A concordance is a list of words similar to an index, where the position of each word – its line number and page number – in a piece of text is indicated. The difference is that in a concordance, all words are considered, not just the important ones. However, a list of common words such as 'and', 'the' and 'is' can be excluded. Create a concordance from a piece of text at your disposal.

11.6   **Menus** Using Example 10.5, make the user interface of the cub system language independent so that it can be used in France, Spain or anywhere with a different language.

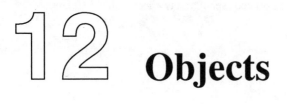

Objects

12.1 What are objects?

Some history

In the history of programming, there have been various movements which have changed the way people write programs, and which led to new and better languages. From Pascal's point of view, the main three are:

- the **structured programming** movement in the 1970s, which promoted the control and data structures we find in Pascal;

- the **modular programming** movement, which emphasized modules or units; and

- the **data abstraction** movement, which concentrated on data types and endeavoured to make them as general, or abstract, as possible.

Pascal can be claimed to be **the** structured programming language and a world-leader in its class. However, it was standardized and fixed without taking into account directly the ideas of the next two waves of change. Instead, Pascal's inventor, Niklaus Wirth, invented new languages which he believed were better able to move with the times. But somehow, Pascal kept its pre-eminent position, largely due to the extensions added by compiler and system designers. Notably, extensions for units and abstract data types have made Pascal dialects such as Turbo Pascal into very powerful languages in their own right.

Oops!

The latest movement to affect languages is **object-oriented programming**. Oops (for object oriented programming and systems) looks at solutions to problems in terms of the objects that need to be defined and manipulated. Objects themselves are record types which contain both data and procedure fields and the procedures (often called methods) can be made the only way of manipulating variables of that type. Furthermore, oops provides for

- **inheritance** of properties from one object to another;
- **late binding** of methods to reflect the latest circumstances.

Once again, the dialects brought out extensions to accommodate the new techniques, and in addition to Turbo Pascal 6.0, there is Object Pascal. However, Standard Pascal can be thought to have missed the boat.

All is not lost

In fact, all is not lost. It is not always necessary to have a built-in language feature to implement a concept, and much can be done in Standard Pascal to adopt the basic ideas of the object-oriented methodology. Since Pascal also does not have units, on which objects are based, we shall use as our basic building block the include file. We have already seen how these are used with ScreenMan: the comments {$I SM1.pas} and {$I SM2.pas} brought into a program the two parts of the windows type and its operations – which indeed is an object!

In this chapter we shall explore the theory behind objects and explain how they can be implemented, to some extent, in Standard Pascal. The example we shall use is ScreenMan. In Chapter 15, further object examples are given for queues, stacks, trees and lists.

12.2   Objects – theory and practice

Defining an object

An object is viewed as a record type which has data fields and **method** fields. The method fields consist of the procedures and functions which operate on the data fields. There are two special kinds of method fields known as **constructors** and **destructors**, which, as their names suggest, are used to create and destroy individual objects. Typically, the constructor procedure is called Init and the destructor called Done. Most objects' definitions also include a method to display the contents of the data fields.

In Pascal, we cannot include method definitions directly in a record, but we can do so with comments.

EXAMPLE 12.1   A Date object _____

An example of an object definition is:

```
TYPE
   date = RECORD
        day : days;
        month : months;
        year : years;
        {METHODS:
        Procedure DateInit;
        Procedure DateRead;
        Procedure DateDisplay;
        Function DateLessThan;}
     end;
```

By convention, we prefix the method name with the object name. In many Pascal extensions, the object name would be required with the dot notation, for example, Date.Read. For clarity, also, we do not list the parameters required by the methods – that comes later.

Following on from the type definition, each of the methods is then expanded as an ordinary procedure or function declaration. That makes two parts to the object declaration. There is a third part – the subsidiary types. In the definition above, we referred to days, months and years: these obviously have to be declared somewhere, and unless there is a prior claim to them in an earlier object, we do it here.

The three parts are then packaged together in one or more 'include' files. Why do we need more than one? The reason is that Pascal requires that the declaration sections be kept in a set order which is: CONST, TYPE, VAR, PROCEDURE. Since both the object and the program might have contributions in all sections, we need to be able to dovetail them in, to keep to one section each.

The full definition of the Date object is therefore in three files, referred to by the section they require.

DateC.Pas

```
{Constants for the Date object}
CONST
   yearmin = 1900;
   yearmax = 2000;
```

DateT.Pas

```
{Types for the Date object}
TYPE
   days = 1..7;
   months = 1..12;
   years = yearmin..yearmax;

   date = RECORD
```

```
            day : days;
            month : months;
            year : years;
            {METHODS:
            Procedure DateInit;
            Procedure DateRead;
            Procedure DateDisplay;
            Function DateCompare;}
          end;
```

DateP.Pas

```
    {Procedures for the Date object}
    PROCEDURE DateInit (var d : date);
      BEGIN
        with d do begin
           day := 1;
           month := 1;
           year := yearmin;
        end;
      END; {DateInit}

    PROCEDURE DateRead (var d : date);
      BEGIN
        with d do
           read(day,month,year);
      END; {DateRead}

    PROCEDURE DateDisplay (d : date);
      BEGIN
        with d do
           write(day,'/',month,'/',year);
      END: {DateDisplay}

    FUNCTION DateLessthan (d1, d2 : date) : boolean;
      BEGIN
        if d1.year < d2.year
        then Datelessthan := true
        else
          if (d1.year=d2.year) and (d1.month < d2.month)
          then Datelessthan := true
          else
             if (d1.year=d2.year) and (d1.month = d2.month)
                and (d1.day = d2.day)
             then DateLessthan := true
             else DateLessthan := false;
      END; {DateLessthan}
```

Including, creating and using objects

Having defined an object type, we can then declare variables of this type, and call the methods to manipulate them. Of course, we first have to include the definitions. To create two dates, we would say:

```
    {$I DateC.pas}

    {$I DateT.pas}

    {$I DateP.pas}
```

```
VAR
    HolsStart, Birthday : Date;
```

We can then use the data fields as normal, with dot notation, and the method fields with the prefix of the object type (Date) and a parameter of the particular object under consideration. For example, we might say:

```
if DateCompare(HolsStart, Birthday) then writeln('Hooray');
```

The beauty of objects is that the code can easily be reused. We are encouraged to write our definitions and procedures in such a way as to make them independent and generally applicable. This raises the standard of our programming overall, and increases our productivity in the long run.

These objects are static, and exist as normal variables with their given scope. We can also create objects at runtime, as described in Chapters 14 and 15.

Inheritance

Given an object type, we can define a new type which is based on it, but which has additional fields and methods added to it. The new type inherits all the methods of the old type, although it may replace some of them. In particular, with new data fields, the new object will need a new constructor method.

Implementing inheritance in Pascal has to be done by creating new include files, and copying over every method, changing what has to be changed and leaving alone what is to be inherited. All the method names must be edited to reflect the new object as the prefix.

EXAMPLE 12.2   Inheriting a Date object _____

For example, consider a version of the Date object which is going to be integrated with ScreenMan. The init, read and display methods will change, but DateLessthan could remain the same. But suppose we wish to add another field to the date which indicates its status, being unset, unknown, half or full. Initially, the date is unset. Later, when it is used in a context where the date should be known but isn't, we can change its state. Further on, we may read in only the year, and have the day and month not known: this is known as a half date.

This change in the data fields would mean that the name and parameters of the new DateLessThan would have to be changed. It so happens in this example that the substance has to be changed too, because of state field. This need not always be the case: there could be inherited methods which do not change inside. The new object becomes:

WinDateC.Pas

```
{Constants for the WinDate object}
{Inherits from Date}
```

WinDateT.Pas

```
{Types for the WinDate object}
{Inherits some subsidiary types from Date}
```

```
      statustype = (unset, unknown, half, full);

      WinDate = RECORD
         day : days;
         month : months;
         year : years;
         status : statustype;
         {METHODS:
         Procedure WinDateInit;
         Procedure WinDateRead;
         Procedure WinDateDisplay;
         Function WinDatesLessthan;}
      end;
```

WinDateP.Pas
```
   {Procedures for the WinDate object}
   PROCEDURE WinDateInit (var d : WinDate);
      BEGIN
         with d do begin
            day := 1;
            month := 1;
            year := yearmin;
            state := unset;
         end;
      END; {DateInit}

   PROCEDURE WinDateRead (var w : windows; var d : WinDate);
      {Decides on whether only a year is given or the whole date}
      var x : integer;
      BEGIN
         with d do begin
            readint(w,x);
            if x > 31 then {only the year} begin
               d.year := x;
               d.state := half;
            end else {must be full date} begin
               d.day := x;
               readint(w,d.month);
               readint(w,d.year);
               d.state := full;
            end;
         end;
      END; {ReadWinDate}

   PROCEDURE WinDateDisplay (var w : windows; d : WinDate);
      BEGIN
         with d do begin
            writeint(w,day); writech(w,'/');
            writeint(w,month); writech('/');
            writeint(w,year);
         end;
      END: {DateDisplay}

   FUNCTION WinDateLessthan (d1, d2 : WinDate) : boolean;
      {Only works if dates are half or full}
      BEGIN
         case d1.state of
            unset, unknown : WinDateLessthan := false;
            half, full :
               if d1.year < d2.year
                  then Datelessthan := true
```

```
            else
              if (d1.state = half) or (d2.state=half)
              then Datelessthan := false
              else
                  if (d1.year=d2.year) and
                  (d1.month < d2.month)
                  then Datelessthan := true
                  else
                      if (d1.year=d2.year) and
                        (d1.month = d2.month) and
                        (d1.day = d2.day)
                      then DateLessthan := true
                      else DateLessthan := false;
    END; {DateLessthan}
```

Is this inheritance?

It is probably overstating the case to call the derivation of WinDate from Date inheritance. Specifically, one of the powers of inheritance is the ability for an object to use its own methods and those of its 'parent' from whom it inherits. Since Pascal has no inheritance mechanism, we have to copy and convert all methods so that they are inherited in spirit, but not in name.

What we have achieved, however, is a disciplined approach to the construction of data types in an object-oriented way.

Delayed binding

The third property of oops is the delayed binding of methods to actual instances of them. Though available in many Pascal extensions, this is beyond the scope of Standard Pascal. If we thought hard, we could probably achieve a reasonable effect using procedural parameters (Section 13.3) along the lines of the delayed binding in the discussion on multi-way sorting in Section 11.1, but that is now beyond the scope of this book.

12.3   ScreenMan again

We have mentioned before that ScreenMan is an object. Let us now study it, and see how it compares to the theory we have so far developed. The first part, SM1.PAS is given here. The Pascal used includes the use of a string extension to enable variable length strings to be read and written. However, passing these to procedures is sometimes problematic, and the type longstring gets around this problem.

ScreenMan is a much more substantial object than dates and exhibits a new property of objects – private and public fields.

```
{   Screen control package Part I
    ==============================

    written in Standard Pascal by J M Bishop, August 1992.

}
{** Add to constants **}
```

```
      space = ' ';
      {PRIVATE}
      charmax = 80;
      linemax = 24;

  {** Add to types **}

  TYPE
  {PUBLIC}
    xrange = 1..charmax;
    yrange = 1..linemax;
    longstring = string[80];
  {PRIVATE}
    lines = packed array[xrange] of char;
    images = array[yrange] of lines;
    xindex = 0..charmax;
    yindex = 0..linemax;
  {OBJECT}
    windows = record
        {METHODS
        PROCEDURE Window   - the Init method
        PROCEDURE Show
        PROCEDURE SnapShot
        PROCEDURE clear
        PROCEDURE whole
        PROCEDURE newline
        PROCEDURE writech
        PROCEDURE writeint
        PROCEDURE writeintln
        PROCEDURE writestr
        PROCEDURE writestrln
        PROCEDURE gotoxy
        PROCEDURE readch
        PROCEDURE readstr
        PROECDURE readint}
        {PRIVATE}
        x, xmin, xmax : xrange;
        y, ymin, ymax : yrange;
        name : string;
      end;
```

Private and public

When defining an object, it may be that there are data fields which it is necessary to declare to hold internal state which is not the concern of the user of the object. This is the case with ScreenMan. The Windows object is provided with 15 methods which together provide all the operations that one wants on windows. The data fields hold the limits of a window and the current cursor position, as well as the window name, and it would be wrong for the user to access or alter these in any way. We therefore mark them out as private. Of course, we cannot enforce this restriction in Pascal, but it is still important to make the distinction.

In the same way, some of the subsidiary types are only used by the methods themselves, and not by the parameters. They are also therefore private.

Finally, it is also possible to have private methods. ScreenMan has a procedure called QuickShow which is used by the reading methods, but should not be called from outside.

Infrastructure

We have all along regarded the windows type as our object, and so it is. Each time we declare a window, we get the 7 new data fields (private though they be) and access to the 15 methods customized for that window. In order for this to operate, the windows object type itself needs an infrastructure. It needs to keep a character matrix of the current contents of all windows. This is declared as a variable in the second part of ScreenMan, and is also private.

The other variable declared here is the snapshot number, which is set to 0 when the whole screen is initialized. The rest of ScreenMan, in SM2.PAS, is:

```
{  Screen control package Part II
   ================================

   written in Standard Pascal by J M Bishop, August 1992.


}
{++ Add to variables}
{PRIVATE}
image : images;
snapno : 1..99;

{** Add to procedures **}

  PROCEDURE window (var w : windows; x1 : xrange; y1 : yrange;
     x2 : xrange; y2 : yrange; s : string);
  BEGIN
    with w do begin
      xmin := x1;
      ymin := y1;
      xmax := x2;
      ymax := y2;
      x := xmin;
      y := ymin;
      name := s;
    end;
  END;

  PROCEDURE Show;
    var i : xrange; j : yrange;
    begin
      for j := 1 to linemax-1 do
        writeln(image[j]);
      for i := 1 to charmax do write(image[linemax,i]);
      readln;
    end;

  PROCEDURE SnapShot;
    var j : yrange;
        f : text;
      name : longstring;
    begin
      name:='snap    ';
      if snapno > 9 then
        name[6] := chr(ord(snapno div 10)+ord('0'));
      name[5] := chr(ord(snapno mod 10)+ord('0'));
      rewrite(f,name);
      for j := 1 to linemax do
        writeln(f,image[j]);
```

```
      close(f);
      snapno := snapno+1;
    end;

PROCEDURE clear (var w : windows);
  var i : xrange; j : yrange;
  begin
    with w do begin
      for j := ymin to ymax do
        for i := xmin to xmax do
          image[j,i] := space;
      x := xmin;   y := ymin;
    end;
end;

PROCEDURE whole (var w : windows);
  begin
    window(w,1,1,charmax,linemax,'');
    clear(w);
    snapno := 1;
  end;

PROCEDURE newline(var w : windows; n : yrange);
  var i : xrange; j,k : yrange;
  begin
    with w do begin
      for j := 1 to n do begin
        if y = ymax then begin
        {scroll}
          for k := ymin to ymax-1 do
            image[k] := image [k+1];
          y := ymax;
          for i := xmin to xmax do image[y,i] := space;
        end else
          y := y + 1;
      end;
      x := xmin;
    end;
  END;

PROCEDURE writech(var w : windows; ch : char);
  begin
    with w do begin
      image[y,x] := ch;
      if x = xmax then newline(w,1)
      else
        x := x + 1;
    end;
  END;

PROCEDURE writeint(var w : windows; int : integer);
  procedure extract(n : integer);
    begin
      if n < 10 then writech(w,chr(n+ord('0')))
      else begin
        extract(n div 10);
        writech(w,chr(n mod 10 + ord('0')));
      end;
    end;

  begin
```

```
            extract (int);
         end;

      PROCEDURE writeintln(var w : windows; int : integer);
         begin
           writeint(w,int);
           newline(w,1);
         end;

      PROCEDURE writestr(var w : windows; s : string);
         var
           i : xrange;
         begin
           with w do
             for i := 1 to length(s) do writech(w,s[i]);
         end;

      PROCEDURE writestrln(var w : windows; s : string);
         var
           i : xrange;
         begin
           writestr(w,s);
           newline(w,1);
         end;

      PROCEDURE gotoxy(var w : windows; tox : xrange; toy : yrange)
         begin
           with w do begin
             x := xmin + tox - 1;
             y := ymin + toy - 1;
           end;
         end;

   {PRIVATE} PROCEDURE quickshow(w : windows);
      var i : xrange; j : yrange;
      begin
        for j := 1 to linemax-1 do
          writeln(image[j]);
          write(w.name,'>');
      end;

      PROCEDURE readch (var w : windows; var ch : char);
         begin
           quickshow(w);
           readln(ch);
           writech(w,ch);
           newline(w,1);
         end;

      PROCEDURE readint(var w : windows; var int : integer);
         begin
           quickshow(w);
           readln(int);
           writeintln(w,int);
         end;

      PROCEDURE readstr(var w : windows; var s : longstring);
         begin
           quickshow(w);
           readln(s);
```

```
        writestrln(w,s);
      end;
```

Name conflicts

All the identifiers defined for this object will be visible to the program that includes it. In some cases, this may cause name conflicts. For example, ScreenMan declares the constant space, because it needs it. If the program also declares space, then there will be a redefined identifier error which will have to be resolved. The rule is to alter the program, and to endeavour to keep the object as stable as possible. Either the definition of space can be removed (since it is only needed once) or if the two definitions mean different things, the name of the program's version will have to be changed.

WHAT WE HAVE LEARNT

---

*We looked at the theory behind objects, then went through the definition of an **object type** and its inclusion into a program, the **creation** of objects and how to use them **Inheritance** was discussed and an example of how to achieve it in Standard Pascal explored. Finally, the whole of the **ScreenMan** package with its rich **windows** object was explained, and we learnt to mark fields and methods as **private** and **public**.*

QUIZ

---

1.   What does oops stand for?
2.   What are the three characteristics of oops?
3.   Find out whether your Pascal compiler will accept declarations in any order. If so, you can keep your objects (and ScreenMan) in one file, not three.
4.   Why do we preface most method names with the object type name?
5.   Write declarations and method calls to read in two dates and print out the one that is earlier.
6.   Repeat question 5 using window-based dates and years only.
7.   Why do read procedures in ScreenMan call QuickShow?
8.   What is the reason for WriteInt having the internal procedure Extract?
9.   Which is the constructor in the windows object?
10. Does the windows object have a destructor? Should it have one?

PROBLEMS

12.1 **Students with objects** Declare a student object type, with fields for a name and date of birth using WinDate for the latter. Now adapt Problem 11.2 to sort a list of ten or so students by date of birth.

12.2 **Object cubs** Adapt the database in Example 11.6 to declare cubs as an object type, which is a composite of object types for each of the individual fields. Ensure that the program still runs.

12.3 **Reuse** If you have completed Problem 12.2, consider how some of the objects might be reused. The Zanyland Education Department keeps records of teachers with their names, dates of births, schools and salaries. Set up a database to handle the usual operations as discussed in Sections 10.5 and 11.6.

13 Advanced Pascal Features

13.1 Variant records
13.2 Conformant array parameters
13.3 Procedural parameters

13.1 Variant records

The information that is gathered together to form a record type could have inherent variations. For example, in a record that has a field for marital status, there may be additional fields for the name and occupation of the spouse. However, if a particular record of this type had the marital status listed as single, then these latter fields would not apply. In fact, it may well be erroneous to store or access them. Pascal provides for this eventuality in a limited way with the concept of records with variants.

Form of a variant record type

A record type may specify one field as a **tag field.** Thereafter, for each value of the tag field, a different group of fields may be specified. Each of these groups is known as a **variant**. The form of a record with variants is:

```
┌─────────────────────────────────────────────────────┐
│  Variant record type                                  │
├─────────────────────────────────────────────────────┤
│   identifier = RECORD                                 │
│      fixed fields                                     │
│      CASE tag-field :   tag-type  OF                  │
│          tag-values  :  (variant  fields);            │
│          tag-values  :  (variant  fields);            │
│                 . . .                                 │
│          tag-values  :  (variant  fields);            │
│      END; {RECORD}                                    │
└─────────────────────────────────────────────────────┘
```

The tag field may be of any of the discrete types, that is, integer, character, boolean, enumerated, or subranges of these. Each value of this type must be listed with a corresponding list of fields. There may be none, one or more fields for each tag value. The fixed fields are always listed first in the record, and are optional. Examples of variant record declarations are:

```
TYPE
    names       = packed array [namerange] of char;
    occupations = 000..999;  {coded}
    status      = (married, divorced, single, widowed);

    person = RECORD
          name  : names;
          birth : dates;
          CASE MaritalStatus : status of
              married  : (spouse  :  names;
                            occupation : occupations);
              divorced : (since : dates);
              single   : (   );
              widowed  : (dependents : integer);
        END;

    kinds = (cartesian, polar);
    coordinates = RECORD
        CASE kind : kinds of
            cartesian : (x,y : real);
            polar     : (theta : angles;
                          radius : real);
        END;
```

When a variable is declared of one of these types, initialization of the tag field becomes important. For example, if we declare:

```
VAR
    P, Q  : person;
    C, D  : coordinates;
```

then valid assignments of values would be:

```
readname(P.name);
readdate (P.birth);
P.MaritalStatus := single;
readname(Q.name);
readdate(Q.date);
```

```
Q.maritalStatus := widowed;
read(Q.dependents);

C.kind := cartesian;
read(C.x, C.y);
D.kind := polar;
read(D.theta, D.radius);
```

Once the tag field has been given a value, only those fields of the corresponding variant are defined. Thus, a variant record provides a secure way of hiding unwanted information. It would not be valid to now refer to P.dependents or C.radius, since these fields are incompatible with their respective records' tag fields.

EXAMPLE 13.1   Roots of a quadratic _____

Problem   Solve the quadratic equation $ax^2 + bx + c = 0$ for given values of a, b and c.

Solution   Solving a quadratic may seem a come-down after the complexity of some of the previous examples, but what we want to do here is to cater for all sorts of roots. The first thing to remember is the formula for the roots of the equation. It is:

$$x = \frac{-b \pm \sqrt{b^2 - 4ac}}{2a}$$

The problem is that the expression inside the square root may be negative, in which case, the roots are complex and are calculated slightly differently. Another check to be made is whether the coefficient a is zero, because then the formula must not be applied.

Algorithm   The algorithm is based on checking the coefficients and the discriminant $b^2 - 4ac$ and performing one of four different calculations. In so doing, a message about the classification of the roots can also be given to the user.

   If the procedure is to be reused, it must be made self-contained. In other words, it must communicate through parameters only. The input parameters will be the coefficients, a, b and c. The output parameters will be the roots. But how are these to be expressed? The number of roots and their meaning will differ according to the discriminant calculated on the basis of the coefficients. To recapitulate, we have the following possibilities:

- no roots;

- one root;

- two real roots (possibly equal);

- two imaginary roots, each with two components.

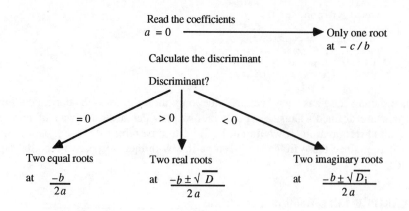

We therefore employ a variant record to express all these variations in a single type.

The definition of the fields for the record follows the list above. Before defining the record, though, we should consider how to represent the imaginary roots. These are given by:

(realpart, impart) and (realpart, –impart)

and we can reuse the type `complex` defined earlier.

Program

```
PROGRAM TestQuadratics (input, output);
  TYPE
     rootsorts = (none, onereal, tworeal, twoimaginary);
     complex   = record
                   realpart,
                   impart   : real;
                 end;
     rootrec   = record
        case sort : rootsorts of
           none            : ( );
           onereal         : (R : real);
           tworeal         : (R1, R2 : real);
           twoimaginary : (i1, i2 : complex);
     end;

  VAR
     a,b,c : real;
     roots : rootrec;

  PROCEDURE quadratic (a, b, c :real; var roots :rootrec);
     VAR
        D    : real;  {discriminant}
        twoa : real;  {optimization}

  BEGIN
     twoa := 2 * a;
     with roots do begin
        if (a = 0) and (b = 0) then
```

```
        sort := none
    else
    if a = 0 then begin
        sort := onereal;
        R :=  -c / b;
    end else begin
        D := b * b - 4 * a * c;
        if D = 0 then begin
            sort := tworeal;
            R1 := -b / twoa;
            R2 := R1;
        end else
        if D > 0 then begin
            sort := tworeal;
            R1 := (-b + sqrt(D)) / twoa;
            R2 := (-b - sqrt(D)) / twoa;
        end else begin
            sort := twoimaginary;
            i1.realpart := -b / twoa;
            i2.realpart := i1.realpart;
            i1.impart := sqrt(-D) / twoa;
            i2.impart := - i1.impart;
        end;
    end;
  end;
END; {Quadratic}

BEGIN
    writeln('***** Solving quadratics ******');
    write('Type the coefficients ');
    readln(a,b,c);
    quadratic(a,b,c,roots);
    with roots do
      case sort of
        none    : writeln('Not a quadratic');
        onereal : writeln('One real root ', R:6:2);
        tworeal : writeln('Two real roots ',
            R1:6:2, '    ', R2:6:2);
        twoimaginary : writeln('Two imaginary roots (',
            i1.realpart:6:2,',',i1.impart:6:2,')    ',
            '(',i2.realpart:6:2,',',i2.impart:6:2,')');
      end;
END.
```

13.2 Conformant array parameters

One of the biggest nuisances in Pascal is the fact that array variables have to be of exactly the same length if they are to be compatible. This means that a general-purpose procedure such as a sort or a matrix inversion can only work for arrays of one size. For any other size, a separate procedure must be provided.

   In the Pascal Standard there is an optional feature which gets around this problem. Parameters that are arrays can be declared in the parameter list with a maximum range for the subscripts. Then, any array variable which has subscripts within this maximum range, and has the same type of elements, will be able to be passed as an actual parameter.

Form of conformant array parameters

A parameter list can also include formal parameters of the form:

Conformant array parameter declaration

```
identifier : array [lowid..highid:subscript type]
                 of element type
```

Then, any array of the same element type with subscripts of the same type which lie within the range `lowid` to `highid` can be passed as an actual parameter to this formal. Multi-dimensional arrays can be specified in the same way.

The important point about this kind of declaration is that the identifiers of the range are treated as variables that can be used but not altered; for the subscripts must consist of identifiers. When the procedure is called, the range of subscripts of the actual array is picked up, and actual values for `lowid` and `highid` filled in. Since a procedure with a conformant array parameter will in all probability need to index through the array, it is good practice to start off by declaring an index variable that will apply, that is:

```
VAR i : subscript type;
```

EXAMPLE 13.2   Searching variable tables _____

Problem   In the program that searched string tables (Example 11.3), all the tables had to be created the same length, that of the longest one. Can this wastage be avoided?

Solution   Use conformant array parameters.

Algorithm   The use of these parameters is indicated in the procedure to read tables. Since we now know how many items to expect for each table, the loop is phrased as a for-loop, not a while-loop.

```
PROCEDURE ReadStringTable (
            VAR n : stringindex;
            VAR T : array[low..high:integer] of names;
            filename : string);
      VAR f : text;

      BEGIN
         reset (f, filename);
         for n := low to high do
            readln(f,T[n]);
         writeln('Table with ', n,
              ' elements read from ', filename);
      END; {ReadStringTable}
```

The three tables are declared on different ranges, but each can be passed to
ReadStringTable or to Search.

Program

```
PROGRAM Searchingtables (input, output);
  CONST
    namemax = 24;
    deptmax = 20;
  TYPE
    positive    = 1..maxint;
    namerange   = 1..namemax;
    names       = packed array [namerange] of char;
    dayrange    = 1..7;
    seasonrange = 1..4;
    deptrange   = 1.. deptmax;
    days        = array [dayrange] of names;
    seasons     = array [seasonrange] of names;
    depts       = array [deptrange] of names;

  VAR
    daytable     : days;
    seasontable  : seasons;
    depttable    : depts;
    word         : names;
    there, stop  : boolean;
    n            : integer;

  PROCEDURE readname (VAR name : names);
    VAR i : namerange;
    BEGIN
      for i := 1 to namemax do
        if eoln then name[i] := ' '
                else read(name[i]);
      readln;
    END; {readname}

  PROCEDURE ReadStringTable (
        VAR n : stringindex;
        VAR T : array[low..high:integer] of names;
        filename : string);
    VAR f : text;

  BEGIN
    reset (f, filename);
    for n := low to high do
      readln(f,T[n]);
    writeln('Table with ', n,
        ' elements read from ', filename);
  END; {ReadStringTable}

  PROCEDURE Search (
        T : array [low..high:positive] of names;
        x : names;
        VAR index : positive;
        VAR result : boolean);


    TYPE
      states = (searching, found, notthere);
    VAR
      i : positive;
```

```
              state : states;
          BEGIN
            state := searching;
            i := low;
            REPEAT
              if x = T[i] then state := found else
              if i = high then state := notthere else
              i := succ(i);
            UNTIL state <> searching;
            CASE state of
              found : begin
                        index := i;
                        result := true;
                      end;
              notthere : result := false;
            END;
          END; {search}

      BEGIN
        writeln('****** Demonstrating conformant ',
                'arrays ******');
        ReadStringTable(7,daytable,'Days');
        ReadStringTable(4,seasontable,'Seasons');
        ReadStringTable(20,depttable,'Depts');

        stop := false;
        repeat
          writeln('Type in a day, a season, a ',
                  'department or QUIT');
          readname(word);
          if word = 'QUIT
          then stop := true
          else begin
            search (daytable, word, n, there);
            if there
            then writeln('This is day No. ', n:1)
            else begin
              search (seasontable, word, n, there);
              if there
              then writeln('This is season No. ', n:1)
              else begin
                search (depttable, word, n , there);
                if there
                then writeln ('This is department No. ',
                              n:1)
                else writeln ('This word is not ',
                              in any of the tables.');
              end;
            end;
          end;
        until stop;
      END.
```

13.3 Procedural parameters

Parameters enable different **values** to be passed to and from procedures, and to be given formal names within the procedures. This same facility can be applied to **actions** by declaring a procedure or function as a parameter. The form of the declaration is exactly the same as that for the heading of the procedure or function itself, that is:

Procedural parameter declaration

```
PROCEDURE name (formal parameter declarations);
FUNCTION name (formal parameter declarations) : type;
```

This is not a facility that is often used in programming, partly because many Pascal systems do not support it. The example most often quoted is in numerical analysis where methods for finding roots of functions, integrating them, differentiating them and so on can be written to be independent of any particular function; the function is then passed to the solving procedure as a parameter. This notion of independence is the key to the need for procedures as parameters. In the context of the examples we have seen so far, the sort procedure could benefit from such a feature.

Multi-way sorting

The classic use of procedural parameters is for multi-way sorting or searching. Although we accomplished this in the case study at the end of Chapter 11, there is no doubt that the method was clumsy and long-winded. It certainly lacked elegance.

Procedure parameters are elegant. Consider once again the selection sorting procedure developed in Section 11.1. It is defined to sort in descending order. This aspect of the sort is confined to the single expression in the middle where the comparison is done, that is:

```
if a[i] < a[chosen] then ...
```

If we make this comparison a call to a boolean function, that is:

```
if inorder (a[i], a[chosen]) then ...
```

then we can declare this function as a parameter to the sort procedure, as in:

```
PROCEDURE sort (var a : somearray;  n : range;
          function inorder (x,y, : items) : boolean);
```

Calling the sort procedure needs actual parameters for the three formals listed, and the following would satisfy:

```
TYPE
   items     = names;
   range     = 1..50;
   somearray = array [range] of items;

VAR
   table : somearray;
   size  : range;

FUNCTION descending (x, y : names) : boolean;
   BEGIN
      descending := x > y;
   END;  { descending}
```

The resulting call would then be:

```
sort (table, size, descending);
```

The power of this facility becomes apparent when we define:

```
FUNCTION ascending (a,b : items) : boolean;
   BEGIN
      ascending := a < b;
   END; {ascending}
```

and can call on the same procedure to order the names in the other direction with:

```
sort (table, size, ascending);
```

Procedures as parameters do not occur in all languages, as they are considered difficult to implement at runtime. However, it is a good idea to gain practice with them, as the concept of parameterized action is central to proper programming in advanced languages. The next example looks at an application of procedural parameters in numerical analysis.

EXAMPLE 13.3   The Newton-Raphson method _____

Problem We would like to be able to find the root of a polynomial equation. For example, we may want to find the specific volume of a particular gas whose state equation at a specific temperature and pressure is given by:

$$f(v) = 70v^3 - 3v^2 + 4v - 16$$

Solution Finding the roots of an equation is an essential task in engineering problems, and we would like to have a method which is reliable and quick. It should be applicable to a wide range of functions and produce real as well as complex roots.

The method we shall use here is the Newton-Raphson method, one of the most popular as it is simple and produces a root relatively quickly. The Newton-Raphson method for finding a root of an equation $f(x) = 0$ relies on having a fairly good initial estimate of the root, and on knowing the derivative $f'(x) = df/dx$.

If x_0 is an estimate of the root, then a better estimate x_1 is:

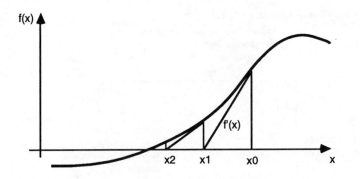

Figure 13.1   Finding a root using Newton-Raphson.

$$x_1 = x_0 - \frac{f(x_0)}{f'(x_0)}$$

This formula is obtained by modelling the curve by its tangent at the point x_0 as shown in the diagram in Figure 13.1. x_1 can then be used to calculate the next and better approximation x_2 and so on, but until when? That is going to depend upon what tolerance can be accepted for the error in the solution. The stopping criterion is given in algorithmic terms by

```
repeat
  ...
until |current estimate - previous estimate| < tolerance,
```

and a typical value for tolerance could be 10^{-6}. However, this is not the whole story for the stopping criterion. If the initial estimate of the root is too far out, the algorithm may never converge – for example, in the figure, suppose the initial estimate had been $2x_0$ rather than x_0. To prevent the possibility of the program being caught in a loop from which it cannot exit, we place a limit on the number of times the loop is executed.

Algorithm   The algorithm for the Newton-Raphson method is given below. To find the specific volume of the gas described above, we must decide on a reasonable starting value ($v = 1$ will do), and know the derivative. It is :

$$f'(v) = 210v^2 - 6v + 4$$

Using the algorithm the program follows easily.

Program

```
PROGRAM SpecificVolume(input,output);
  VAR
      imax        : integer;
      i           : 0..100;
      tolerance,
      x, x0       : real;
```

Newton-Raphson method

Input initial estimate for the root,
the tolerance and
the maximum number of iterations

Until convergence
or maximum iterations reached

Set old estimate
to new estimate
Calculate new estimate
for root

Reason for exiting?

Maximum iterations
reached

Converged

Output 'no convergence'

Output new estimate
for the root

```
PROCEDURE initialize;
   BEGIN
      writeln('******Newton-Raphson root-finding ',
              program******');
      writeln('for the specific volume of a gas');
      writeln('          3      2');
      writeln('Solves 70v - 3v + 4v - 16 = 0');
      writeln;
      write('Initial estimate for root:');
      readln(x);
      write('Required error limit:');
      readln(tolerance);
      write('Maximum number of iterations permitted:');
      readln(imax);
      i := 0;
      writeln(' i        x');
      writeln(i:4, x:10:6);
   END; {initialize}

FUNCTION gas (x : real) : real;
   BEGIN
      gas := (70 * x * x * x - 3 * x * x + 4 * x - 16);
   END;
FUNCTION gasdiff (x : real) : real;
   BEGIN
      gasdiff := 210 * x * x - 6 * x + 4;
   END; {fdiff}

PROCEDURE NewtonRaphson (var xold, xnew : real;
            var i : range;
            imax : range;
            tolerance : real;
```

```
                  monitor : boolean;
                  function f (x : real) : real;
                  function fdiff (x : real) : real);
        BEGIN
          REPEAT
            i := i + 1;
            xnew := xold;
            xold := xnew - f(xnew) / fdiff(xnew);
            if monitor then writeln(i:4, xold:10:6);
          UNTIL ((abs(xold - xnew) < tolerance)
                    or (i = imax));
        END;   {NewtonRaphson}

      BEGIN
        initialize;
        NewtonRaphson (x, x0, i, imax, tol, true,
                        gas, gasdiff);
        if (i = imax)
        then writeln('Failed to converge: x = ',
                        x:10:6, '   x0 = ',x0:10:6,'  i = ', i:3)
        else writeln('Root is:', x:10:6, '     ',
                        i:3, ' iterations required');
      END.
```

Testing

```
******Newton-Raphson root-finding program******
for the specific volume of a gas
                       3      2
Solves 70v - 3v + 4v - 16 = 0

Initial estimate for root: 1
Required error limit: 1E-6
Maximum number of iterations permitted:   100
    i     x
    0  1.000000
    1  0.735577
    2  0.619165
    3  0.595125
    4  0.594157
    5  0.594155
    6  0.594155
Root is:  0.594155       6 iterations required
```

To see the method in real action, we tried an initial guess of 100: this eventually converged, but took 17 steps. The root can be verified as correct by substituting in the equation.

The beauty of procedural parameters is that we can solve a completely different equation now by simply providing two new functions. We have no need to know how Newton-Raphson works. All we have to do is set up the parameters correctly and check the output.

WHAT WE HAVE LEARNT

We discussed Pascal features which are very powerful but little used in practice. All three are aimed at providing variability in a program. **Variant records** *enable a record to take on different forms, and we looked at typical examples where this feature would be useful.* **Conformant array parameters** *enable procedures to be defined without reference to the size of the actual arrays that will be passed. We looked at the mechanics of handling this variation and the extensions needed to the parameter list syntax. Finally* **procedural parameters** *were introduced with the concrete example of a comparison function used to provide multi-way sorting.*

QUIZ

---

1. Can fields in different options of a variant record have the same names?
2. Consider the person record in Section 13.1. If we declare

        var x : person;

        x.maritalstatus := married;

    how many fields does x have and what are their names?
3. Define a variant record for the dates with status as explained in Example 12.2.
4. In the ReadStringTable procedure of Example 13.2, where are the identifiers low and high declared?
5. Define a procedure called P having two array parameters A and B which may have different array bounds but have the same item type.
6. Define a procedure called Q having two array parameters C and D which may have different item types but have the same array bounds.
7. In section 13.3, if equality was an option for the function inorder as well as ascending and descending would it be necessary to define another function?
8. Write the necessary additional Pascal to call the Newton-Raphson procedure to find the root of:
    $$x^3 - 3x^2 + 2 = 0.$$

PROBLEMS

13.1   **Better searching** Add to the Searchingtables program of Example 13.2 a sorting procedure which is defined for conformant arrays of names. Use it to sort each table of words after it is read in. Given that the tables are then in alphabetical order, can you think of a way in which the search procedure could be optimized to detect more quickly that a word is not in the table?

13.2 **Improved marks** In the Sortingmarks program of example 11.2, we postulated that it would be useful to be able to sort on the name field or on the marks field of the table of students. Using a function as a parameter, as described in Section 13.3, extend the program to print out two lists – one in alphabetical order of name, and one in descending order of marks.

13.3 **Secant method** The Newton-Raphson method depends on a guess of the root, and on knowing the derivative of the function. An alternative root finder is the **secant** method. If x_1, x_2 ($x_1 \neq x_2$) are estimates of the root, then a better estimate is:

$$x_3 = \frac{x_1 f(x_2) - x_2 f(x_1)}{f(x_2) - f(x_1)}$$

The formula is obtained by modelling the curve $f(x)$ by the secant through the points x_1, x_2 and taking the geometric relationship between the two triangles thus formed.

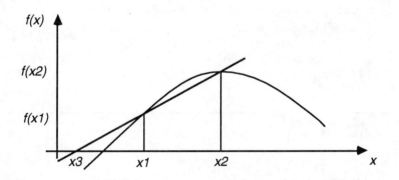

Write a procedure similar to provide this method and use it to solve the problems posed in Example 13.3 and quiz question 8.

14 Pointers and Lists

14.1 What are pointers?

In Pascal, every variable declared in the VAR section is given a name – its **identifier**. Identical items can be grouped in an array, so that one name can stand for a whole list of items. Each item is known by a **designator** comprising the array name and a subscript to that array, and can be accessed directly by its designator. The drawback of arrays is that the number of items must be known in advance and, once set, it cannot be expanded. This can lead to situations such as shown in Figure 14.1 where much of the array is empty.

Pascal provides for lists of varying size to be created. Each item in a list is created separately and linked to the next by means of a pointer. A pointer by itself can point to the first item. The example list would then be represented as in Figure 14.2.

If another item needs to be added to the list, another **node** and pointer are created and linked up. When no longer required, nodes can be removed from lists. Moreover, this adding and removing does not have to be done at the start or end of the list – it can be done anywhere within the list, simply by reorganizing the pointers.

list

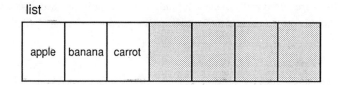

Figure 14.1   Array with unused items.

list

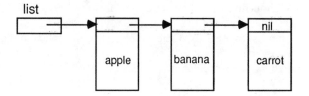

Figure 14.2   Linked list with pointers.

The cost of using pointers

The price that one pays for such flexibility is twofold. First, there is the **overhead** of one pointer per node, plus one for the start of the list. A pointer usually takes up at least as much space as an integer. If the data in the nodes requires more space than the pointer – and it usually does – then the overhead is not significant. However, one would not use pointers to hold lists of small items such as characters: it would be more economical to waste space at the end of a packed array than to provide the pointers.

The second part of the cost of pointers is a **lack of accessibility**. Each element of an array is directly accessible by means of its subscript; not so for nodes in a pointer list. They can only be accessed by starting at the name of the list and following a chain of pointers until the required node is reached. Thus, once again, one would not use pointers if diverse items in the list need to be accessed all the time, as is the case in a sort. But if the list is to be processed sequentially most of the time, then a linked list is not a drawback.

The form of pointer declarations

The syntax for declaring a pointer type is simply:

Pointer type

        identifier = ^ type;

The caret symbol ^ serves to indicate that pointers are involved. Alternative symbols for pointers are @ and ↑.

14.2 Linked lists

There are four steps to setting up and accessing a linked list using pointers. We give them all in general form here and then explain them using an example. Throughout the forms, the term `nodes` in italics stands for whatever record type is to constitute the list. Consequently, the term `tonodes` is used for the type that points to `nodes`. Other identifiers in italics have a similar importance, that is, they convey the general sense of the item, but could be any identifier required by the particular circumstances.

Four steps in defining a linked list

1. *Define the node and pointer types.*

```
TYPE
    tonodes =  ^ nodes;
    nodes   = RECORD
                 link  :  tonodes;
                 other data fields
              END;
```

The nodes are records with an extra field for the link to the next node.

2. *Declare the header.*

```
VAR
    list  : tonodes;
```

This will define a variable which can be used to point to a dynamically created node. As yet it has no value, that is:

list

Pascal has a special pointer value called `nil` which can be assigned to pointer variables to indicate specifically that they point nowhere. This value can be tested for, and is conventionally used as the link value for the last node in a list. Pointers are considered to be bound to their node type, but `nil` is a pointer literal and is compatible with all pointer types.

3. *Create space for a new node.*

```
new (list);
```

Space large enough for a node of the correct type is taken from an area in the Pascal system known as the **heap**. The address of this area is put into the pointer variable mentioned. This produces:

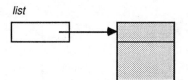

list

4.   *Access fields in the node.* If the node is a record, access to a field is via the
        dot notation, plus the carat, to indicate that a pointer must be followed
        first.

```
list^.field
```

EXAMPLE 14.1   Party people

In the example in Section 8.4, various people were to be invited to a party, and
they were listed as families, for example:

> Tom & Pat
> Nigel & Judy & William & Michael

Each family, therefore, is a list of people, and the list is of variable size. We
could set up such a list with the declarations:

```
TYPE
   topeople = ^people;
   people   = record
                   next : topeople;
                   name : names;
           end;
VAR
   family, guest : topeople;
```

As each name is read in, a space for a new name can be created (together with its
pointer), and linked up to the others. The loop to do this would be:

```
family := nil;
repeat
   new(guest);
   readname (guest^.name);
   guest^.next := family;
   family := guest;
until eoln;
```

Working through this sequence for Nigel, Judy, William and Michael, we see that
the list is created as in Figure 14.3.
        After a brief resumé of the properties of pointers, we shall see how to
access the nodes and print them out. You may notice that the names have been
inserted in the list in reverse order. A means of linking them in a more obvious
order is discussed in the next chapter.

family

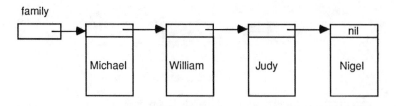

Figure 14.3 Four people in a list.

14.3 Properties of pointers

Pointer values and operators

Pointer values are generated identifiers. The nodes that a pointer may point to are kept in the area of memory called the **heap**. Therefore, a valid pointer value is any address in the heap. It is not possible to have pointers pointing to a variable or area of memory, other than one created through the procedure `new`. The only pointer literal is the special value `nil`.

Pointer values can be assigned and compared for equality. They can also be followed down to their nodes, or **dereferenced**, by using the caret (or other pointer symbol). Thus, if `head` is a pointer, `head^` represents the node it points to. Such indirect names are legitimate wherever variables of that type are legitimate. Thus, given the two pointers and nodes:

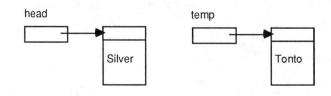

the assignment:

```
head^ := temp^;
```

will copy the entire contents of the node pointed to by `temp` into the node pointed to by `head`. Pictorially, we have:

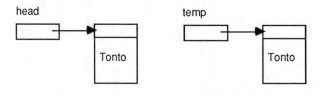

This is quite different to saying:

```
head := temp;
```

which would only copy the pointer, giving:

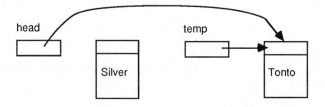

In this case, note that the node originally pointed to by `head` would be inaccessible after the assignment, unless the pointer to it had previously been copied somewhere.

Pointer procedures

There are two special procedures for pointers: `new` and `dispose`. `new` acquires an area from the heap, as already described, and `dispose` can be used to return unwanted nodes to the heap. The system may then be able to reuse that space.

Pointer values cannot be read or written. Input and output of fields of nodes they point to are subject to the input and output provisions of their own types.

14.4   Scanning a list

Once a list is created, it can be scanned by following the pointers. Notice that we can only scan the list in the direction in which the pointers were created. Two reasons for scanning a list are to print its contents, and to find a particular element.

Printing a list

For the list created in Example 14.1, we could print out the names with the following loop:

```
VAR
   family, current : topeople;

current := head;
while current <> nil do begin
   writename (current^.name);
   current := current^ .next;
end;
```

which would give us Michael, William, Judy, Nigel. If we wanted the list in reverse order, which in this case is the original order, we can use recursion to achieve the required effect, that is:

```
PROCEDURE PrintList (head : topeople);
   BEGIN
      if head <> nil then begin
         PrintList(head^.next);
         writename (head^.name);
      end;
   END;
```

This procedure is identical in form to the one used to reverse a number while printing it to a new base (Example 8.8).

Searching a list

The second common operation on a list is to find a node with a particular value. Here we can adapt the simple linear searching algorithm mentioned at the end of Section 11.2.

```
Get a value to search, x
current := family;
while (current <> nil) and (current^.name <> x) then
   current := current^.next;
if current := nil then value not found
else required node is pointed to by current.
```

However, there is a potential problem with the double condition in the while statement: if the current pointer is nil, then the expression current^.name is invalid. Thus, it is better to express search-loops using state indicators.

EXAMPLE 14.2   Winning a raffle _____

Problem At a party, everyone is given a numbered raffle ticket. At the end of the party, a number is drawn and the person with that number wins a prize, as well as the family winning a prize. Write a program using pointers to implement the draw and print out the winning person and winning family.

Solution The algorithms developed so far can be integrated into a program, together with an enlarged people record.

Data structure The data structure for people needs a new field – that of a raffle ticket number. We also would like to make provision for different families, and link them all up together. The data structure we need will look like Figure 14.4.

Algorithm There are two records here: one forms a list of families, with each of these nodes being the head of a list of familiar people nodes. Thus, reading and printing the whole structure involves two different types of nodes and pointers, which will be handled by different procedures. Printing is done by recursion so that the lists can be unravelled into the order in which they were read in.

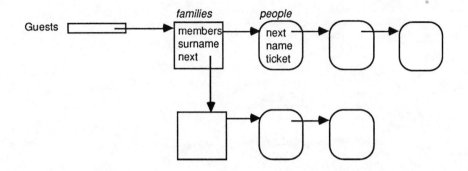

Figure 14.4   Data structure for guests at a party.

Searching is similarly a two-level process, and we use the state indicator approach as suggested above.

Program The program expects data from a file, with each family separated by a blank line and ticket numbers preceding the names. A sample data file is:

```
Bishop
456 Nigel
777 Judy
123 William
921 Michael

Sears
888 Michael
401 Annette
595 Jackie

Mullins
707 Matthew
662 Celeste
901 Tammie
111 Kirsten
```

Once the data has been read in, it is printed out and then a lucky number is requested.

```
PROGRAM Party (input, output);
TYPE
    names       = string[20];
    tickets     = integer;
    topeople    = ^people;
    people      =  record
          next  : topeople;
          name  : names;
          ticket: tickets;
       end;
    tofamilies  = ^families;
    families    = record
```

```
          next     : tofamilies;
          surname : names;
          members : topeople;
       end;

VAR
   guests, winningfamily : tofamilies;
   winner : topeople;
   lucky : tickets;
   data : text;

PROCEDURE ReadFamily (var p : topeople);
   var member : topeople;
   BEGIN
     p := nil;
     repeat
       new (member);
       with member^ do readln(data,ticket,name);
       member^.next := p;
       p := member;
     until eoln(data);
     readln(data);
   END; {ReadFamily}

PROCEDURE ReadGuests (var f : tofamilies);
   var group : tofamilies;
   BEGIN
     f := nil;
     repeat
       new(group);
       readln(data,group^.surname);
       ReadFamily(group^.members);
       group^.next := f;
       f := group;
     until eof(data);
   END;

PROCEDURE PrintFamily (p : topeople);
   BEGIN
     if p <> nil then begin
       PrintFamily(p^.next);
       with p^ do writeln('      ',name,'      ',ticket);
     end;
   END;

PROCEDURE PrintGuests(f : tofamilies);
   BEGIN
     if f <> nil then begin
       PrintGuests(f^.next);
       writeln(f^.surname);
       PrintFamily(f^.members);
     end;
   END;
   PROCEDURE SearchGuests (guests : tofamilies; x : tickets;
                    var p : topeople; var win : tofamilies);
   var
     state : (searching, found, notthere);
     f : tofamilies;
   BEGIN
     state := searching;
     f := guests;
```

```
      repeat
        if f = nil then state := notthere else
        begin
          p := f^.members;
          repeat
            if p = nil then state := notthere else
            if p^.ticket = x then   state := found else
            p := p^.next;
          until state <> searching;
          if state = found then win := f
          else f := f^.next;
          if state = notthere then state := searching;
        end;
    until state <> searching;
  END; {SearchGuests}

BEGIN
  writeln('**** The party prizes *****');
  reset(data,'Party.data');
  ReadGuests(guests);
  writeln('The guests are:');
  PrintGuests(guests);
  write('What is the lucky number? ');
  readln(lucky);
  SearchGuests(guests, lucky, winner, winningfamily);
  if winner = nil then writeln('No winner tonight') else
  writeln(winner^.name, ' of the ',
     winningfamily^.surname, ' family is the winner.');
  readln;
END.
```

Testing Typical output would be:

```
**** The party prizes *****
The guests are:
Bishop
     456 Nigel
     777 Judy
     123 William
     921 Michael
Sears
     888 Michael
     401 Annette
     595 Jackie
Mullins
     707 Matthew
     662 Celeste
     901 Tammie
     111 Kirsten
What is the lucky number? 401
Annette of the Sears family is the winner.
```

WHAT WE HAVE LEARNT

*The pointer mechanism allows us to create space for data while the program executes. Pointer variables point (usually) to records on the **heap** and these can themselves be linked together with their own pointers into **lists**. We learnt to distinguish between a pointer variable, P, the variable it points to, P^, and fields of that variable, P^.field. We looked at standardized procedures to scan a list performing some operation on each item, such as printing; and to search a list for an item with a given value.*

QUIZ

1. Give two advantages of pointers.
2. Give two disadvantages of pointers.
3. What does the `new` procedure do?
4. If a and b are pointers, what is the difference in effect of the following two assignments?

    ```
    a := b;
    a^ := b^;
    ```

5. Why do pointers usually point to records?
6. Can a pointer point to records of different types during the course of a program's execution?
7. In Example 14.1 give specific statements to add another person called Peter to the list.
8. Draw a diagram showing the new list after question 7.
9. After a call to `ReadGuests` in Example 14.2, what would the following print out?

    ```
    writeln(guests^.next^.next^.members^.next^.name);
    ```

10. What procedure returns unneeded space to the heap?

PROBLEMS

14.1 **Age groups** Expand Example 14.2 to include the age of each guest in the data. Then create separate lists of children, teenagers and adults and print them out on request.

14.2 **Variable classes** Problem 9.7 on class marks at Zanyland University would have had to have a built-in upper bound for the class size. Redo the solution using a linked list instead of an array to store the data.

14.3 **More archiving** Example 10.4 developed procedures to archive arrays onto a file. Adapt the procedures to archive linked lists, and test that they work.

14.4 **Cubs again** The case study in Section 10.5 on the cubs database uses an array to store the data in between runs. Discuss the advantages and disadvantages of using a linked list instead.

15 Classic Data Structures

15.1 Introducing data structures

We conclude our study of Pascal by looking ahead to a second computer science course, and the study of data structures. The data structure that we built up in Example 14.2 was an *ad hoc* one, designed for the purpose. Another problem might require a very different data structure. In computer science, though, there are several recognized data structures that crop up again and again in solutions to problems. They have names and defined properties, and in a sense can be regarded as an extension of the basic data types of a language.

The four structures that can be considered classic are:

- stack

- queue

- tree

- linked list.

Each of these has properties relating to the following:

1. Relationship to other nodes;

2. Composition of a header node;

3. Point of addition of nodes – front, back or anywhere;

4. Point of deletion of nodes – front, back or anywhere;

5. Direction of scanning – none, forwards, backwards or other.

The linked list has already been touched on in the previous chapter, but actually has additional properties that we can study.

Representation

Data structures can be represented as either arrays or as nodes connected by pointers. The decision as to which method to employ depends on two factors. A pointer representation has the advantage that the number of nodes in the structure can be completely flexible: with an array representation, the maximum number would have to be fixed. On the other hand, pointer-based structures require links, and these increase the overall size of the structure.

There is no inherent complexity related to the programming in either case, and we shall present both representations, endeavouring to show the underlying algorithms as independent of the representation. In so doing, we create **abstract data types** which have recognizable forms and properties, and can only be used as specified.

Objects

The classic data structures lend themselves very well to an object-oriented approach, and we shall develop our programs in this style. One of the main benefits from adopting an oops approach, even in Standard Pascal, is that one is encouraged to develop programs as modules. In our case, the modules are include files, but they share the desirable property of reusability with the units and objects that make use of Pascal extensions.

15.2 Stacks

Informally, a stack is defined as its name suggests: it is a list of nodes where new nodes are added on to and removed from one end. In order to reflect this property, we tend to use a different terminology from that introduced for lists, and refer to the beginning of the stack as the **top**. A stack is also often drawn upright, as in Figure 15.1(a), although it can be drawn on its side as in 15.1(b).

Stack properties

Formally, we can detail the properties of a stack according to the criteria stated above as:

1. Nodes are arranged in sequence.

2. There is one end, the **top**.

3. Nodes are added to the **top**.

4. Nodes are removed from the **top**.

5. The stack cannot be scanned: only the **top** node is visible.

Thus a stack can also be known as a LIFO or Last-In-First-Out list.

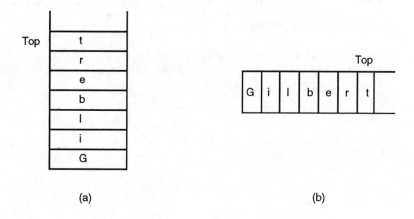

(a)   (b)

Figure 15.1   Diagrams of stacks.

The stack abstract data type

We are now in a position to define the stack as a data type. Since we are mindful
of the two alternative representations for stacks, we shall start off by defining it in
abstract terms, using the familar forms notation.

```
Stack

TYPE stacks,
    {requires a definition of items}
PROCEDURE Push (var s : stacks; x : items);
PROCEDURE Pop (var s : stacks; var x : items);
PROCEDURE Top (s : stacks; var x : items);
PROCEDURE StackInit (var s : stacks);
FUNCTION  StackEmpty (s : stacks) : boolean;
```

This form describes all the public types and procedures required by anyone using
the stack type. The Push procedure takes the item *x* and pushes it on to the top of
the stack. The Pop procedure returns the top item, 'popping' the stack at the same
time, while the Top procedure returns just the top item, without popping the stack.

The `StackInit` procedure clears a stack, and the `StackEmpty` function determines whether there are any items on the stack. The last two will probably appear in other data structures, so we use the prefix notation; `Push`, `Pop` and `Top` can be considered to be unique to stacks and are left as is.

To emphasize that the abstract definition is usable without knowing anything about the representation, we present an example at this stage.

EXAMPLE 15.1   Reversing a string _____

Problem Reverse a string of any length.

Solution   Stacks have the property that they can be used to reverse a sequence. By using eoln and `StackEmpty` as terminators, we do not have to know the length of the string in advance.

Program

```
PROGRAM Reverse (input, output);
   {$I Starr1.pas}

   TYPE
      items = char;
   VAR
      s : stacks;
      ch : items;
   {$I Starr2.pas}

   BEGIN
      writeln('***** Testing the stack data type *****');
      writeln('Type in a string');
      StackInit (s);
      while not eoln do begin
         read(ch);
         push(s,ch);
      end;
      writeln('The string reversed is:');
      while not StackEmpty(s) do begin
         pop(s,ch);
         write(ch);
      end;
   END.
```

Testing Expected input and output would be:

```
***** Testing the stack data type *****
Type in a string
The curfew tolls the knell of parting day.
The string reversed is:
.yad gnitrap fo llenk eht sllot wefruc ehT
```

Stacks using arrays

The first and obvious implementation of a stack is as an array. One consideration with an array implementation is that the maximum size of the stack must be fixed in advance (the array's upper bound). If this is exceeded, an error condition occurs, and we have to decide how to handle it. The simplest way at this stage is to do nothing. We check for a possible overflow or underflow (popping when empty), but simply regard the call as a null operation. To do more would require more parameters and spoil the impact of the stack design as we are putting it across.

The full object definition is:

```
{STACK object using an array Part I - File Starr1.pas
   REQUIRES type items to be defined}
{PRIVATE}
   CONST
      maxstack = 100;
      nul = 0;
   TYPE
      stackrange = 1..maxstack;
      stackindex = 0..maxstack;
{PUBLIC}
      stacks
      {PROCEDURE Init
      PROCEDURE Pop
      PROCEDURE Push
      PROCEDURE Top
      FUNCTION Empty}
{PRIVATE}
         = RECORD
            head : stackindex;
            data : array[stackrange] of items;
            end;

{STACK object using an array Part 2 - file Starr2.pas}

PROCEDURE StackInit(var s : stacks);
   BEGIN
      s.head := nul;
   END; {Init}

PROCEDURE Push (var s : stacks; x : items);
   {Has no effect if the stack is full}
   BEGIN
      with s do
         if head < maxstack then begin
         head := succ(head );
         data[head] := x;
         end;
   END; {Push}

PROCEDURE Pop (var s : stacks; var x : items);
   {Has no effect if the stack is empty}
   BEGIN
      with s do
         if head <> nul then begin
         x := data[head];
         head := head - 1;
         end;
   END; {Pop}

PROCEDURE Top (s : stacks; var x : items);
   {Has no effect if the stack is empty}
```

```
      BEGIN
        with s do
        if head <> nul then
            x := data[head];
      END; {Pop}

   FUNCTION StackEmpty (s : stacks) : boolean;
     BEGIN
        StackEmpty := s.head = nul;
     END; {Empty}
```

Notice that the insides of the record for a stack are private: the user may not manipulate the head index or any of the data items except via the procedures provided as public.

Stacks using pointers

Since a stack is such a simple structure, without the possibility of inserting items in the middle, the only advantage of using a pointer implementation is to obtain complete flexibility of the size of the stack. The above object definition can be very simply translated into a pointer version thus:

```
{STACK object using pointers Part I - File Stapoi1.pas
   REQUIRES type items to be defined}
{PRIVATE}
   TYPE
      tonodes = ^nodes;
      nodes = RECORD
                 next : tonodes;
                 data : items;
              END;
{PUBLIC}
      stacks
      {PROCEDURE Init
      PROCEDURE Pop
      PROCEDURE Push
      PROCEDURE Top
      FUNCTION Empty}
{PRIVATE}
               = tonodes;

{STACK object using an array Part 2 - file Stapoi2.pas}

PROCEDURE StackInit(var s : stacks);
   BEGIN
      s:= nil;
   END; {Init}

PROCEDURE Push (var s : stacks; x : items);
   var n : tonodes;
   BEGIN
      new(n);
      n^.data := x;
      n^.next := s;
      s:= n;
   END; {Push}
```

```
PROCEDURE Pop (var s : stacks; var x : items);
   var n : tonodes;
   BEGIN
        n := s;
        x := s^.data;
        s := s^.next;
        dispose (n);
   END; {Pop}

PROCEDURE Top (s : stacks; var x : items);
   BEGIN
      x := s^.data;
   END; {Pop}

FUNCTION StackEmpty (s : stacks) : boolean;
   BEGIN
      StackEmpty := s = nil
   END; {Empty}
```

In many ways, the pointer implementation is simpler. There are no error conditions to consider, and there is no header node as such, since we are only carrying around one pointer.

If this version is used in a program, then the declaration:

```
VAR
   mystack : stacks;
```

creates a single pointer variable of type tonodes, from which the stack will start.

Uses of stacks

Stacks are useful for recording the state of a computation as it unfolds. A typical example is the evaluation of expressions which involve precedence and nesting. A stack is also the data structure that implements recursion. In a language like Pascal, it is usually possible to use recursion with its implicit stack rather than an explicit stack. The next data structure is probably more useful in practice.

15.3 Queues

Although stacks are the simplest structures we have, their property of reversibility is not always useful. A more common data structure is one where the items can be removed in the same order in which they were inserted. Such a structure is known as a queue or FIFO list (First In First Out).

In order to implement this property, a queue has to have two ends, indicating the front and back. New items are added on to the back, and items are removed from the front. Queues are usually drawn sideways, as in Figure 15.2(a). However, an innate property of queues is that they move forward: as an item is removed from the front, so all the other items behind it move up one. We can see immediately that such moving in an array implementation would be inefficient, and so we can already consider an alternative depiction of a queue as a

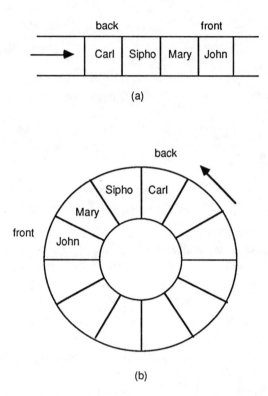

Figure 15.2   Diagrams of queues.

circle. Here there is a fixed number of slots in the circle and the queue moves around it, as in Figure 15.2(b).

Queue properties

Formally, we can detail the properties of a queue as:

1. Nodes are arranged in sequence.

2. There are two ends, the **front** and **back**.

3. Nodes are added to the **front**.

4. Nodes are removed from the **back**.

5. The queue can be scanned from the front to the back.

The queue abstract data type and object

We are now in a position to define the queue as a data type. As for stacks, we shall start off by defining it in abstract terms.

Bounded Queue

```
TYPE
    queues;
    {requires a definition of items}
PROCEDURE QueueAdd (var q : queues; x : items);
PROCEDURE QueueRemove (var q : queues; var x : items);
FUNCTION  QueueEmpty (q : queues) : boolean;
PROCEDURE QueueInit (var q : queues; size : integer);
FUNCTION  QueueFull (q : queues) : boolean;
```

This form describes all the public types and procedures required by anyone using the queue type. The QueueAdd procedure (sometimes known as Enqueue) adds an item to the back. QueueRemove takes the item off the front (providing such an item exists). This is sometimes known as Dequeue. QueueEmpty does the obvious, but QueueInit has an extra parameter: a property of queues is that they can be bounded, and we can specify the bound here. In an array implementation, the bound specified would have to be less than the maximum size of the array. In order to make use of the user-specified bound, we have a QueueFull function as well.

Property 5 above indicated that we should be able to scan the queue, perhaps doing something to each item. For example, we may wish to print the queue out, or search for a particular item. Without more sophisticated language features, it is difficult to generalize the scanning operation. We therefore have to allow the user access to the queue itself. This can be done in a controlled way by insisting that all scanning operations be written as procedures and added to the queue's 'include' file. In the example that follows, we assume that a QueueDisplay operation has been so defined.

EXAMPLE 15.2   Doctor's waiting room _____

Problem A doctor has a small waiting room with a small number of seats. Patients can come in and wait there, but once the seats are full, they tend to go away and come back later. Simulate this behaviour, so that the doctor can decide if it is essential to build a bigger waiting room.

Solution We can set up a queue with a maximum size and randomly let patients arrive and be seen by the doctor. The state of the queue can be continuously displayed and when it is full, a signal can be made, and arrivals ignored until there is space again.

Algorithm We can simulate what is happening with the following algorithm:

Simulation

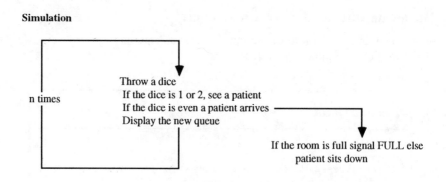

There is a 50% chance at each iteration that a patient will arrive (signified by checking whether the dice throw is even) and there is a 30% chance that the doctor will be ready to see another patient (dice is 1 or 2). There is also a 30% chance that nothing will happen (dice is 3 or 5). We run the simulation for a set number of times and watch what happens.

Program

```
PROGRAM DoctorSimulation (input, output);
  TYPE
    items = integer;
          {a sequence number of the time of arrival}

{$I Qarr1.pas}
VAR
  chairs : queues;
  nchairs, i , patient, n : integer;
  dice : integer; {1..6}
  seed : real;

{$I Qarr2.pas}

PROCEDURE Throw (var d : integer);
  BEGIN
    seed := seed*27.182813 + 31.425917;
    seed := seed - trunc(seed);
    d := trunc(seed*6)+1;
  END; {Throw}

PROCEDURE Instructions;
  BEGIN
    writeln('***** The Doctor''s Waiting Room *****');
    write('How many chairs? ');   readln(nchairs);
    write('How many iterations? '); readln (n);
    writeln('Arrive on 2 4 6');
    writeln('Be seen on 1 2');
    writeln;
    writeln(' I  Throw');
    writeln('              <--------');
  END; {Instructions}
```

```
        BEGIN
            Instructions;
            QueueInit(chairs, nchairs);
            QueueAdd(chairs,1);
            seed := 1.234567;
            for i := 2 to n do begin
                Throw(dice);
                write(i:2,' : ',dice:1,' : ');
                QueueDisplay(chairs);
                if dice in [1,2] then QueueRemove(chairs,patient);
                if not odd (dice) then
                    if QueueFull (chairs)
                        then writeln(' ':60,'FULL')
                        else QueueAdd (chairs, i);
            end;
        END.
```

Testing A run could look like this:

```
***** The Doctor's Waiting Room *****
How many chairs? 6
How many iterations? 30
Arrive on 2 4 6
Be seen on 1 2

 I   Throw
                <--------
 2 : 6 : !_ 1_!    !____!    !____!    !____!    !____!    !____!
 3 : 2 : !_ 1_!    !_ 2_!    !____!    !____!    !____!    !____!
 4 : 5 : !_ 2_!    !_ 3_!    !____!    !____!    !____!    !____!
 5 : 1 : !_ 2_!    !_ 3_!    !____!    !____!    !____!    !____!
 6 : 5 : !_ 3_!    !____!    !____!    !____!    !____!    !____!
 7 : 4 : !_ 3_!    !____!    !____!    !____!    !____!    !____!
 8 : 2 : !_ 3_!    !_ 7_!    !____!    !____!    !____!    !____!
 9 : 5 : !_ 7_!    !_ 8_!    !____!    !____!    !____!    !____!
10 : 5 : !_ 7_!    !_ 8_!    !____!    !____!    !____!    !____!
11 : 4 : !_ 7_!    !_ 8_!    !____!    !____!    !____!    !____!
12 : 4 : !_ 7_!    !_ 8_!    !_11_!    !____!    !____!    !____!
13 : 2 : !_ 7_!    !_ 8_!    !_11_!    !_12_!    !____!    !____!
14 : 5 : !_ 8_!    !_11_!    !_12_!    !_13_!    !____!    !____!
15 : 4 : !_ 8_!    !_11_!    !_12_!    !_13_!    !____!    !____!
16 : 5 : !_ 8_!    !_11_!    !_12_!    !_13_!    !_15_!    !____!
17 : 2 : !_ 8_!    !_11_!    !_12_!    !_13_!    !_15_!    !____!
18 : 5 : !_11_!    !_12_!    !_13_!    !_15_!    !_17_!    !____!
19 : 4 : !_11_!    !_12_!    !_13_!    !_15_!    !_17_!    !____!
20 : 1 : !_11_!    !_12_!    !_13_!    !_15_!    !_17_!    !_19_!
21 : 3 : !_12_!    !_13_!    !_15_!    !_17_!    !_19_!    !____!
22 : 6 : !_12_!    !_13_!    !_15_!    !_17_!    !_19_!    !____!
23 : 4 : !_12_!    !_13_!    !_15_!    !_17_!    !_19_!    !_22_!
                                                                 FULL
24 : 6 : !_12_!    !_13_!    !_15_!    !_17_!    !_19_!    !_22_!
                                                                 FULL
25 : 3 : !_12_!    !_13_!    !_15_!    !_17_!    !_19_!    !_22_!
26 : 1 : !_12_!    !_13_!    !_15_!    !_17_!    !_19_!    !_22_!
27 : 3 : !_13_!    !_15_!    !_17_!    !_19_!    !_22_!    !____!
28 : 4 : !_13_!    !_15_!    !_17_!    !_19_!    !_22_!    !____!
29 : 2 : !_13_!    !_15_!    !_17_!    !_19_!    !_22_!    !_28_!
30 : 2 : !_15_!    !_17_!    !_19_!    !_22_!    !_28_!    !_29_!
```

Queues using arrays

The best array implementation for a queue is a circular one. The back of the queue starts at 1, and gradually moves up to the maximum size. Once there, the next position considered for insertion is 1 again, provided a remove has taken place and there is no live data there. Because of this, the conditions for full and empty are no longer based on whether the indicators are 0 or max, but on a count of the number of live items. The full object definition for a queue is:

```
{QUEUE object using an array Part I - File Qarr1.pas
   REQUIRES type items to be defined}
{PRIVATE}
   CONST
      maxqueue = 100;
   TYPE
      queuerange = 1..maxqueue;
      queueindex = 0..maxqueue;
{PUBLIC}
      queues
      {PROCEDURE QueueAdd
      PROCEDURE QueueRemove
      FUNCTION QueueEmpty
      PROCEDURE QueueInit
      FUNCTION QueueFull}
{PRIVATE}
            = RECORD
               front, back : queueindex;
               live : queueindex;
               size : queuerange;
               data : array [ queuerange] of items;
            end;
{QUEUE object using an array Part 2 - file Qarr2.pas}

PROCEDURE QueueInit(var q : queues; n : integer);
   {Overrides size requested if it is too large}
   BEGIN
      q.front := 1;
      q.back := 0;
      q.live := 0;
      if n <= maxqueue then q.size := n else q.size :=
maxqueue;
   END; {QueueInit}

PROCEDURE QueueAdd (var q : queues; x : items);
   {Has no effect if the queue is full}
   BEGIN
      with q do
         if live < size then begin
            back := (back + 1) mod maxqueue;
            data[back] := x;
            live := live + 1;
         end;
   END; {QueueAdd}

PROCEDURE QueueRemove (var q : queues; var x : items);
   {Has no effect if the queue is empty}
   BEGIN
      with q do
         if live >= 1 then begin
            x := data[front];
```

```
        front := (front+1) mod maxqueue;
        live := live - 1;
      end;
  END; {QueueRemove}

FUNCTION QueueEmpty (q : queues) : boolean;
  BEGIN
    QueueEmpty := q.live = 0;
  END; {Empty}

FUNCTION QueueFull(q : queues) : boolean;
  BEGIN
    QueueFull := q.live = q.size;
  END; {QueueFull}
```

Notice that as for a stack the insides of the record for a queue are private. The QueueDisplay procedure depends on the type of items being queued. For the chairs of Example 15.2, QueueDisplay is:

```
PROCEDURE QueueDisplay(q : queues);
  var i : queueindex;
      pos : queuerange;
  BEGIN
    with q do begin
      pos := front;
      for i := 1 to live do begin
        write('!_',q.data[pos]:2,'_!   ');
        pos := (pos+1) mod maxqueue;
      end;
      for i := live+1 to size do
        write('!____!   ');
    end;
    writeln(out);
  END; {QueueDisplay}
```

Queues using pointers

As with stacks, queues cannot be altered except at the ends, so the only advantage of using a pointer implementation is to obtain complete flexibility of the size of the queue. However, unlike the stack where one pointer was sufficient, and this was simply called the stack, here we need two pointers to represent the queue, and we keep them in a record. Notice that we still provide a border facility, so that a queue can stop growing. The above object definition can be very simply translated into a pointer version thus:

```
{QUEUE object using pointers Part I - File Qpoi1.pas
   REQUIRES type items to be defined}
{PRIVATE}
  TYPE
    tonodes = ^nodes;
    nodes = RECORD
               next : tonodes;
               data : items;
            END;
{PUBLIC}
    queues
    {PROCEDURE QueueAdd
    PROCEDURE QueueRemove
```

```
               FUNCTION QueueEmpty
               PROCEDURE QueueInit
               FUNCTION QueueFull}
      {PRIVATE}
                    = RECORD
                        front, back : tonodes;
                        live, size : 0..maxint;
                      END;

      {QUEUE object using pointers Part 2 - file Qpoi2.pas}

      PROCEDURE QueueInit(var q : queues; n : integer);
         {Overrides size requested if it is too large}
         BEGIN
            q.front := nil;
            q.back := nil;
            q.live := 0;
            q.size := n;
         END; {QueueInit}

      PROCEDURE QueueAdd (var q : queues; x : items);
         {Has no effect if the queue is full}
         var n : tonodes;
         BEGIN
            with q do
               if live < size then begin
                  new (n);
                  n^.data := x;
                  n^.next := nil;
                  if back = nil then
                     front := n
                   else
                      back^.next := n;
                  back := n;
                  live := live + 1;
               end;
         END; {QueueAdd}

      PROCEDURE QueueRemove (var q : queues; var x : items);
         {Has no effect if the queue is empty}
         VAR n : tonodes;
         BEGIN
            with q do
               if live >= 1 then begin
                  x := front^.data;
                  n := front;
                  front := front^.next;
                  dispose (n);
                  live := live - 1;
               end;
         END; {QueueRemove}

      FUNCTION QueueEmpty (q : queues) : boolean;
         BEGIN
            QueueEmpty := q.live = 0;
         END; {Empty}

      FUNCTION QueueFull(q : queues) : boolean;
         BEGIN
            QueueFull := q.live = q.size;
         END; {QueueFull}
```

Notice the sequence used in the add procedure, that is:

```
new (n);
n^.data := x;
n^.next := nil;
if back = nil then
        front := n
else
        back^.next := n;
back := n;
```

There are two different linking conditions. If the queue is empty, then we have to adjust front as well as back. If the queue already has items in it then we have to link the new item on and move back.

For completion we give the QueueDisplay procedure for Example 15.2 using pointers:

```
PROCEDURE QueueDisplay(q : queues);
    var p : tonodes;

    BEGIN
      p := q.front;
      for i := 1 to q.live do begin
         write(out,'!_',p^.data:2,'_!    ');
         p := p^.next;
      end;
      for i := q.live+1 to q.size do
         write(out,'!____!    ');
      writeln(out);
    END; {QueueDisplay}
```

The Doctor program will run without change if the Qpoi1.pas and Qpoi2.pas files are included instead of the array ones.

15.4 Trees

Both stacks and queues are linear structures because they have a single relationship with the next element. Trees are quite different because each node may be related to several others. A tree starts with a root and branches out until the leaves are reached. Data may be stored at every node or only at the leaves.

Trees are very versatile structures and the relationship between the root, branches and leaves has many parallels in real life. Typical trees are shown in Figure 15.3.

Tree properties

In general, the properties of the tree data structure are:

1. A tree consists of a root node and zero or more subtrees.

2. The tree is accessed from the root.

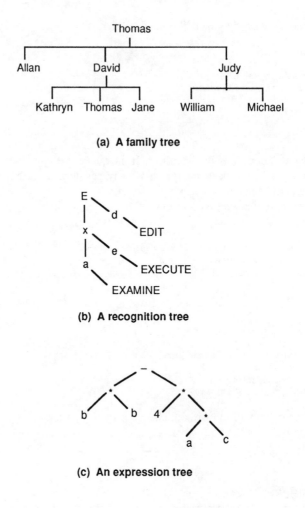

(a) **A family tree**

(b) **A recognition tree**

(c) **An expression tree**

Figure 15.3   Typical trees.

3. Nodes may be added anywhere.

4. Nodes may be removed from anywhere.

5. The tree can be scanned in various orders, known as preorder, inorder
   and postorder.

Theoretically, there is no restriction on how many branches any one node in a tree
may have. However, computer science practice has developed along the lines of
regarding two branches as a workable number. Trees with this restriction are
known as **binary trees** and we shall restrict our discussions to them. In fact, any
tree can be converted by a simple algorithm into a binary tree, so what follows is
generally useful. The algorithm for this transformation would be covered in a
second computer science course.

On a tree, there is a relationship between the values on the nodes, both vertically and horizontally. Items are not placed anywhere: they are placed in a fixed relationship. For example, in Figure 15.3(a), nodes have a child and sibling relationship. Thus, if David had another child, it would be linked on to the right of Jane. In Figure 15.3(b) nodes are related by common spelling. Thus, if we added another word, say Extract, then it would be placed to the right of the x, causing a change in the position of Execute. Essentially, the relationship between keys indicates whether a new node is to be added to the left or the right of the current node. This distinction will be taken into account when designing the procedure to add a node.

The binary tree abstract data type and object

Having decided to restrict ourselves to binary trees, we can define the abstract data type as:

Binary Tree

```
TYPE
   Trees;
   {requires the definition of
      type items and type keys}
PROCEDURE TreeInit (var t : trees);
PROCEDURE TreeAdd (var t : trees; x : items; ontheleft:boolean);
PROCEDURE TreeSearch (t : trees; k : keys;  var node : trees);
PROCEDURE Preorder (t : trees; PROCEDURE visit (p : trees));
PROCEDURE Inorder (t : trees; PROCEDURE visit (p : trees));
PROCEDURE Postorder (t : trees; PROCEDURE visit (p : trees));
```

The definitions need some explanation. `TreeInit` will, as usual, clear the tree and get it ready for insertions. `TreeAdd` will take a single item and insert it as the left or right branch, depending on the third parameter. `TreeSearch` will search the tree and look for a particular key, returning the start of the subtree with that key. The reason why we return the subtree and not the contents of the node is that we may wish to carry on searching from there.

The remaining three procedures are known as **traversals** and are the means by which we scan a tree. Because the tree is not linear, there is more than one way of visiting each node in turn. The three classic traversals differ in terms of the order of visiting the root node of each tree and subtree. These are:

- Preorder – visit root, preorder left subtree, preorder right subtree;

- Inorder – Inorder left subtree, visit root, inorder right subtree;

- Postorder – Postorder left subtree, postorder right subtree, visit root.

For example, given the simple tree of Figure 15.3(c), then the three traversals give us:

```
- * b b * 4 * a c
```

```
b * b - 4 * a * c
b b * 4 a * c * -
```

It is clear that for different purposes one or other of the traversals will be more appropriate. In this case, inorder gives us the expression as originally put in, and postorder gives us the familiar postfix form, where the operators come after their two operands. Preorder does not mean much here. In general, for alphabetically ordered trees, inorder will return the sorted version of the data.

What about the procedure shown in the parameter lists for the traversals, that is, visit? We are using here the procedural parameters feature of Pascal, described in Section 13.3. It allows us to describe the traverse operation without worrying about what the visit entails at each node. The call of a traverse would specify the actual procedure to be used at that point, for example Display or Print or AddOnetoKey, or whatever.

We have not included in the definition an operation for removing a node: this is slightly more complicated than the others, and we shall leave it to CS2.

EXAMPLE 15.3   File directory

Problem   A file directory with multiple levels is to be stored and accessed with queries such as find a directory, list the directories, and so on.

Solution   The directories can be stored on a tree. Is it possible to use a binary tree? Yes, if we regard the left link as giving the first file in a directory one level down, and the right link as giving other files at the same level. For example, we might have:

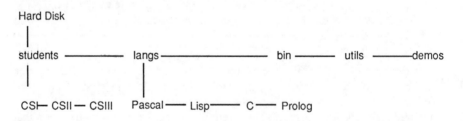

How does the input data look? Well, we start off with the hard disk as root, and then add nodes depending on commands as follows:

F	Find name – finds a directory with the given name
M	Make a new directory
E	Enter a directory
D	Display the whole directory

New directories are added after the current position.

Example   To create the directory above, the following sequence of commands would be feasible. Others could also produce the same structure.

M	Hard Disk
E	
M	students
E	
M	CSI
M	CSII
M	CSIII
F	students
M	langs
M	bin
F	langs
E	
M	Pascal
M	Lisp
M	C
F	bin
M	utils
M	demos
F	C
M	Prolog
D	

Algorithm   What tree operations will help to implement this solution? Making a directory is the same as executing an add operation. The tree parameter must be supplied as the current position on the tree: this is maintained by the user. The link indicator is set to the right (that is, false). Entering a directory sets the link indicator to true, because the intention is that the next add will refer to the left link. Finding is directly implemented by Treesearch.

Displaying the directories needs some thought. We do not wish to get involved in a graphical 2-D display, and would prefer simply to list each directory, with its subdirectories in an indented list. This is preorder format. To obtain the indenting, we add another parameter to our visit procedure which is incremented each time we follow a left link (that is, go down a level).

Program   The program to create and display such a directory is very short. It assumes nothing about the tree abstract data type, other than that which we defined in the design above.

```
PROGRAM DirectoryManager (input,output);

TYPE
   names = string[20];
   keys = names;
   items = RECORD
      key : keys;
      size : integer;
      END;
{$I Treepoil.pas}

VAR
   dir, current : trees;
   entry : items;
```

```
            command : char;
            newlevel : boolean;
            name : names;

        PROCEDURE Visit(t : trees; indent : integer);
            BEGIN
                writeln(' ':indent,t^.data.key);
            END; {Visit}
    {$I Treepoi2.pas}

    BEGIN
        writeln('***** Directory manager *****');
        writeln;
        TreeInit(dir);
        entry.key := 'Hard Disk';
        entry.size := 0;
        TreeAdd(dir,entry,true);
        newlevel := true;
        current := dir;
        repeat
            write('>'); readln(command,name);
            entry.key := name;
            entry.size := 0;
            case command of
                'F' : TreeSearch(dir,name,current);
                'M' : begin
                            TreeAdd(current,entry,newlevel);
                            newlevel := false;
                        end;
                'E' : newlevel := true;
                'D' : Preorder(dir);
                'Q' : ;
            end;
        until command = 'Q';
    END.
```

Testing If we run the commands suggested above, we shall get the following display at the end:

```
Hard Disk
    students
        CSI
        CSII
        CSIII
    langs
        Pascal
        Lisp
        C
        Prolog
    bin
    utils
    demos
```

Further extensions to this program are discussed in the problems at the end of the chapter.

Implementing binary trees

The obvious implementation for a binary tree is based on a node with two pointers. There is no sense in using an array, since the elements are not related to each other in a +1 manner, as was the case for stacks and queues. Because searching is now an issue, we keep the key field of the data separately in the node. All of the procedures (except TreeInit and TreeAdd) make use of recursion. They regard the empty tree as the base case, and operate by reducing the problem to the base case.

```
{TREE object using pointers Part I  - File Treepoil.pas
   REQUIRES types items and keys to be defined}

  {PRIVATE}
    TYPE
      tonodes = ^nodes;
      nodes = record
                 left, right : tonodes;
                 key : keys;
                 data : items;
               end;
  {PUBLIC}
    trees
      {PROCEDURE TreeInit
       PROCEDURE TreeAdd
       PROCEDURE TreeSearch
       PROCEDURE Preorder
       PROCEDURE Inorder
       PROCEDURE Postorder}
       = tonodes;

{TREE object using pointers Part 2  - File Treepoi2.pas}

  PROCEDURE TreeInit (var t : trees);
    BEGIN
       t := nil;
    END; {TreeInit}

PROCEDURE TreeAdd (var t : trees; x : items; branch :
boolean);
    BEGIN
       if t = nil then new (t) else
       case branch of
          true : begin new(t^.left);  t := t^.left; end;
          false: begin new(t^.right); t := t^.right; end;
       end;
       t^.data := x;
       t^.left := nil;
       t^.right := nil;
    END; {TreeAdd}

PROCEDURE TreeSearch (t : trees; k : keys; var node :
trees);
    BEGIN
       if t^.data.key = k then node := t else
       if t <> nil then begin
          TreeSearch(t^.left,k,node);
          TreeSearch (t^.right,k,node);
       end;
    END; {TreeSearch}
```

```
PROCEDURE Preorder (t : trees);
  PROCEDURE Pre (t : trees; pos : integer);
  BEGIN
    if t <> nil then begin
      visit(t,pos);
      Pre(t^.left,pos+4);
      Pre(t^.right,pos);
    end;
  END;
BEGIN
  Pre(t,0);
END; {Preorder}

PROCEDURE Inorder (t : trees);
  BEGIN
    if t <> nil then begin
      Inorder(t^.left);
      visit(t,0);
      Inorder(t^.right);
    end;
  END; {Inorder}

PROCEDURE Postorder (t : trees);
  BEGIN
    if t <> nil then begin
      Postorder(t^.left);
      Postorder(t^.right);
      visit(t,0);
    end;
  END; {Postorder}
```

Ordered trees

In every tree there must be some inter-node relationship that is used to decide
whether a new node is added to the left or to the right. A common relationship is
alphabetical or numerical ordering. A tree can be set up with each node having
the property that all nodes to its left have keys that are less, and all nodes to its
right have keys that are more. If the tree is then traversed in inorder, or
'flattened', then a sorted version of the input data is the result.

We can therefore define a new operation for the tree as follows:

Ordered Binary Tree

```
INHERITS Binary Tree and adds
  PROCEDURE TreeOrderAdd(t : trees; x : items);
```

TreeOrderAdd will take an existing tree and find the correct place for the item,
before adding it on.

EXAMPLE 15.4   Treesort _____

Problem   Illustrate tree sorting.

Solution   As described above, we create an ordered binary tree and then flatten it.

Algorithm   The procedure that needs to be added to the tree object files is TreeOrderAdd. The basis for finding the position is to do a traverse of the tree, but to stop as soon as the correct leaf is found. In other words, the left and right links are followed, depending on whether the keys are less or more, and when a nil link is found, that is the correct place.

Procedure   The procedure encloses the recursive traverse. It will not work for empty trees, and assumes that it has been primed by the user reading in and adding the first entry via TreeAdd.

```
PROCEDURE TreeOrderAdd (tree : trees; entry: items);
   var found : boolean;

  PROCEDURE Position (tree : trees);
  BEGIN
     if not found then begin
        if entry.key < tree^.data.key then begin
           if tree^.left <> nil then position(tree^.left)
           else begin
              TreeAdd(tree,entry,ontheleft);
              found := true
           end
        end else begin
           if tree^.right <> nil then position(tree^.right)
           else begin
              TreeAdd(tree,entry,ontheright);
              found := true;
           end;
        end;
     end;
  END; {position}

  BEGIN
     found := false;
     Position(tree);
  END; {TreeOrderAdd }
```

This procedure is added to the Treepoi2.pas file, and then the following program can run:

Program
```
PROGRAM TreeSort (input,output);
TYPE
   names = string[20];
   keys = names;
   items = RECORD
        key : keys;
      END;
{$I Treepoi1.pas}
```

```
VAR
   tree : trees;
   entry : items;

PROCEDURE Visit(t : trees; indent : integer);
   BEGIN
      writeln(' ':indent,t^.data.key);
   END; {Visit}
{$I Treepoi2.pas}

BEGIN
   writeln('***** Tree Sorter *****');
   writeln;
   writeln('Type in names ending with ^N');
   tree := nil;
   readln(entry.key);
   TreeAdd(tree,entry,true);
   while not eof do begin
      readln(entry.key);
      TreeOrderAdd(tree,entry);
   end;
   writeln('The sorted data is');
   Inorder(tree);
   readln;
END.
```

Testing A run of the program would produce:

```
***** Tree Sorter *****

Type in the names ending with ^N
Charlie
Adam
Bob
Peter
June
Carol
Lyn
The sorted data is
Adam
Bob
Carol
Charlie
June
Lyn
Peter
```

15.5 Linked lists again

The lists discussed in Chapter 14 were very simple, but had the odd property that they stored data backwards. This was not a problem, since we used recursion to return the data in the correct order when needed. What we were really creating was a stack – a very neat data structure because it has only one header. If we would prefer to store the data in the correct order, then we need two headers – one for the front and one for the back, as in a queue.

In fact, linked lists can be more general than either a stack or queue and can permit operations to occur not just at the ends.

Linked list properties

Formally, we can define the properties of a list as:

1. Nodes are linked together linearly in both directions, forwards and backwards.

2. There are two ends to the list – the front and the back.

3. Nodes can be added anywhere in the list.

4. Nodes can be deleted anywhere in the list.

5. The list can be scanned forwards or backwards.

The list abstract data type and object

The formal definition of the full-blown list type is:

```
List

TYPE lists
{REQUIRES definitions of items and keys}
    front,
    back : positions;
    size : integer;
PROCEDURE ListInit (var list : lists);
PROCEDURE AddBefore (var list:lists; pos:positions; x:items; k:keys);
PROCEDURE AddAfter (var list:lists; pos:positions; x:items; k:keys);
PROCEDURE Remove (var list:lists; pos:positions; x:items; k:keys);
PROCEDURE ListSearch (var list:lists; pos:positions; x:items; k:keys);
PROCEDURE ListScan (list : lists);
```

ListInit will initialize the list, setting the front and back to nil, and the size to zero. Unlike the other data structures, we allow the user of the object to have access to the first and last pointers of the list. The type position is used to indicate a single node in the list, since the list type itself will probably be a more substantial record. We do not, however, reveal exactly what type this is, and so maintain a degree of protection.

When inserting items, we may find that we wish to do this before or after where we are currently in the list: both options are catered for. However, removing an item is done on the current item. Searching is similar to TreeSearch, as it returns a position where a key is found. However, we have added a refinement in that we can search for a node that has more than an equality relation. By searching for less or more, we can maintain an ordered list based on the key. Scanning is similar to the tree traversals in that it deals with the entire list, calling the visit procedure for every node.

EXAMPLE 15.5   Photograph line up_____

Problem   A photographer is going to photograph a class of students, and wants them neatly arranged in heights. The plan is to have the taller people in the back rows, and for each row to slope down from the centre. Given a class of students and their heights, we would like a plan of where each should stand.

Example   Each row should be lined up like this.

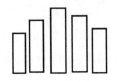

Solution   We start by creating a single line of everyone in height order. Then, starting at the tallest, we peel off however many we want per row, and create a new list starting in the middle and adding alternately to the right and left. Suppose we label the people A,B, ... Then a row of seven people would be arranged thus:

GECABDF

Algorithm   The algorithms make very good use of the list methods defined above. First, we consider how to create a list in height order:

Create an ordered list

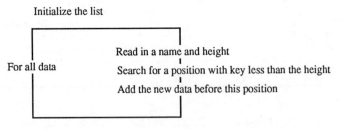

The result will be a list with the front pointing to the tallest person.

Now we consider how to peel off a row and create the left–right effect. For ease of computation, we assume that the row will have an odd number of people.

Adding to the back equates to AddAfter(back) and adding to the front becomes AddBefore(front). We can print out or display the line, by calling ListScan and providing write as the visit procedure. Then, we can erase the line and start with a new one. Erasing a list at the moment involves taking each node in turn and removing it: this operation could be made a method in itself.

Create a left–right sorted list

Initialize the line
Remove the front of the main list
Add it to the line

Remove the front of the main list
Add it to the back of the line
Remove the front of the main list
Add it to the front of the line

n/2 times

Program   As before, the program is surprisingly clean and short, since all the work is done in the well-defined list object methods.

```
PROGRAM Photograph (input, output);

{Creates a layout for a photograph where each row of people
has the tallest in the middle. Must have data in file
students.data and the number of people must be a multiple
of rowsize.}

  CONST
    rowsize = 7;
  TYPE
    keys = real;   {metres}
    items = record
          name : string;
          height : keys;
        end;

    {$I Listpoi1.pas}
  VAR
    row : integer;
    students : lists;
    data : text;

  PROCEDURE Visit (s : items);
    BEGIN
      writeln(' ':10,s.name:20,s.height:5:2);
    END; {Visit}

  {$I Listpoi2.pas}

  PROCEDURE LineUp (var students : lists);
    var s : items;
    p : positions;
    BEGIN
      reset(data,'Students.data');
      ListInit(students);
      while not eof(data) do begin
        readln(data,s.height, s.name);
        ListSearch(students,s.height,p,less);
        AddBefore(students,p,s,s.height);
      end;
      writeln('The students in height order are:');
      ListScan(Students);
```

```
            readln;
        END; {LineUp}

    PROCEDURE PickOff (var students:lists; n, row : integer);
        var i : integer;
        line : lists;
        s : items;
        h : keys;

        BEGIN
            writeln('Row ',row);
            ListInit(line);
            Remove(students,students.front,s,h);
            AddAfter(line,line.back,s,h);
            i := 0;
            while i < n div 2 do begin
                i := i + 1;
                Remove(students,students.front,s,h);
                AddAfter(line,line.back,s,h);
                Remove(students,students.front,s,h);
                AddBefore(line,line.front,s,h);
            end;
            ListScan(line);
            writeln; readln;
            for i := 1 to n do
                Remove(line,line.front,s,h);
        END; {Pickoff}

    BEGIN
        writeln('**** The Class Photo *****');
        LineUp(students);
        row := 0;
        while Students.size > 0 do begin
            row := row +1;
            PickOff (students,rowsize, row);
        end;
    END.
```

Testing   Suppose we have the following data file:

```
1.80 Danie du Toit
1.58 Petra le Roux
1.90 Stefan Wessels
1.55 Henrietta Botha
1.81 Mary Peel
1.75 Craig Leeming
1.71 Size Shongwe
1.77 Diamond Chabalala
1.40 Tiny Claasens
1.79 Michael Bishop
1.76 Robert Browne
1.69 Elizabeth Rogers
1.68 Lucy Mullins
1.50 Adrian de Villiers
```

The program would process this and produce the following arrangement:

```
**** The Class Photo *****
The students in height order are:
            Stefan Wessels 1.90
                Mary Peel 1.81
```

```
       Danie du Toit 1.80
      Michael Bishop 1.79
   Diamond Chabalala 1.77
       Robert Browne 1.76
       Craig Leeming 1.75
        Size Shongwe 1.71
     Elizabeth Rogers 1.69
        Lucy Mullins 1.68
       Petra le Roux 1.58
     Henrietta Botha 1.55
   Adrian de Villiers 1.50
        Tiny Claasens 1.40
```

Row 1

```
       Craig Leeming 1.75
   Diamond Chabalala 1.77
       Danie du Toit 1.80
      Stefan Wessels 1.90
          Mary Peel 1.81
      Michael Bishop 1.79
       Robert Browne 1.76
```

Row 2

```
       Tiny Claasens 1.40
     Henrietta Botha 1.55
        Lucy Mullins 1.68
        Size Shongwe 1.71
     Elizabeth Rogers 1.69
       Petra le Roux 1.58
   Adrian de Villiers 1.50
```

The program has the restriction that the number of students must be a multiple of the row size, but this is a minor detail.

Implementing linked lists

We have assumed that the lists will be implemented using pointers. Since insertion and deletion are allowed anywhere, it would be messy to use an array. We have also committed ourselves to supplying a front and back pointer, and to maintaining the size of the list.

There are still, however, several choices to be made in the implementation. The first issue is whether we go for a singly-linked list or a doubly-linked list. A singly-list list will have links going from the front pointer to the last node, where the pointer will be nil. The list's back pointer will point here too. Graphically, we have:

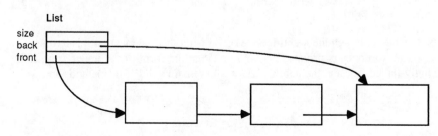

The advantage of this implementation is that it uses up the minimum of extra space (one pointer per node). However, it is not so easy to insert nodes before another node, and scanning the list backwards will require recursion.

An alternative is to spend an extra pointer per node and to link the list in both directions. This gives us:

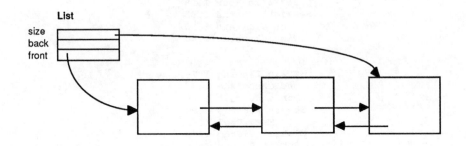

This is the most flexible arrangement, and is not all that difficult to maintain.

The declarations for a doubly-linked implementation of linked lists are:

```
{LISTS object using pointers Part I - File Listpoil.pas
   REQUIRES types items and keys to be defined}

   TYPE
   {PUBLIC}
     conditions = (equal, less, more);
          positions
   {PRIVATE}
     = ^ nodes;
     nodes = record
       forward, backward : positions;
       key : keys;
       data : items;
       end;
   {PUBLIC}
     lists
       {PROCEDURE ListInit
        PROCEDURE AddBefore
        PROCEDURE AddAfter
        PROCEDURE Remove
        PROCEDURE ListSearch
        PROCEDURE ListScan}
       = RECORD
          front, back : positions;
          size : integer;
       END;
```

Notice that although the identifier `position` is public, the fact that it is defined as a pointer to nodes is private. We could change the form of the nodes (say, to a singly-linked list) and the public parts would remain valid. The methods are:

```
{LISTS object using pointers Part II - File listpoi2.pas}

PROCEDURE ListInit (var list : lists);
```

```
        BEGIN
            list.front := nil;
            list.back := nil;
            list.size := 0;
        END; {ListInit}

    PROCEDURE AddBefore
        (var list : lists; pos : positions; x : items; k : keys);
        VAR node : positions;
        BEGIN
            new(node);
            node^.data := x;
            node^.key := k;
            node^.forward := nil;
            node^.backward := nil;
            if list.size = 0 then begin
                list.front := node;
                list.back := node;
            end else if pos=nil then begin
                node^.backward := list.back;
                list.back^.forward := node;
                list.back := node;
            end else if pos = list.front then begin
                node^.forward := list.front;
                list.front^.backward := node;
                list.front := node;
            end else begin
                node^.forward := pos;
                node^.backward := pos^.backward;
                pos^.backward^.forward := node;
                pos^.backward:=node;
            end;
            list.size := list.size + 1;
        END; {AddBefore}

    PROCEDURE AddAfter
        (var list : lists; pos : positions; x : items; k : keys);
        var node : positions;
        BEGIN
            new(node);
            node^.data := x;
            node^.key := k;
            node^.forward := nil;
            node^.backward := nil;
            if list.size = 0 then begin
                list.front := node;
                list.back := node;
            end else if (pos=nil) or (pos=list.back) then begin
                node^.backward := list.back;
                list.back^.forward := node;
                list.back := node;
            end else begin
                node^.backward := pos;
                node^.forward := pos^.forward;
                pos^.forward^.backward := node;
                pos^.forward:=node;
            end;
            list.size := list.size + 1;
        END; {AddAfter}
```

```
PROCEDURE Remove (var list : lists;
   pos : positions; var x : items; var k : keys);
   BEGIN
      x := pos^.data;
      k := pos^.key;
      if pos=list.front then begin
         list.front^.forward^.backward := nil;
         list.front := list.front^.forward;
      end else if pos=list.back then begin
         list.back^.backward^.forward := nil;
         list.back := list.back^.backward;
      end else begin
         pos^.backward^.forward:=pos^.forward;
         pos^.forward^.backward:=pos^.backward;
      end;
      dispose(pos);
      list.size := list.size-1;
   END; {Remove}

PROCEDURE ListSearch(list : lists; k : keys; var pos :
positions; condition : conditions);
   VAR state : (searching, notthere, found);
   okay : boolean;
   BEGIN
      pos := list.front;
      state := searching;
      REPEAT
         if pos = nil then state := notthere
         else begin
            case condition of
               equal : okay := pos^.key = k;
               less : okay := pos^.key < k;
               more : okay := pos^.key > k;
            end;
            if okay then state := found else
            pos := pos^.forward;
         end;
      UNTIL state <> searching;
   END; {ListSearch}

PROCEDURE ListScan(list : lists);
   VAR pos : positions;
   BEGIN
      pos := list.front;
      while pos <> nil do begin
         visit(pos^.data);
         pos := pos^.forward;
      end;
   END; {ListScan}
```

In the add and remove procedures, we consider three different cases, depending
on whether the list is empty or we are dealing with an end, whereupon the front
and back pointers need special attention. In the general case, the insertion of a
node follows the symmetric pattern:

```
node^.backward := pos;
node^.forward := pos^.forward;
pos^.forward^.backward := node;
pos^.forward:=node;
```

and deletion is done by:

```
pos^.backward^.forward:=pos^.forward;
pos^.forward^.backward:=pos^.backward;
```

WHAT WE HAVE LEARNT

*We learnt about the properties and implementation for four class data structures – stacks, queues, trees and linked lists. A **stack** was defined with five methods, used in an example (reversing a string) and then implemented with arrays and with pointers. A **queue** was defined as circular and bounded with five methods, used in an example (doctor's waiting room) and then implemented with arrays and with pointers.*

*Trees were discussed in general, specialized to a binary tree, defined with six methods, used in an example (file directory) and implemented with pointers. The tree type was further refined to an ordered tree with an additional method and used in a treesort example. **Linked lists** were defined with six methods, used in an example (photograph line up) and implemented using pointers.*

QUIZ

1.   Which data structures allow any nodes to be deleted?
2.   If insertion had to be allowed anywhere, which data structure should I use?
3.   Which data structures cannot be scanned?
4.   What happens if we try to pop an empty stack?
5.   Why did we decide on representing the queue as a circle?
6.   Draw a tree for the headings in this chapter.
7.   On Figure 15.3 (b), show where the command Exit would be added.
8.   Why do linked lists need two different Add procedures?
9.   What are the advantages of doubly linked lists?
10.   Is the root of a tree a record?

PROBLEMS

15.1   **Palindromes again** Solve the palindrome problem (Problem 9.8) using a stack rather than recursion.

15.2   **Maximum queue** Set up the solution for Example 15.2 with pointers and no bounds, and find the maximum size that queue attains over 100 patients.

15.3 **File directory** Run Example 15.3 and understand it!

15.4 **Reserved words** Create a tree storage system for the Pascal reserved words listed in Appendix 1, and develop a recognizer for detecting if a word is reserved or not.

15.5 **Advanced cubs** Consider using a binary tree in the cubs database. What would be the advantages? Reimplement the program using the tree given in Section 15.4.

15.6 **Sorted lists** Is it possible to sort a linked list? How would it be done? Add a sorting method to the list object of Section 15.4.

Predeclared Words

Reserved words

and	end	nil	set
array	file	not	then
begin	for	of	to
case	function	or	type
const	goto	packed	until
div	if	procedure	var
do	in	program	while
downto	label	record	with
else	mod	repeat	

Predefined identifiers

Constants

true	false	maxint

Types

boolean	char	integer	real
text			

File variables

input	output

Functions

abs	arctan	chr	cos
eof	eoln	exp	ln
odd	ord	pred	round
sin	sqr	sqrt	succ
trunc			

Procedures

dispose	get	new	pack
page	put	read	readln
reset	rewrite	unpack	write
writeln			

Directives

forward

Syntax diagrams

These diagrams provide a precise description of the syntax of Pascal. The rounded boxes indicate keywords or operators, and the rectangular boxes refer to other diagrams. To use the diagrams to find the syntax of a construct, look for a keyword, and then follow the arrows, filling in the rectangular boxes with the appropriate construct.

Letter

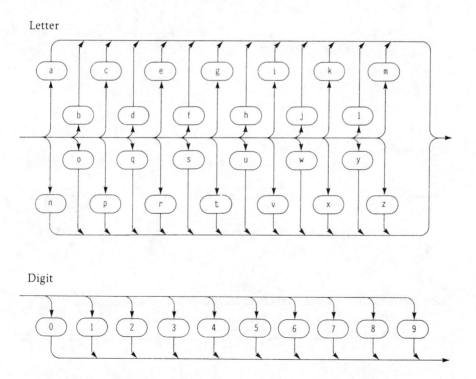

Digit

The publishers wish to thank Springer-Verlag for permission to reproduce this appendix from *Pascal User Manual and Report* 3rd edition by K. Jensen and N. Wirth.
© 1985 Springer-Verlag New York Inc.

Identifier and Directive

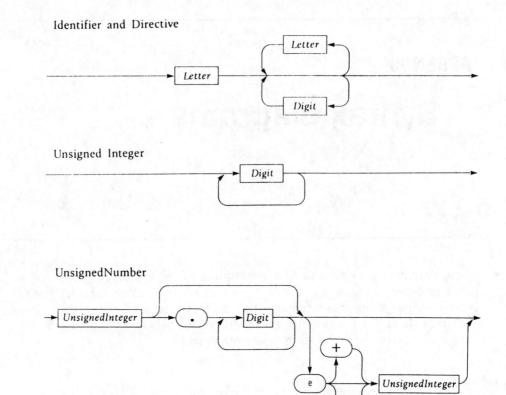

Unsigned Integer

UnsignedNumber

CharacterString

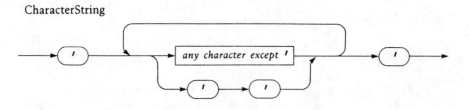

ConstantIdentifier, VariableIdentifier, FieldIdentifier, BoundIdentifier, TypeIdentifier, ProcedureIdentifier and FunctionIdentifier

Identifier

Unsigned Constant

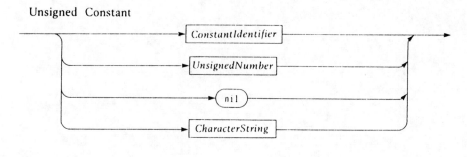

Constant

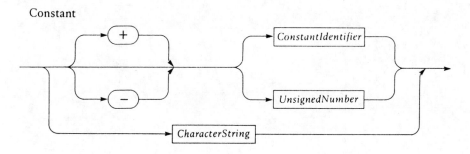

Variable

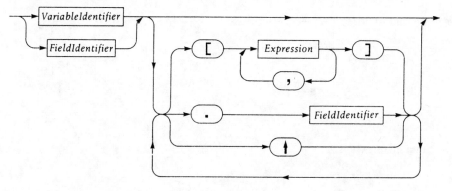

Factor

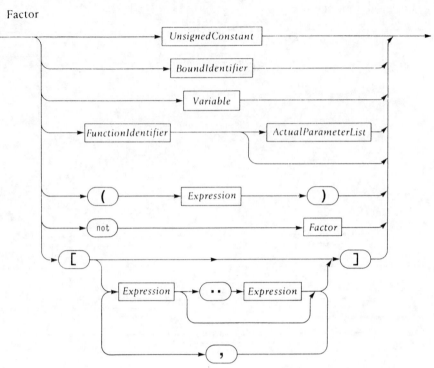

Term

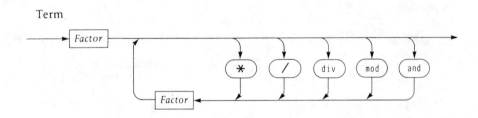

SimpleExpression

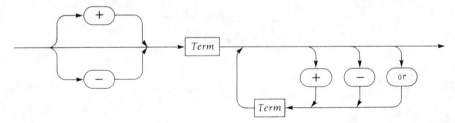

Expression

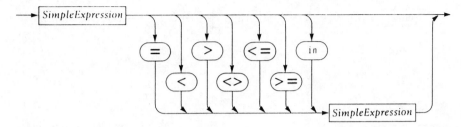

ActualParameterList

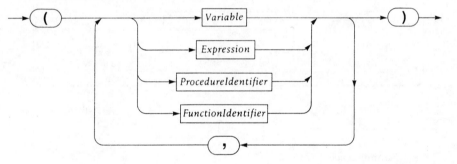

WriteParameterList

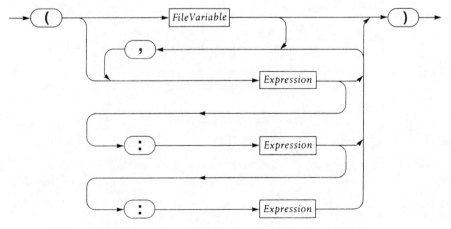

IndexTypeSpecification

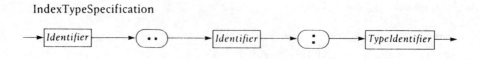

ConformantArraySchema

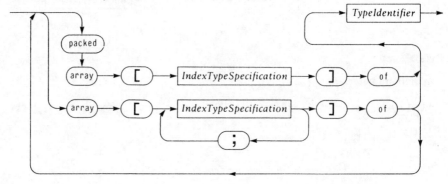

FormalParameterList

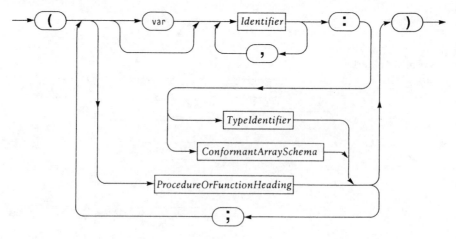

ProcedureOrFunctionHeading

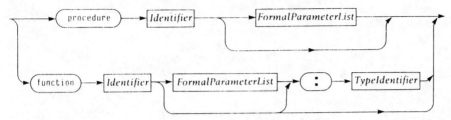

OrdinalType

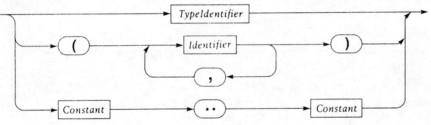

Type

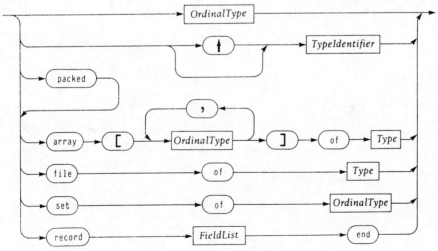

FieldList

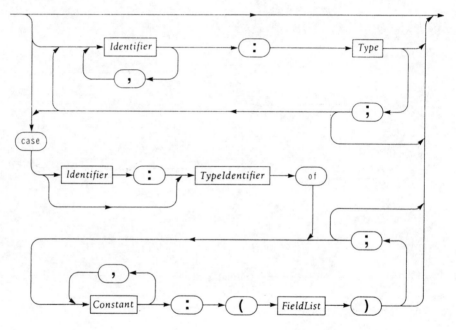

Statement

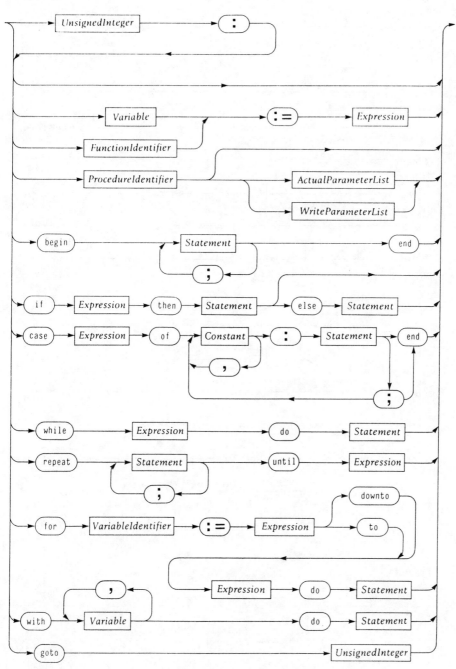

Block

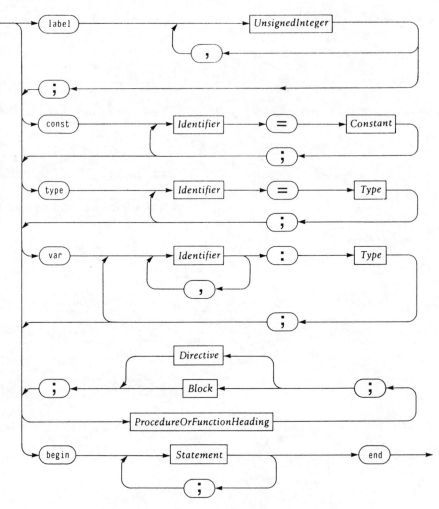

Program

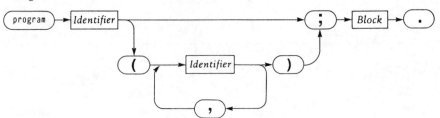

Answers to Quizzes

1. The hardware, software and devices that are available will limit a computer's capabilities.

2. Multi-programming involves several programs sharing time on a single computer.

3. A microcomputer usually has all the necessary software and devices to make it a general-purpose tool; a microprocessor is usually designed and programmed for a single embedded application; a personal computer is another name for a microcomputer, but with the emphasis being on software which is used in the home and office (such as spreadsheets, word processors, games); there are different sorts of chips – memory chips, processor chips and so on, and several go into a single microprocessor.

4. Mips (millions of instructions per second) or Megaflops (millions of floating point operations per second) are most usual.

5. RAM is random access memory for reading and writing, whereas ROM is for read-only access.

6. A compiler translates a program in a high-level language like Pascal into the machine code of the computer.

7. Unambiguous, precise, finite, self-checking and brief notation.

8. A compilation error indicates an error in the formulation of a construct in a language, whereas an execution error indicates an error in the logic of the program.

9. The cursor keys replace the mouse if needed.

10. Machine language consists of the codes which directly drive the hardware instructions of the computer.

QUIZ 2

1. The declarations always come before statements.
2. The last END is followed by a fullstop.
3. The string must be broken into two parts, separated by a comma.
4. No. The first statement will write 'Hello' as it is, while the second will write 'Hello' on the right hand side of 20 spaces.
5. The result is 0.25, which is a real number. To print it out, we could use :4:2, or anything greater than 4, with 2 decimal places.
6. Named constants contribute towards the readability of a program. Changes to constants need only be made in one place, reducing the chance of errors.
7. The first loop would print nothing because there is no range between 9 and 0. The second loop will print 7 stars.
8. Although the statements under the for-statement are indented, there is no `begin-end` bracketing them. Therefore the loop applies only to the first statement, and we get:

    ```
    1 2 3 4 5 ***** ***** … +
    ```

    The five numbers are printed. Then the value of `number` is not defined, and the second loop could go on for ever, or not at all. The plus may or may not get printed.

    The way to fix the problem, is to add the `begin-end` as was the intention.
9. The number of spaces needed before the start of the name is 40 less half the name's length. Suppose the length of your name is 8 letters. Then we would say:

    ```
    writeln(space:40-4,name);
    ```
10. The first even number is 2, otherwise known as twice one. If we run the loop from 1 to 20 and print out twice the loop variable each time, we are done.

    ```
    for i := 1 to 20 do write(i * 2 : 5);
    ```

QUIZ 3

1. Yes, a procedure call is a statement.
2. No, writeln is a predefined procedure. It can actually be redefined as something else (though this would be unwise).
3. Comments are used at the end of procedures to repeat the name; in declarations to amplify the units; and in conjunction with ordinary statements that may be too complex to stand on their own.
4. The `price` parameter must be set to a space. A typical call might be:

    ```
    VaryBox (10,5,'-','|',' ');
    ```
5. `Price` was declared as a character so that it would be restricted to a fixed size, and so that it could be replaced by a space, as in the previous question.

6. The following are not valid identifiers:

`second_value`	underscores not permitted in Standard Pascal
`1stvalue`	an identifier must start with a letter
`Hello!`	identifiers may not contain special characters
`end`	end is a keyword
`water-level`	identifiers may not contain hyphens
`Number of lines`	identifiers may not contain spaces.

7. The following two calls are invalid:

`Mountain (10,10)`	the second parameter must be a character.
`Mountain (6)`	there must be two parameters.

8. Yes, comments can extend over several lines.

9. The following will result in syntax errors.

`K = 1,000`	cannot use a comma in a number.
`Prize = D50`	D50 is not a valid constant – must just use 50.
`2ndPrize = D25`	Identifier must start with a letter. D25 not valid.
`i,j,k`	k is being redefined.
`start, end`	end is a keyword.

10.

identifier

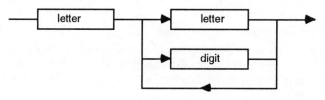

QUIZ 4

1.
```
VAR
    roman      : char;
    distance   : 100..10000;
    weight     : real; {0.5 to 10 kg, probably}
    age        : 4..19;
    minute     : 0..59;
    balance    : real; {0 to something very large}
```

2.
```
VAR
    h1, m1, s1, h2, m2, s2, ht, mt, st : integer;

        BEGIN
          ht := h2;
          mt := m2;
          st := s2;
          h2 := h1;
          m2 := m1;
          s2 := s1;
          h1 := ht;
```

```
        m2 := mt;
        s2 := st;
    END;
```

3. Screen creep occurs when prompts for data cause the screen to scroll too rapidly. It can be avoided by keeping prompts and answers on the same line.

4. There is always scope for named constants. The range of 5..15 could be specified as going from some minimum year to some maximum. The constant 1.1 in the call to histo is obscure: it actually refers to the 10% extra interest on the growth plan. It would also be better specified as a constant with an explanatory comment. The 100 is a dimensionless figure related to percentages, and can stay as it is.

5. A write–readln sequence has several advantages. The write on its own ensures that screen creep is minimized, as the reply will appear on the same line. The readln then forces the return key to be pressed, which is a normal reflex for users, and also serves to terminate the data. (Numbers are terminated by a space, tab or return).

6. In this program several data values are to be read per line, so write–read is more appropriate. A space will terminate most numbers, and when the user sees that the end of a line is near, the return can be pressed instead.

7. The output will be

    67   98   91

8. This one is up to you!

9. I think that the computer should trap the use of an uninitialized variable, as it traps invalid subranges. However this is seldom done.

10. In order to read numbers with units simply, we must insist that a space separates the number and the unit, for example 65 kgs. In addition, in order to skip the units, if that is required, each data item must be on its own line, and the return key with readln be used to skip the units.

QUIZ 5

1. If a key-value appeared more than once, it would not be clear as to which statement should be followed.

2. The loop variable must be initialized and its value must be altered during the course of the loop.

3. Suitable trailer values would be:
    - for ages of people, a zero might do, but if babies are included then a negative number is needed;
    - air temperatures in Celsius range from about −20 to 50. A value of 99 would be quite impossible;
    - years can often be restricted to start from 1900, say, and projected only as far as 2050 or so, leaving 0 as a suitable trailer.

4.

> ### RSP – Instructions
>
> This is the guessing game for two players. I can play you. We each choose one object – rocks, scissors, paper. Then we see whose object dominates, and that person wins. Domination is determined as follows:
>
> > rock can smash scissors,
> >
> > scissors can cut paper,
> >
> > paper can wrap up a rock.
>
> I shall make my choice secretly, and you enter yours on the keyboard as R S or P. Good luck!

5.   The loop uses the first number as the starting point for the highest. It can also be the starting point for the lowest number.

```
read(highest);
lowest := highest;
for i := 2 to n do begin
  read(number);
  if number > highest then highest := number;
  if number < lowest then lowest := number;
end;
```

6.   Pre can only have one of the values, so once one is found, there is no sense in checking further; the statements should be connected with `else` :

```
if pre = 'm' then write('milli') else
if pre = 'c' then write('centi') else
if pre = 'K' then write('kilo');
```

7.   The then-part consists only of the statement `temp := x`, since there is no `begin-end` bracketing the indented statements. So `temp` will sometimes get set to x and the other two statements will always be executed, the last with unpredictable results in some cases.

8.   The variable `total` has not been set to zero before the loop begins.

9.   The program should halt with an execution error.

10.
```
VAR
   symbol : char;
   rate : real;

case symbol of
   'F' : rate := francsperdolly;
   'M' : rate := marksperdolly;
   '£' : rate := poundsperdolly;
   '$' : rate := dollarsperdolly;
end
```

QUIZ 6

1. The properties that define a data type are: range of values; notation for constants; input and output capabilities; operators; procedures and functions.

2. `write(-maxint)` will get close.

3. Assuming that the field width for integers is 10 characters, we have:

    ```
    1948~~~~~~194800
    ```

    Notice that the values are written close up to each other, unless field indicators or explicit spaces are inserted.

4. `mod` is not defined for negative divisors.

    `exp` cannot raise a negative number to a real power.

    `ln` is not defined for negative values.

    `arctan` – no restriction.

5.
    ```
    possiblyleap := (day = 29) and (month = 2);
    ```

6. The expression does not constrain the interval as required. We need `and` not `or`.

7. `Temp` has not been initialised to zero.

8. To adapt the for-loop, we must run it over all the readings, expressed as integers from 1 to 600, and divide by ten when printing.

    ```
    total := 0;
    for sec := 1 to 600 do begin
       write(sec / 10:4:1);   read(temp);
       total := total + temp;
    end;
    ```

    Other possibilities using conditional loops are:

    ```
    total := 0;                        total := 0;
    sec := 0.1;  sec := 0.1;
    while sec < 60.1 do begin          repeat
       write(sec:4:1);                    write(sec:4:1);
       read(temp);                        read(temp);
       total := total + temp;             total := total + temp;
          sec := sec + 0.1;               sec := sec + 0.1;
    end;                               until sec > 60.0;
    ```

    Notice that equality on real numbers is avoided.

9. In a computer with 11 digits of precision, the 9-digit constant can be stored comfortably. Writing it out with a field width of 10:6 will give ~~3.141593. However, in a - digit computer, the full constant will not even be stored. Only 3.141 will fit. Therefore, writing it out with 10:6 will yield ~~3.141000.

10.
    ```
    shift := trunc(time) div + 1;
    ```

QUIZ 7

1. It could be one of several possibilities. My computer uses ESC N.
2. No, they should have the same effect, since input is the default input file.
3.
```
VAR
    fin : text;
    lines : integer;
BEGIN
    reset (fin);
    lines := 0;
    while not eof(fin) do begin
       readln(fin);
       lines := lines + 1;
    end;
END;
{The answer is in lines}
```

4. Over to you.
5. Yes, it will work, except that on many systems we must remember to close the output file, in this case g.
6.
```
VAR screen : window;

BEGIN
    whole (screen);
    gotoxy (screen, 32,12);
    writestr(screen,'Judy Bishop');
END;
```

7. The first parameter to the window procedure is the name of the window, and the next four are its upper left and bottom right coordinates. The order of the coordinates is $x1$, $y1$, $x2$, $y2$.
8. We put a loop running from 1 to 4 around the existing loop. This will print four rows of the four labels.
9.
```
VAR Top, Bottom : windows;

window (Top, 1,1,80,12);
window (Bottom, 1,13,80,24);
```

10. A number is terminated by a space as well as by a return. If a file has extra spaces or returns after its last number, a reading loop will not correctly identify a number as the last one, and will look for one after the extra spaces. The absence of such a number will cause a read-past-end-of-file execution error.

QUIZ 8

There is no Quiz 8.

QUIZ 9

---

1. No, real numbers cannot appear in subranges;

2. Yes, subscripts can be negative integers.

3. A row of a matrix (the first dimension) can be regarded as a variable in its own right and passed as a parameter.

4. No, unfortunately, an array cannot be the result of a function.

5. The first will print winter in 10 characters, that is `Winter     !` and the second will print `Winter!` .

6. `PROCEDURE P (a, b : integer; var c : real; d : real);`

7. Yes, and it is sometimes convenient to do so.

8. No, they are both in the same declaration level.

9. The program is going to print four rows of something. The printing involves calling `modify`, writing out the values of the two main variables `row` and `length`, and then calling the procedure `line`. `modify` looks at its input parameter, `v`, and creates a value for its output parameter, `x`, accordingly. `line` on the other hand, writes out the `row` value a certain number of times, depending on its input parameter. Put altogether, we get:

   ```
   1    0
   2    3 2 2 2
   3    6 3 3 3 3 3 3
   4    12 4 4 4 4 4 4 4 4 4 4 4
   ```

10. Yes. They can be accessed as if it were a multi-dimensional array.

QUIZ 10

---

1. No, values of an enumerated type must be identifiers.

2. No, unfortunately enumerated types cannot be read or written.

3. Yes, records can be assigned.

4.
   ```
   VAR
       x : of the type of the file

   BEGIN
       reset(f);
       rewrite(g);

       WHILE not eof(f) do begin
           read(f,x);
           write(g,x);
       END;
       {Perhaps, close(g)}
   ```

5. No, there will be confusion between the fields referred to in the statement that follows.

6. No, only sets of discrete values are allowed.

7. Enumerated types cannot consist of integers – only newly declared identifiers.

    • enumerated types cannot be read with the read procedure.

    • `Coinset` is a type, so we cannot use it with the `in` operator. We must define, declare and initialise a set for the coins, such as:

    ```
    TYPE
      change = set of coins;
    VAR
      pocket : change;
    pocket := [ ];

    if n in pocket then ...
    ```

8.
    ```
    TYPE
      illness = set of symptoms;
    ```

9. `flu * cold`

10. `chr(ord(ch) - ord('a') + ord('A'))`

QUIZ 11

1. 35 will be found on the first probe.

2. The search will consider the numbers in this order (assuming that in odd divisions the extra number goes to the left): 41, 25, 35.

3. 500

4. 10

5. Selection sort: 41.66 minutes. Quicksort: 0.76 seconds.

6. Binary search requires that the items be sorted; linear search does not mind.

7. Linear search will take on average 500 probes. Quicksort will need 10 000 comparisons to sort, followed by 10 probes to find the number. A comparison is roughly equivalent to a probe, so it looks as though the straight search wins.

8.
    ```
    (j + k) div 2
    ```

9. If x is not in the array, then the loop will run on uncontrollably.

10. There is a limit, imposed by the maximum size of an array permitted in your system's memory. It may limit the sort to thousands or maybe even hundreds of elements.

QUIZ 12

1. Object Oriented Programming Systems

2. Objects, inheritance and late binding.

3. Turbo Pascal will.

4. So as to distinguish them from similar methods in other objects.

5.

```
VAR
    date1, date2 : date;

if DateLessThan (date1, date2) then
    DateDisplay (date1) else DateDisplay (date2);
```

6.

```
VAR
    wd1, wd2 : WinDate;
    W : windows;

if WinDatesLessThan (wd1, wd2) then
    WinDateDisplay (W, wd1) else WinDateDisplay (W, wd2);
```

7. QuickShow is a streamlined version of Show that also prints out the prompt symbol '>' and waits at that position on the screen for a reply.

8. Extract is a recursive procedure to create a digit-by-digit version so that it can be processed by writech.

9. Window itself is the constructor.

10. As it stands the Windows object does not have a destructor. Since it only represents a boundary on a screen, it is unlike that it would need a destructor.

QUIZ 13

1. No, all fields in a record must be distinct.

2. There are five fields: name, birth, MaritalStatus, spouse and occupation.

3.

```
TYPE
    realdate = record
        case status : statustype of
            unset, unknown : ( );
            half : year : years;
            full : d : dates;
        end;
    end;
```

4. low and high are defined in the procedure parameter list as part of the definition of the conformant array T.

5. If the bounds may differ in the actual arrays, then we need to have different names for calling them during the execution of P.

```
PROCEDURE P (A : array[low1..high1  : integer] of type1;
             B : array[low2..high2 : integer] of type2);
```

6. Since the types are different, two different entries in the parameter list are needed.

```
PROCEDURE Q (A : array[low1..high1  : integer] of type1;
             B : array[low2..high2 : integer] of type2);
```

7. No, all types can be compared for equality using the equality operator =.

8. First of all we need two functions, one for the equation, and one for its derivative. These are:

```
FUNCTION equation (x : real) : real;
   BEGIN
      equation := x*x*x - 3*x*x + 2;
   END; {equation}

FUNCTION equationdiff (x : real) : real;
   BEGIN
      equationdiuff := 3*x*x - 6*x;
   END; {equation diff}
```

Then to call the solver, we could use

```
NewtonRaphson (x, x0, i, 50, 1E-6, equation, equationdiff);
```

QUIZ 14

14.1   The number of variables does not have to be decided in advance. Complex linked data structures can be easily created.

14.2   There is an overhead to be paid for the links. The variables are no longer directly accessible by index.

3.   New(p) creates space for a new variable of the type defined by p's pointed-to type, and sets p to point to it.

4.   The first assignment copies the pointers so that they will both now point to the same physical place. The previous heap variable pointed to by b will be lost. The second assignment copies the contents of b's variable over into a's, so that the contents of a's will now be lost.

5.   In most cases, we wish to create lists of variables on the heap, and each will need its own pointer. Therefore the heap variables have at least two fields: one the link pointer, and one for actual values.

6.   No, pointers are reserved for the type of variable specified in the declaration.

7.
```
new (guest);
guest^.name:= 'Peter       ';
guest^.next := family;
family := guest;
```

8.

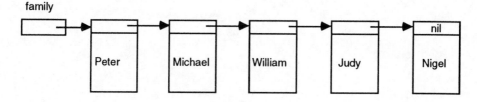

9. William. Remember that the list is stored backwards, so that `guests` will point to the Mullins family, and the first member of each family will be the last one entered.

10. `Dispose(p);`

QUIZ 15

1. Trees and linked lists.

2. Linked lists and possibly trees, depending on the relationships between nodes.

3. Stacks.

4. In our implementation, nothing.

5. A queue 'moves along' and whether we use an array or pointer representation, we need to constrain this property.

6. We give here the first four sections.

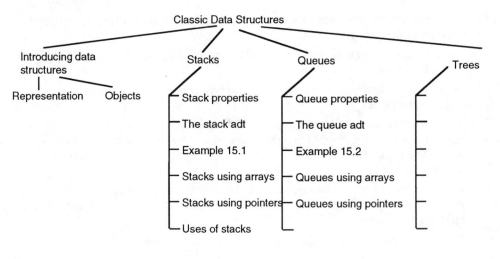

7.

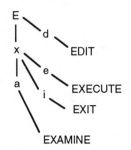

8. When scanning a linked list, we may end up one past the particular node we are interested in. Thus we would need to add before where we are. In other cases, we wish to add after.

9. In a doubly linked list, scanning is more efficient in either direction, and one can backtrack. For example, if we go beyond the point we are interested in, we can easily go back, and then add after. In this case we could make do with only one Add procedure.

10. No, it is usually just a pointer.

Answers to Selected Problems

CHAPTER 3

3.1 **Printing names** As a sample, the procedure for 'm' would look like this:

```
PROCEDURE m;
   BEGIN
      writeln('******');
      writeln('     *');
      writeln('  ****');
      writeln('     *');
      writeln('******');
   END; {m}
```

Given that the other letters' procedures are similarly defined, then the program might look like this:

```
PROGRAM William (input, output);
   BEGIN
      W; i; l; l; i; a; m;
   END.
```

The important point to grasp in this example is the concept of the identifier for a procedure. We have assumed that the procedures have single letter names. This might be confusing if we wanted to use these names somewhere else (for example, as a loop variable), so instead we could choose names such as `printm`, `printi` and so on. Then the program would be:

```
PROGRAM William (input, output);
   BEGIN
      printW; printi; printl; printl;
      printi; printa; printm;
   END.
```

Can you see whether there would be a problem with writing the name 'Susan' in this way? *Two* procedures for 's' would have to be defined, and they would have to have different names. Prints and prints are the same name, since Pascal does not regard cases as different.

3.4 **Times tables** . There are three nested loops here. The outermost one runs down the page for each group of tables. It goes from 1 to 4, there being 4 groups of 3. The next loop goes down the lines of each group, from 1 to 12. The final loop goes across the page for the three tables in a group. In addition, each group must have three headings printed. It therefore makes sense to parcel up the printing of a group into a procedure, with two parameters indicating the first and last tables. A suitable program would be:

```
PROGRAM OldenDays (input, output);
  VAR
    down : 1..4;

PROCEDURE PrintThreeAcross (first, last : integer);
  VAR
    across, line : 1..12;
  BEGIN
    for across := first to last do
      write(across:2, ' times table    ');
      writeln;
      for line := 1 to 12 do begin
        for across := first to last do
          write(line:2, ' x ',across:2, ' = ',
                        line*across:3,' ':5);
        writeln;
      end;
  END; {PrintThreeAcross}

BEGIN
  writeln('******* Times Tables up to 12 *****');
  for down := 1 to 4 do begin
    PrintThreeAcross ((down-1)*3+1,down*3);
    writeln; writeln;
  end;
END.
```

CHAPTER 4

4.3 **Fibonacci** The program is really quite simple:

```
PROGRAM Fibonacci (output);
  VAR
    first,
    second,
    sum    : 1..100;  {say}
    i          : 3..10;     {say}
  BEGIN
    writeln('****** First 10 Fibonacci numbers ******');
    first := 1;
    second := 1;
    write(first, '   ', second);
    for i := 3 to 10 do begin
```

```
        sum := first + second;
        write ('   ', sum);
        first := second;
        second := sum;
    end;
    writeln;
END.
```

CHAPTER 5

5.2   **Rainfall figures** The solution to this problem involves a mixture of the algorithms for summing numbers and for finding the largest one, and the mixture is all wrapped up in loops for the weeks and days. It is vital to have a clear picture of the algorithm before proceeding to the program. The positioning of the checks and loops is shown in the pseudo-code chart:

Calculate rainfall

Initialize wettest day total and number
Initialize driest week number

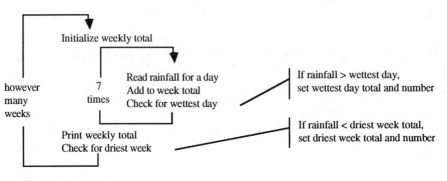

Print wettest day number
Print driest week number

Notice that the checking for the wettest day and driest week involves keeping track of two variables – the actual rainfall and the day or week number. In order to find the maximum rainfall for the wettest day, the total can be initialized to zero; for the driest week, the initializing is not so clear and it is necessary to choose something impossibly large.

Recording the wettest day also has its problems because in the loop, the day number will run from 1 to 7, but ultimately, the wettest day must be recorded in the range 1 to 28. To perform this mapping, the week number must be taken into account.

5.3   **Golf scores** The solution to the Golf Course problem is based on finding the lowest number; the handling of the handicap and par are very much side issues. Obviously, the algorithm for finding the highest number (Example 5.2) can be adapted to find the lowest.

A point to note is how the question suggests that the prompts, data and results should all appear on a single line. This will require deft use of write, read, and writeln. What follows is a suitable main program, omitting the procedures that it calls. Notice how the use of procedures makes the main program really easy to read.

```
PROGRAM GolfScorer (input, output);
  CONST
      par              = 30;
      NoofHoles        = 9;
      maxplayers       = 6;
      maxscore         = 100;
  VAR
      player,
      winner        :  1 .. maxplayers;
      handicap,
      total,
      result,
      winningresult :  0 .. 100; {say}

  BEGIN
    writeln('***** Golf Scoring Program ******');
    writeln;
    PrintHeading;
    player := 1;
    ReadHandicap;
    ReadandTotalShots;
    PrintOutcome;
    winner := player;
    winningresult := result;
    FOR player := 2 to Noofplayers do begin
       ReadHandicap;
       ReadandTotalShots;
       PrintOutcome;
       CheckforWinner;
    END;
    AnnounceWinner;
  END.
```

5.7 **Rabbits!** Two things happen every three months: the children become adults, and new children are born. As formulated here, everything happens in pairs, so we can base our calculations on pairs, too. The program is centred around a simple while loop, which stops when we run out of room. The results you should get are:

```
***** Rabbit populations *****

We assume that a pair of rabbits of 3 months or over
produces 2 more rabbits every 3 months.

In 27 months there will be more than 500 rabbits.
```

CHAPTER 7

7.3 **File splitter** We give here the full Pascal version of the program.

```
PROGRAM Splitter (input, output, all, pos, neg);
   VAR
      all, pos, neg : text;

   PROCEDURE printfile (VAR f : text);
      VAR n : integer;
      BEGIN
         reset(f);
         WHILE not eof(f) do begin
            read(f, n);
            write(n, '    ');
         END;
         writeln;
      END; {Printfile}

   BEGIN
      writeln('****** Splitting a file ******');
      writeln;
      writeln('For the data file connect to all.file');
      writeln('For the positives file connect to pos.file');
      writeln('For the negatives file connect to neg.file');
      reset(all, 'all.file');
      rewrite(neg, 'neg.file');
      rewrite(pos, 'pos.file');
      WHILE not eof(all) do begin
         read(all, n);
         if n >= 0
         then write(pos, n, '    ')
         else write(neg, n, '    ');
      END;
      close(pos);   close(neg);
      printfile(pos);
      printfile(neg);
   END.
```

Since the printing is done for both files, it is profitable to put it in a procedure. Notice, however, that the file parameter has to be declared as VAR. If the separate files are not needed later on, they could have been left as local files, unconnected to any device and existing only during the run of the program.

7.4   **Comments** This, and the next problem, are typical character processing programs. Characters are read from a file, one by one, examined, processed and written out again. The programs are made more interesting by the introduction of the notion of a paragraph; at each new paragraph, after a blank line, the counters and conditions can begin anew.

The body of the comments program is governed by a single boolean variable, inacomment, which records whether we are processing a comment or not. Depending on the value of this condition, the occurrence of a { or } at specific points will either be correct or an error. This is all shown in the program.

```
PROGRAM  Comments (input, output, data, results);
   VAR
      data, results      : text;
      ch                 : char;
      inacomment,
      endofparagraph     : boolean;
      commentcount,
```

```
          noncommentcount    : 0 .. maxint;

PROCEDURE CheckforOpenComment;
   BEGIN
      if ch = '{' then
         if inacomment {already}
         then writeln(results, '*** { found in a comment'
         else inacomment := true;
   END;  {CheckforOpenComment}

PROCEDURE CheckforCloseComment;
   BEGIN
      if ch = '}' then
         if not inacomment
         then writeln(results, '*** } no opening comment')
         else inacomment := false;
   END;  {CheckforCloseComment}

PROCEDURE CountandWrite;
   BEGIN
      if inacomment
      then commentcount := commentcount + 1
      else begin
         noncommentcount := noncommentcount + 1;
         write(results, ch);
         if eoln(data) then writeln(results);
      end;
   END; {CountandWrite}

PROCEDURE CheckforParagraph;
   {Detects a blank line}
   BEGIN
      if eoln(data) then readln(data);
      if eoln(data) then begin
         readln(data);
         endofparagraph := true;
         if inacomment then writeln(results,
                     '*** No ending bracket');
         writeln(results);
      end;
   END;   {CheckforParagraph}

BEGIN
   writeln('****** Comment checker ******');
   writeln;
   write('For data file, connect to comments.dat');
   write('For results file connect to comments.out');
   reset(data,'comments.dat');
   rewrite(results,'comments.out');
   WHILE not eof(data) do begin
      endofparagraph := true;
      commentcount := 0;
      noncommentcount := 0;
      inacomment := false;
      while not endofparagraph do begin
         read(data,ch);
         CheckforOpenComment;
         CountandWrite;
         CheckforCloseComment;
         CheckforParagraph;
      end;
```

```
            writeln('Comment is ', trunc(commentcount * 100 /
                    (commentcount + noncommentcount)):1,
                    '% of the text');
    END;
END.
```

CHAPTER 9

9.8 **Palindromes** The recursive function is:

```
FUNCTION IsPalindrome (s : phrase; left, right : range) : boolean;
    BEGIN
        if left >= right   {the stopping condition}
        then IsPalindrome := true
        else
            if s[left] = s[right]
                then IsPalindrome := IsPalindrome(s,left+1,right-1)
                else IsPalindrome := false;
    END; {IsPalindrome}
```

It would be called by an expression such as `IsPalindrome(data, 1, n)`.

CHAPTER 10

10.4 **Training schedules**. Assume that the data looks like this:

```
100 AHF
123 JHU
99 U
77 JHAF
213 BAF
190 AB
180 AJHUF
170 JHUF
110 BHAF
115 AHF
```

We need to keep a set of employee numbers for each course, and a set of all courses taken. This is done with the data structures:

```
CONST
    numbermax   = 250;
TYPE
    courses     = char;
    coursesets  = set of courses;
    numbers     = 000..numbermax;
    numbersets  = set of numbers;
VAR
    classlist   : array[courses] of numbersets;
    taken       : coursesets;
```

The algorithm then consists of reading in a number followed by courses until an end of line, and for each course, we add the number to the set in the array indexed by its character. The important statement is:

```
classlist[c] := classlist[c] + [number];
```

To get the full set of courses taken, we construct the union of all courses read in, as in

```
taken := taken + [c];
```

The rest of the program is concerned with printing out the sets neatly, four numbers to a line. The program is suprisingly simple. A striking feature of it is that the procedures do not use parameters. This is because there are only two main data structures, they are used from all parts of the program, and it would be superfluous to keep passing them in and out of the procedures. We do, of course, declare all other variables locally where they are needed.

```
PROGRAM Trainingschedule (input, output);
  CONST
     numbermax      = 250;
     space          = ' ';
  TYPE
     courses            = char;
     coursesets     = set of courses;
     numbers        = 000..numbermax;
     numbersets     = set of numbers;

  VAR
     data           : text;
     classlist      : array[courses] of numbersets;
     taken          : coursesets;

  PROCEDURE InitializeSets;
   VAR c : courses;
   BEGIN
     for c := 'A' to 'Z' do
       classlist[c] := [ ];
     taken := [ ];
   END; {InitializeSets}

  PROCEDURE ReadEmployee;
   VAR c : courses;
       number : numbers;
   BEGIN
    read(data,number);
    write(number);
    read(data,c); write(c:5); {the space}
    while not eoln(data) do begin
        read (data,c); write(c);
        classlist[c] := classlist[c] + [number];
        taken := taken + [c];
    end;
    readln(data); writeln;
   END; {ReadEmployee}

  PROCEDURE PrintClassLists;
   var c : courses;

     PROCEDURE PrintSet(class : numbersets);
       CONST numbersperline = 4;
```

```
          VAR n : numbers;
              i : 1..numbersperline;
          BEGIN
            i := 1;
            for n := 0 to numbermax do
               if n in class then begin
                  write(n:8);
                  if i = numbersperline
                  then begin
                       writeln;
                       i := 1;
                  end else i := i + 1;
               end;
          END; {PrintSet}

       BEGIN
          writeln;
          writeln('Class Lists');
          for c := 'A' to 'Z' do
             if classlist[c] <> [ ] then begin
                writeln('Course ',c);
                PrintSet(classlist[c]);
                writeln;
             end;
          writeln;
          write('Courses used were :');
          for c := 'A' to 'Z' do
             if c in taken then write(c,space);
          writeln;
       END; {PrintClassLists}

    BEGIN
       writeln('**** Employee Training Statistics ****');
       reset (data, 'train.dat');
       InitializeSets;
       writeln('Number  Courses');
       WHILE not eof(data) do
          ReadEmployee;
       PrintClassLists;
    END.
```

A sample run would give:

```
**** Employee Training Statistics ****
  Number      Courses
    100        AHF
    123        JHU
     99        U
     77        JHAF
    213        BAF
    190        AB
    180        AJHUF
    170        JHUF
    110        BHAF
    115        AHF

Class Lists
Course A
      77       100       110      115
     180       190       213
Course B
     110       190       213
```

```
Course F
        77       100       110       115
       170       180       213
Course H
        77       100       110       115
       123       170       180
Course J
        77       123       170       180

Course U
        99       123       170       180

Courses taken were :  A B F H J U
```

10.5 **Better training schedules** The major sticking point for this extension is that we cannot use Pascal sets to store names. There are two ways of going about the solution. We could abandon sets as inadequate, and use linked lists or arrays of strings instead. Adding each employee onto the class list is then no longer the simple:

```
classlist[c] := classlist[s] + [employee]
```

but will necessitate extending the list or array. Printing is not really more difficult. However, if we are to work out how many employees are doing the same combination of any two courses, then we want to hold on to the sets, because they will enable us to use intersection to ascertain the answers.

The second approach is to keep the employee numbers and use them in the class lists, but to maintain an additional list of names for each number. All the calculations are done on the numbers, and only the printing process need change to print out names instead. If the names list is kept as an array, indexed by number, then in fact the only change will be in printset where write(n:8) becomes:

```
write(namelist[n]:8);
```

10.6 **AD and BC dates** For the input, it would be nice if the dates could remain in the traditional format. However, if the read statement is used for the number, the BC or AD part will have to be separated from the year by a space. Alternatively, the number could be read character by character and converted to an integer by a procedure.

For storing the dates, there are two possibilities. Either the year can be an integer, and a separate field of, say,

```
TYPE eras = (BC, AD);
```

could indicate what era it refers to, or we could investigate storing BC dates as negative numbers. Either way, there will be an impact on the operations. Using negative numbers might make the arithmetic easier, but the other option might be easier for writing. Try them both!

10.8 **Population increase** The technique of keeping a running maximum is now quite familiar. The interest in this example comes from the use of a record to keep the data pairs. This contributes considerably towards keeping the program tidy, and to ensuring that the pairs always move together.

The program below also goes to some lengths to produce decent output in a file, echoing the data as it comes in and printing out the increase each year. Notice that the test data is carefully chosen so that the answer can be easily checked.

```
PROGRAM Population (input, output);
  TYPE
    years = 1970 .. 2000;
    populationcounts = 0 .. maxint;
    readings = record
                  year   : years;
                  people : populationcounts;
               end;
  VAR
    data, results    : text;
    thisyear, lastyear,
    year1, year2     : readings;
    increase,
    greatestsofar    : real;

  PROCEDURE process (var R : readings);
    BEGIN
      with R do begin
        readln(data, year, people);
        write(results, year:4,people:12);
      end;
    END; {process}

BEGIN
  writeln('***** Population Statistics *****');
  writeln;
  write('For the data file connect to stats.data');
  reset (data, 'stats.data');
  rewrite (results, 'stats.out');
  write('For the results file connect to stats.out');
  writeln(results, 'Zanyland Population Statistics');
  writeln(results);
  writeln(results,'Year    Population      %Increase');
  greatestsofar := 0;
  process (lastyear);
  writeln(results);
  WHILE not eof (data) do with thisyear do begin
    process (thisyear);
    increase := (people - lastyear.people)
                   /lastyear.people * 100;
    writeln(results, increase:10:2,'%');
    if increase > greatestsofar then begin
      greatestsofar := increase;
      year1 := lastyear;
      year2 := thisyear;
    end;
    lastyear := thisyear;
  END;
  writeln(results);
  writeln(results,
      'The greatest percentage increase was ',
      greatestsofar:6:2,'% between ',year1.year:4,
      ' and ',year2.year:4);
  writeln('See the file for the results');
END.
```

The data and results are:

```
1970    1400000
1971    1410000
1972    1420000
1973    1440000
```

```
1974    1450000
1975    1460000
1976    1470000
```

```
Zanyland Population Statistics
```

Year	Population	%Increase
1970	1400000	
1971	1410000	0.71%
1972	1420000	0.71%
1973	1440000	1.41%
1974	1450000	0.69%
1975	1460000	0.69%
1976	1470000	0.68%

```
The greatest percentage increase was    1.41% between 1972
and 1973
```

10.11 **Sieve of Eratosthenes** The algorithm will use set difference to take values out of the sieve, and set union to construct the set of primes.

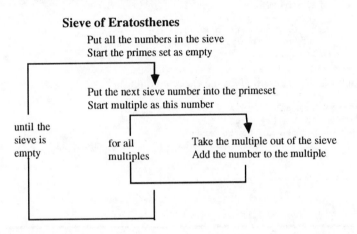

Sieve of Eratosthenes

Put all the numbers in the sieve
Start the primes set as empty

Put the next sieve number into the primeset
Start multiple as this number

until the sieve is empty   for all multiples   Take the multiple out of the sieve / Add the number to the multiple

Although we know the size of the base set, conditional rather than counting loops will be needed. In the outer one, the stopping condition will be the sieve being empty, which may occur before the last number needs to be considered.

Of course, the primes do not have to be put into a set themselves – they could just be written out, but this way there is more illustration of set manipulation!

```
PROGRAM Eratosthenes (input, output);
   CONST
      maxset = 255;
   TYPE
      baserange = 0..maxset;
      sets = set of baserange;
   VAR
      sieve, primes : sets;
      n, next,
      multiple, count : baserange;

BEGIN
   writeln('****** Primes using a sieve ******');
   write('Primes up to (<= ', maxset:1, ')? ');
```

```
         repeat
            readln(n);
         until  (n >= 2) and (n <= maxset);
         sieve := [2..n];
         primes := [   ];
         next := 2;
         count := 0;
         REPEAT
            if next in sieve then begin
               primes := primes + [next];
               count := count + 1;
               multiple := next;
               while multiple <= n do begin
                  sieve := sieve - [multiple];
                  multiple := multiple + next;
               end;
            end;
            next := next + 1;
         UNTIL sieve = [   ];
         writeln('The ', count:1, ' primes up to ',
                    n:1, ' are:');
         for next := 2 to n do
            if next in primes then write(next:1,'   ');
         writeln;
      END.
```

Running the program gives the expected output:

```
****** Primes using a sieve ******
Primes up to (<= 255)? 50
The 15 primes up to 50 are:
2    3    5    7    11    13    17    19    23    29    31    37    41
43    47
```

CHAPTER 13

13.1   Better sorting. A sorting procedure for a conformant array of names would be declared as:

```
PROCEDURE sortnames (VAR T : array[low..high : positive] of names);
```

and the standard procedure would need to refer to `low` and `high` instead of 1 and `n`. The procedure would then be called by

```
sortnames (daytable);
sortnames (seasontable);
sortnames (depttable);
```

If the tables being searched are known to be in alphabetical order, then as soon as the search has gone past the possible place for x, it can stop. The change comes in the loop as follows:

```
REPEAT
    if x = T[i] then state := found else
    if (x > T[i]) or (i = high) then state := notthere else
    i := succ(i);
UNTIL state <> searching;
```

13.2   **Improved marks**. Following the method outlined in Section 13.3, we need to declare a function for each type of ordering that we want, and link these in to a procedural parameter in the sort. The actual functions will be:

```
FUNCTION namesordered (s1, s2 : students) : boolean;
   BEGIN
      namesordered := s1. name < s2.name;
   END;

FUNCTION marksordered (s1, s2 : students) : boolean;
   BEGIN
      marksordered := s1.mark > s2.mark;
   END;
```

The sort procedure is delared as

```
PROCEDURE sortclass (VAR C : classes; n : classrange;
              FUNCTION inorder (a,b : students) : boolean));
```

and the comparison statement in the inner loop becomes

```
if inorder(C[i], C[smallest]) then ...
```

The calls to the sort would be:

```
sortclass (class,n,namesordered);
sortclass (class,n,marksordered);
```

If we wanted to keep the different lists, then we could declare some new variables and sort into them instead, for example:

```
VAR
    namelist: classes;

namelist := class;
sort (namelist, n, namesordered);
```

13.3   **Secant method** The algorithm, given below, is very similar to the Newton-Raphson method. What we need to do now is to package the algorithm up in a self-contained procedure or function. We start by defining the interface required:

      Uses   : 2 initial estimates, tolerance, maximum iterations
      Returns   : 2 final estimates, iterations taken

From this, we can devise a list of parameters and a procedure header, and proceed to write the procedure. Since there is more than one result from the method, we need a procedure and not a function.

An important consideration when writing procedures to implement iterative (that is, looping) numerical methods is whether they should print out temporary results or not. In some cases, a program is working and only the result of the method is required, but in many cases, it may be useful or necessary to have the intermediate results printed out. In order to provide this flexibility, we add one more parameter, called monitor, which is used to govern the output of the values as the loop progresses. If monitor is true, then the values are printed, and if it is false then they are not.

The Secant Method

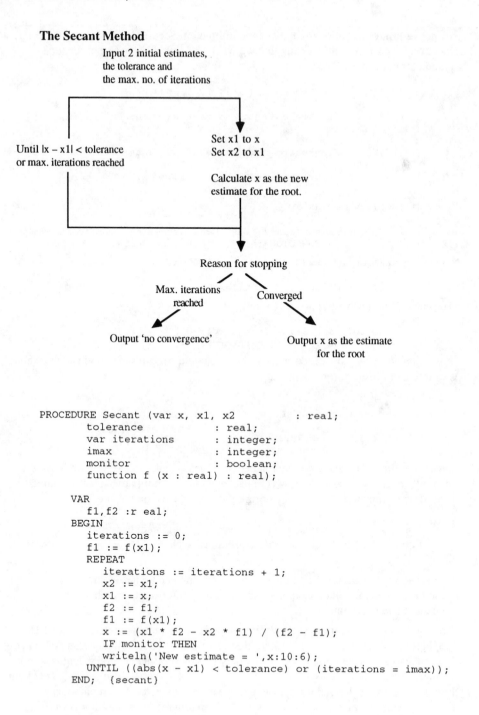

Input 2 initial estimates,
the tolerance and
the max. no. of iterations

Set x1 to x
Set x2 to x1

Until |x − x1| < tolerance
or max. iterations reached

Calculate x as the new
estimate for the root.

Reason for stopping

Max. iterations
reached

Converged

Output 'no convergence'

Output x as the estimate
for the root

```
PROCEDURE Secant (var x, x1, x2        : real;
         tolerance           : real;
         var iterations      : integer;
         imax                : integer;
         monitor             : boolean;
         function f (x : real) : real);

    VAR
        f1,f2 :r eal;
    BEGIN
        iterations := 0;
        f1 := f(x1);
        REPEAT
            iterations := iterations + 1;
            x2 := x1;
            x1 := x;
            f2 := f1;
            f1 := f(x1);
            x := (x1 * f2 - x2 * f1) / (f2 - f1);
            IF monitor THEN
            writeln('New estimate = ',x:10:6);
        UNTIL ((abs(x - x1) < tolerance) or (iterations = imax));
    END;  {secant}
```

The program will follow the Newton-Raphson one almost exactly. Compare the results obtained with those for the other method.

Index

A

abs 107, 122
accuracy 121, 126
Ada 10
algorithm development 13
algorithms 9
  choice of 266
  notations 13
  performance 263
and 112
animating 260
apostrophe 23
archiving 228
arctan 123
arithmetic limits 126
arrays 194
  as an abstraction 197
  conformant 293
  form of 194
  multi-dimensional 206
  properties of 196
ASCII 115
assembler 1
assignment 67

B

base number writing 178

BASIC 10

binary search 259
  procedure 261
  animation 260
bits 5
block 175
Boole, George 109
booleans 109
bottom-up 18
buffer variable 138, 228
bytes 5

C

C programming language 10
call statement 43, 49
cardinality 233
case statement 85
char 48
character set 118
characters 31, 115
  and loops 35
chips 3
COBOL 10
comment 54
compilation 1
  errors 11, 56
compiler 7
compound interest 124